SHERARD COWPER-COLES is one of the most respected authorities on foreign affairs in the country. He has held a series of senior diplomatic posts, both in the UK and overseas, most recently as the British Ambassador in Kabul and as the Foreign Secretary's Special Representative for Afghanistan and Pakistan. He is the author of *Cables from Kabul*, which was published to critical acclaim in 2011. He lives in London.

Also by Sherard Cowper-Coles

CABLES FROM KABUL

SHERARD COWPER-COLES

Ever The Diplomat

Confessions of a Foreign
Office Mandarin

Harper
Press

Harper*Press*
An imprint of HarperCollins*Publishers*
77–85 Fulham Palace Road,
Hammersmith, London W6 8JB
www.harpercollins.co.uk

This Harper*Press* paperback edition published 2013
1

First published in Great Britain by Harper*Press* in 2012

A catalogue record for this book
is available from the British Library

ISBN 978-0-00-743601-9

Typeset in Minion with Giovanni display by
G&M Designs Limited, Raunds, Northamptonshire
Printed and bound in Great Britain by
Clays Ltd, St Ives plc

MIX
Paper from
responsible sources
FSC   FSC™ C007454

FSC™ is a non-profit international organisation established to promote
the responsible management of the world's forests. Products carrying the
FSC label are independently certified to assure consumers that they come
from forests that are managed to meet the social, economic and
ecological needs of present or future generations,
and other controlled sources.

Find out more about HarperCollins and the environment at
www.harpercollins.co.uk/green

For Harry, Rupert,
Minna, Freddy, Myles and Louise

British Embassy Tel Aviv

Sherard Cowper-Coles
H.M. Ambassador

192 Hayarkon Street, Tel Aviv 63405
Tel. +972 (0)3 725 1244 Fax. +972 (0)3 527 1572
e-mail: sherard.cowper-coles@fco.gov.uk
Website: www.britemb.org.il

Foreign and Commonwealth Office

Sherard Cowper-Coles
Principal Private Secretary

London SW1
Telephone: 0171 270 2059 Facsimile: 0171 270 2144
Mobile: 0385 221324

Sherard Cowper-Coles
H.M. Ambassador

British Embassy
P. O. Box 94351
Riyadh 11693

Tel. : +966 (0) 1 488 0077 Ext. 2202
Fax : +966 (0) 1 488 3125
Mobile : +966 (0) 50546 4861
E-mail : sherard.cowper-coles@fco.gov.uk
Website : www.britishembassy.gov.uk/saudiarabia

Sherard Cowper-Coles
Scrutineer

Foreign and Commonwealth Office
London SW1A 2AF

Telephone: 071-210-6841
Facsimile: 071-210-6073

**British Embassy
Kabul**

Sir Sherard Cowper-Coles
KCMG LVO
HM Ambassador

15ᵗʰ St. Roundabout
Wazir Akbar Khan
PO Box 334
Kabul

Switchboard   +93 (0)700 102 000
Direct   +93 (0)700 102 201
FTN: 8404 2201
E-mail: Sherard.Cowper-Coles@fco.gov.uk
Website: www.fco.gov.uk

SIR SHERARD COWPER-COLES KCMG LVO

Mr. Sherard Cowper-Coles
First Secretary (Chancery)

British Embassy,
Washington D.C.

Tel: (202) 462-1340

Foreign &
Commonwealth
Office

Sir Sherard Cowper-Coles KCMG LVO
Foreign Secretary's Special
Representative for Afghanistan and
Pakistan

W2.83, King Charles Street
London SW1A 2AH

Tel +44 (0)20 7008 4260
Mob +44 (0)7810 637916
Fax +44 (0)20 7008 3039
Sherard.Cowper-Coles@fco.gov.uk
sherard.cowpercoles@mobileemail.vodafone.net
www.fco.gov.uk

**British Embassy
Kabul**

Sir Sherard Cowper-Coles
Minister

15th Street Roundabout
Wazir Akbar Khan
Kabul

Tel: +93 (0) 7980 18708

sherard.cowpercoles@
mobileemail.vodafone.net

www.fco.gov.uk

Sherard Cowper-Coles
Conseiller aux Affaires Politiques

Ambassade de Grande-Bretagne
35, rue du Faubourg St-Honoré
75383 Paris Cedex 08

Téléphone : 01 44 51 32 07/8
Télécopie : 01 44 51 34 85

شيـرارد كوبـر-كولز
سفير صاحبة الجلالة البريطانية

هاتف : ٧٧ ٠٠ ٤٨٨ ١ (٠) ٩٦٦ تحويلة ٢٢٠٢
فاكس : ٣١٢٥ ٤٨٨ ١ (٠) ٩٦٦
جوال : ٤٨١١ ٥٤٦ ٥ (٠) ٩٦٦
sherard.cowper-coles@fco.gov.uk :بريد الكتروني
موقعنا على الانترنت : www.ukm.org.sa

السفارة البريطانية
ص.ب ٩٤٢٥١
الرياض ١١٦٩٣

شرارد كوبر كولى
سفير دولت شاهى انگلستان

سركـ پازده وزير اكبر خان
پوست بكس: ٣٣٣
كابل

سفارت انگلستان
كابل

موبايل:
سويج پرزو:
دايركت:
فن اى ان:
پوست الكترونيكى: Sherard.Cowper-Coles@fco.gov.uk
وب سايت: www.fco.gov.uk

שגרירות בריטניה תל אביב

שראד קופר-קולס
שגריר

רחוב הירקון 192 תל אביב 63405
טל. 1244.5 725-03 פקס. 1572 527-03
e-mail: sherard.cowper-coles@fco.gov.uk
www.britemb.org.il

شرارد كوبر كولز
ـ سكرتير ثان (أعلام)

السفارة البريطانية
القاهرة ت ٢٠٨٥٢/٩

٣٩ شارع محمد مظهر شقة ٤
الزمالك ــ ت ٨٠٢٠٢٩

Sherard Cowper-Coles
Second Secretary (Information)

British Embassy
Cairo
Tel. 20852 - 9

39, Mohamed Mazhar Str.
1st. Floor - Flat 4
Zamalek Tel. 802029

英國外交及聯邦事務部
香港科主管

古 沛 勤

倫敦 SW1A 2AH
電話: 071-270-2647   傳眞: 071-270-3387

Sherard Cowper-Coles
Head of Hong Kong Department

Foreign and Commonwealth Office
London SW1A 2AH

Telephone: 071-270-2647
Facsimile : 071-270-3387

Contents

List of Illustrations

FCO Letter of Appointment
'Thatcher's Thesaurus'

Middle East Centre for Arab Studies. *Photograph by a local Lebanese photographer*

TRH The Prince and Princess of Wales, and President and Mrs Sadat. *Photograph by a member of the crew of HM Yacht* Britannia

Foreign Office Planning Staff. © *Brian Harris/The Times/NI Syndication*

Permanent Under Secretary's office. *Photograph by an FCO photographer*

Congressman Kennedy. *Photograph by a member of his staff*

Mrs Thatcher. *Photograph by a member of Blair House staff*

Governor Patten. © *Roger Hutchings/In Pictures/Corbis*

Hong Kong Handover Ceremony. © *Reuters/Jason Reed*

President's House, Jerusalem. *Photograph by a member of the President's staff*

Crown Prince Abdullah, the Prince of Wales and the author. *Photograph by a Saudi court photographer*

Crown Prince Abdullah, Prime Minister and the author. *Photograph by a Saudi court photographer*

All other photographs are from the author's private collection and were taken either by him or by friends, colleagues or family members

Preface

This book is really a long love letter to an institution – the Foreign Office – for which I worked for some three decades. From the age of twenty-two until I was fifty-five, I was a British diplomat. Formally, I was a member of Her Majesty's Diplomatic Service, with a commission from the Queen. But for me diplomacy was much more than a job, or even a profession: it was my way of life. It was what I got up for in the morning, and what I went to sleep at night thinking about. For thirty-three years, I looked forward almost every working day to going into the office, or embassy, or wherever work took me. I was never bored. And I didn't just enjoy being a diplomat. I also believed that what I did as a diplomat mattered in small but important ways. From Ireland to Israel, and Arabia to Afghanistan, in Paris or Washington, in long hours in London worrying about Europe's future or Hong Kong after the handover, I tried as a minor cog in HMG's foreign policy machine to make the world work better. I met the people who helped or hindered our efforts. I went to the places where foreign policy happened. I cared about the issues. And at the end of it all I wanted to share some of the highlights and low points, as I remembered them. I wanted to give the reader a flavour of what diplomats really do, and of what being a diplomat actually feels like. But mostly I wanted to show why I had enjoyed it all so much.

I kept no proper diary. The random private papers I did keep are now buried beyond easy recovery in barns and attics in Britain and France. I have made no use of official documents. But what I do have is memories: plenty of them, good and bad, of the tough times and the bright spots, of the fun I had, but also of the horrors I witnessed and of the mistakes we made. Of the people too, conscientious mostly, committed and often courageous, but some charlatans as well and others with more reptilian qualities. I have set down, place by place, post by post, the best and worst of those memories. All are the truth as I remember it, but not always the whole truth. The story stops at the edge of private turmoil. It alludes only in passing to the disreputable deal-making over top jobs that led me to choose early retirement, five years sooner than expected.

As with my first book, *Cables from Kabul*,* I have asked myself whether publishing an account of my experiences so soon after I left the public service was consistent with my obligations to my former employer. But Diplomatic Service Regulations state that 'The FCO welcomes debate on foreign policy … The FCO recognises that there is a public interest in allowing former officials to write accounts of their time in government. These contributions can help public understanding and debate … there is no ban on former members of the Diplomatic Service writing their memoirs … but obligations of confidentiality remain …'

Like *Cables*, this book is the fruit of a conversation with my future agent, Caroline Michel, at a dinner at the Irish Embassy in London in 2009. It was Caroline who first suggested that I had a book or two in me. It was she who told me to set down my memories and share them. I shall be forever grateful to her for sticking so faithfully to that judgement.

I am also immensely grateful to the team at HarperPress who have given such enthusiastic and wholly professional support to this project: in particular my editor and friend, Martin Redfern, a diplomat if ever there was one, whose quiet judgement has often saved me from error, and who has driven the whole thing forward with determination and discrimination; to project editor Kate Tolley for putting the book together with efficiency and taste; and to Helen Ellis, publicist sans pareil, Minna Fry and the whole of the HarperPress gang.

I owe my research assistant, Max Benitz, a particular debt of gratitude for his hard work in establishing what really happened, in tracking

---

* London: HarperPress, 2011.

down key documents or photographs, and in offering many excellent suggestions, all done with remarkable accuracy and to time. I have also been extraordinarily lucky in my copy-editor, Peter James, an Oxford contemporary, and in having had the help of the king of indexers, Douglas Matthews.

Two people have given me exceptional support and encouragement as I conceived and wrote this book: my friend Charles Richards and my wife Jasmine. I must also thank a number of former colleagues, including Nigel Cox and Andrew Patrick, for help and suggestions with different parts of the text. As with *Cables from Kabul*, we have had outstanding help and support from the Cabinet Office in clearing the text around Whitehall: I am very appreciative.

The mistakes which remain are my responsibility alone.

Ealing, July 2012

Foreign and Commonwealth Office
London SW1 A 2AH

Telephone 01- 233 5216

S L Cowper-Coles Esq
Fig Street Farm
Sevenoaks
Kent
TN14 6HP

Your reference

Our reference

Date 15 April 1977

Dear Cowper-Coles,

You will by now have heard from the Civil Service
Commission that you have been declared successful for
the Administrative Grades of the Diplomatic Service
subject to the satisfactory completion of enquiries
into health and other matters. This is excellent
news.

The introductory course for new entrants begins on
5 September and we should like you to start with us
then. Please let me know if you foresee any difficulty about this. We shall, of course, be writing
to you again before September, but if you would like
to raise any points with me in the meantime, please
do not hesitate to get in touch.

Yours sincerely,

Antony Ford

A Ford
Personnel Policy
Department

nk

Chapter 1

The Third Room

The walk down Whitehall, from Trafalgar Square to the vast Italianate palazzo of the Foreign Office, seemed so long. I passed the statues of Sir Walter Raleigh and the generals* on the green in front of the Ministry of Defence with hardly a glance in their direction. I ignored the Cenotaph. My stomach was knotted with excited dread. I was worried I would be late. It was just like starting at a new school, right down to my new suit and shoes, my empty briefcase and my freshly filled fountain pen.

Nervously, I turned right down King Charles Street, under the bridge which joins in stone but not in style the two great departments of the British state – the Foreign and Commonwealth Office and HM Treasury – then right again, through the main-entrance arch of the Foreign Office. A single security guard waved me in across the quadrangle, to the steps in the far left-hand corner. Up I climbed, through the great double doors. Two grand ladies peered down from behind a high counter. I told them that I was a newly appointed member of the Diplomatic Service. I had been instructed to report by 10 a.m. to the Recruitment Section of the Personnel Policy Department. Gently they told me that I had come to the wrong place. 'PPD' was across the other side of Whitehall, in the Curtis Green building (now Cannon Row police station). If I didn't hurry, I would be late. More nervous than ever, I retraced my steps, and eventually found the official whom I had been told to see.

The formal 'fast stream' induction course was not until the following month, and lasted only two weeks: we were taught not much more than

---

* Sir Walter has since been relocated, but the generals remain.

how to use the Foreign Office telephone directory. But four members of the 1977 entry of seventeen young diplomats had been told to start work earlier. After minimal formalities, we were led back across Whitehall, and taken to our new departments in the labyrinth still known formally as the Old Public Offices. The Foreign Office believed in on-the-job training.

It was Monday 22 August 1977, and I had been told that I had been accepted into the Diplomatic Service only in April that year. I had graduated from Oxford in June. In July, out of the blue, had come a letter saying that I had been appointed desk officer for Ireland in the FCO's Republic of Ireland Department. I was needed two weeks earlier than the official start date. I asked how I should prepare. Read three books, I was told: *Ireland since the Famine** by the Provost of Trinity College, Dublin, F. S. L. Lyons; Tim Pat Coogan's history of the IRA;† and, best of all, Robert Kee's two-volume history of Irish nationalism, *The Green Flag*.‡ The few brief weeks between being a student and having a grown-up job had passed in a flash, mainly on my uncles' farm in Devon. I immersed myself in the emotion-filled history of Britain's engagement with Ireland. In my mind's eager eye, deepest Devon became rural Ireland. I could hardly believe my luck: I was being paid to think about issues and events in which I would anyway have taken an interest. And I had learned the first and last lesson of diplomacy: know your history. It had been a narrow escape – had I not passed the Foreign Office selection process, I might instead have become a barrister or a merchant banker.

That selection process had had its moments. Sitting the initial Qualifying Tests with hundreds of others in Oxford's cavernous Examination Schools had felt like retaking the Eleven-plus – with the same rather arbitrary pattern of success and failure. Some very bright people had fallen at that first fence, while some notorious dunces had somehow scraped through. The next stage was a series of extended interviews and of subjective and objective tests – the infamous

---

* London: Weidenfeld & Nicolson, 1971.

† London: Pall Mall Press, 1970.

‡ London: Weidenfeld & Nicolson, 1972.

'country-house weekend', in a nondescript office block, long since demolished, just off Trafalgar Square. It was based on the techniques Britain had used in wartime to find capable officers, and it worked. The interview with the psychologist felt a bit weird. The invitation to 'chat among yourselves' while we were observed was even more artificial. But writing descriptions of oneself by a best friend and by a worst enemy was fun. So, in a masochistic way, was the Final Selection Board, in front of a group of grand officials high up over Horse Guards Parade. Less fun was the Positive Vetting. A creepy former Palestine Police officer asked if I had ever been drunk or in debt, and did not believe me when I said I had never taken drugs. A written questionnaire enquired whether I kept a radio transmitter, and how many of my friends were Communists ('For the purpose of this form, the term "Communist" is taken to include the term "Fascist"') – quite a few I had to say. Somehow I got through.

That first week in the Foreign Office began on a high note. My Oxford contemporary Bobby McDonagh* had just started in the Irish Foreign Ministry at Iveagh House in Dublin. I decided I had to ring him up, to tell him that I was the new Desk Officer for his country in London. 'Guess what, Bobby,' I said proudly, 'I have been appointed desk officer for Ireland.' 'Aw, that's nuthin', boasted Bobby, in his seductive Irish accent. 'I'm the Desk Officer for the whole of Africa and Asia.' It was a good introduction to the blarney and bravado of one of the world's smaller but more effective foreign services.

A second encounter was harder work. The First Secretary at the Irish Embassy in London, Dick O'Brien, invited me to lunch, at the Gay Hussar in Greek Street. I remember little of what was said at the lunch – although a great deal was said, mainly by Dick. As we ranged back over the eight years since the Troubles had flared up again, and far back beyond that, Dick wouldn't concede a single point: it was good that I had studied my history and had taken a close interest in Northern Ireland ever since British troops had been put back on the streets in August 1969. I was flattered that Dick, an experienced first secretary,

---

* Later Irish Ambassador to London. It was he who introduced me to my agent, Caroline Michel.

should have taken me, a newly appointed third secretary with no diplomatic experience, even half seriously. I suddenly realised that, in the eyes of those with whom I was dealing professionally, my job – my formal position and title – counted for more than I thought they did, or necessarily should. I was now an official representative of my country and my government. What I said or did would be seen or heard in that light. Diplomatic titles, the elaborate protocols of international intercourse, concealed – and eased – substantive exchanges, of information and opinion.

After a good lunch with plenty of wine, Dick insisted on three brandies each. I staggered back into King Charles Street at four in the afternoon, incapable of further work. If this was diplomatic entertainment, I was not sure how much of it I could take.

But I had a real job to do. As what was then called a 'Grade 8' new entrant, a third secretary, I was taking over from an experienced first secretary, Alan Goulty, an Arabist in his early thirties with several overseas postings under his belt. I would have to work hard to fill his shoes. Alan taught me straight away the two unwritten rules of the Foreign Office. The first – never knock on any doors – is meant to reflect complete trust among diplomats, but still leads to many embarrassing incidents. The second – call everyone by his or her first name, except ministers, ambassadors and the Permanent Under Secretary – seemed revolutionary in 1977: at twenty-two, I had great difficulty in addressing a fifty-nine-year-old deputy under secretary as 'Antony', let alone 'Tony'. The only other occupant of my first office, sitting opposite me, was a diplomat even more experienced than Alan Goulty. Michael Hodge had joined the Prison Commission as a clerk, but, having proved himself at policy work, had transferred after only a year to the Foreign Service (as it was then) as a junior diplomat I dealt with Ireland (or the Republic of Ireland as the Diplomatic Service formbook taught us to call it: 'Irish Republic' implied a republic embracing the whole island). Michael handled overseas interest in Northern Ireland – mainly forty million Americans claiming Irish descent. Michael gave me more wise advice than he will ever remember, about drafting, about what he called officemanship, about good and bad postings, and about good and bad ambassadors. As an incentive to stay the course, Michael shared his memories of foreign service, ranging from repatriating, in a shoe box, the remains of a British citizen killed in Uganda whose cremation Michael had had to perform, to travelling the Gulf as personal assistant to the Political Resident, Sir Geoffrey Arthur, during the last year – 1971 – of Britain's quasi-colonial presence there.

Together, Michael and I made up what was called the 'Third Room' of the standard Foreign Office political department of the time. In the hierarchy above us, in rooms of their own (presumably the second and first rooms, though we never used the term), sat the Assistant (or deputy head of the department) and the Head of Department.

A fourth room contained two alarmingly efficient Foreign Office secretaries. Both took shorthand, but not from someone as junior as me. In a fifth and final room two clerks slaved away, carefully registering all the department's papers, before placing them on files established according to a centralised system overseen by the Chief Registrar of the Foreign Office – the high priest of the cult of the file. Apart from the fact that most, but by no means all, papers were now typed, little can have changed since Victorian times.

I had my first lesson in pushing paper: the approved way to attach one paper to another was to punch a hole in the top left-hand corner of each, half an inch in from the top and side, and then to pass a tag through the holes. Paperclips become detached, or attached to the wrong papers; staples are a fiddle to unpick. In the Foreign Office then, as now, the India tag, aka the Treasury tag, ruled supreme: two small metal, later plastic, bars, joined by a miniature red cord. With the India tag went the key instrument of bureaucratic order: the hole punch – always in short supply, often purloined, never to be let out of sight, the only property I have ever 'liberated' from the Foreign Office.

My first Assistant (and therefore boss) was a kind and careful official, Peter Wallis, who had come to the Foreign Office via HM Customs & Excise. He took endless trouble to improve my drafts. We used special blue drafting paper, with wide margins for corrections. In those leisurely days, almost everything we wrote was prepared first in draft, in type or handwriting. Most serious pieces of work on Britain's relations with Ireland started on my desk, as a draft by me. As that draft moved up the chain, it would change beyond recognition. But, as the new boy in the Department, I was the bureaucratic focus for Britain's bilateral relationship with Ireland. I was the continuity person, the official responsible for knowing which plates we had in the air at any one time, and for keeping them there. It was at once exhilarating and intimidating. After university, the most difficult thing, by far, was dealing with a dozen real problems at once, rather than the single subject of that week's essay.

We were told that the core of our job was influencing foreigners, in the British interest. In order to do so, we needed first to understand them, and then to put our messages in terms that would have the best chance of being absorbed and acted upon by those we were trying to persuade to do what HMG wanted them to do. Clear thinking equalled clear writing. And clear writing was most effective in explaining to ministers in London the realities of any particular foreign policy challenge, and of ensuring that the instructions resulting from our analysis had some effect. All this explained why the Foreign Office attached so much importance to 'drafting', and why, in my first job in London, and my second in Cairo, each of my bosses took such trouble to go through my drafts and improve them. And at the heart of all this – the lifeblood of any decent diplomatic machine – was and is the telegram: a collective classified message, as tautly drafted as possible, sent from overseas posts to London, and vice versa.

That was why in the autumn of 1977 we new entrants to the Diplomatic Service were told, only half jokingly, that, like the fountains in Trafalgar Square, Foreign Office officials operated only from ten till six. We didn't need to arrive in King Charles Street before ten o'clock, because that gave time for the distribution, around the Office and Whitehall, of the overnight telegram traffic pouring into London via the former Diplomatic Wireless Service station at Hanslope Park, near Milton Keynes. The first thing we did each morning was read the telegrams.

I soon learned that Foreign Office life is a continual merry-go-round of postings, for yourself and for your colleagues. After only a few weeks Peter Wallis was posted, on promotion, to Ankara. He was succeeded by one of the most accomplished eccentrics of the Foreign Office of that time – an official who was anything but careful.

Trevor Mound was a minor hero to my generation in the Foreign Office. In idiosyncratic fashion, he encapsulated one of the attributes the writer and diplomat Sir Harold Nicolson had said were essential for success in diplomacy: a sense of proportion, but leavened with a sense of humour. Trevor never ever panicked. And he always saw the funny, often absurd, side of everything.

The son of a small Worcestershire farmer, Trevor had joined the Army as a private soldier without going to university. He had begun in the Guards, but before long he had been commissioned into the Parachute Regiment. Well over six feet tall, he had the erect bearing of the Foot Guard he had once been. A long thin face was framed by a sweep of reddish hair on top, and a small pointed ginger beard at the bottom, set off by twinkling blue eyes and an ever present smile. He could easily have been a late-nineteenth-century French novelist-adventurer. He was always immaculately turned out, in hand-made black jodhpur boots and deep-cut three-piece suits, with all sorts of extra features, including more pockets than anyone could ever use, and cuff buttons that really undid. Every day Trevor wore a cream silk shirt and a blue-red-blue Brigade tie, even though most of his military service had in fact been with the Paras. He had an OBE after his name, but would never say for what. There was an air of charmingly seductive mystery about him. Much married (or so he liked us to think), he loved women, fine wine and fun.

Trevor had joined the Diplomatic Service late, as a retired major. He had had a succession of tough postings, culminating in Beirut as we closed the Embassy at the height of the Lebanese Civil War. The last telegram Trevor had received in Beirut before he smashed up the cipher machine with the hammer provided in every embassy for just that purpose had been 'You are instructed to proceed with closing down the Embassy in accordance with Volume 12 of Diplomatic Service Procedure.' His reply to London had been 'DSP already incinerated. But shutting down any way. Signed Mound.'

Back in London, financial pressures, including multiple alimony payments, had obliged Trevor to let out his own house and live in the top floor of the Foreign Office building as a resident clerk. In return for a reasonably generous allowance, and a one-bedroom flat in SW1, with stunning views over St James's Park, resident clerks were expected to man the phones – and monitor the overnight telegram traffic – one night a week, and one weekend in six. Trevor used often to invite me up to his eyrie after work, for gin and tonic and a gossip. He used his flat to entertain generously and widely. With that in mind, he had persuaded the Foreign Office Home Estates Department that his bad back – the result, he said, of an awkward parachute landing in Malaya – required that a double bed be installed in his bedroom in the Clerkery, at some expense, and even greater effort for the workmen obliged to propel the bed up the narrow staircase. Sometimes Trevor would invite his latest 'lady friend' (as he used to call them) and any other guests to climb, quite illegally, out of the window of the Clerkery, to enjoy a drink on the roof of the Foreign Office, as the sun went down behind Buckingham Palace at the other end of the Park.

Over those talks with Trevor, I learned much about diplomatic life. The Army had trained him as a Cantonese speaker, although, when the Foreign Office had subjected him to its language-aptitude test on join-ing, he had been judged incapable of learning any foreign language. But Trevor's first diplomatic love was China, and it was in Shanghai that he and I would next meet, eight years later. Perhaps because of his Chinese, Trevor's English handwriting resembled an exotic, almost cuneiform, script. His written expression was anyway economical in the extreme. At least decrypting his written comments in the margins of my drafts gave me a chance to see him and talk. Trevor offered several pieces of career advice. One was that, if you wanted to rise to the top of 'the Office' (as he always called it), spend as little time as possible in distant or dangerous postings. Colleagues in faraway embassies were soon forgotten, accidentally or deliberately. It was naive to think that the reward for a tough posting would be a plum one. The ambitious knew that walking the corridors in Whitehall or in the Brussels near-abroad did far more for one's career than working the far bazaars of Asia, Africa or Latin America. It was advice that Trevor, with his love of China, did not himself follow. He ended his career, serenely happy, as consul-general in Marseilles, untroubled by the anxious ambition that ate away at so many others. Trevor showed that striving too hard in the Diplomatic Service did not always lead to the best postings. In fact, as he once observed on seeing a hopeless colleague sent to govern a balmy Caribbean island, ours was a good service in which to fail.

Another piece of Trevor's advice I also followed only partially. Abroad, Trevor said, as the British representative, one had to cut a dash. That meant always wearing a hat, so as to stand out from the crowd of other diplomats.

None of his colleagues would have wanted to describe Trevor as lazy. But he didn't believe in exerting more effort than was strictly necessary to get the job done. The time saved from this remarkable economy of effort was devoted to various good causes: lunch, an early drink after work, and, in the Office, the composition of limericks. One of the best celebrated the IRA 'dirty protests' in HM Prison Maze and the involvement of the Roman Catholic Primate of All Ireland, Cardinal Ó Fiaich (correctly pronounced O'Fee). One couplet had the Cardinal's name rhyming with 'dabbling in IRA muck'.

Trevor's boss, and the Head of our little department, could hardly have been more different. Philip Mallet had been educated at Winchester and Balliol. He bore the burden of at least two immensely distinguished forebears in the public service: his father, Sir Victor Mallet, had ended his career as ambassador to Rome, while a cousin, Sir Louis Mallet, had served as permanent under secretary of state for India. He must have complained at having been obliged to accept a green young third secretary as his main desk officer. At first sight, Philip was Foreign Office premier grand cru. In my first week, he took me to lunch at his club in St James's. I must have passed the test, because he later included me in the dinners he gave for foreign diplomats at his house in Chelsea. In the autumn, he would appear on Monday mornings with apples for us all from his orchards in Kent.

But, despite his ancestry, or perhaps because of it, Philip and the Office had never quite got on as they should have done. He was too well mannered to complain, but one could see that he had not had the promotion his talent deserved. I was too inexperienced to understand quite why: he worked hard, his judgement was good and his understanding of Irish issues profound. I suspect it was something to do with his manner, and perhaps self-confidence. He was particularly upset when an especially high-handed minute from the Foreign Secretary's office landed on his desk. Usually, notes from the Foreign Secretary's private secretaries were models of periphrastic circumlocution: 'The Secretary of State was grateful for your advice, but wonders whether it would be possible to examine an alternative ...' But that wasn't the style of the new young Foreign Secretary, Dr David Owen. The memorandum to Mallet read, rather brutally, something like: 'The Secretary of State has seen your minute, and does not like this advice at all ...'

In a sardonic way, Philip saw the funny side of it. After the Republic of Ireland Department, his final posting would be as high commissioner to Guyana. He said that his main contribution in Georgetown had been to redraft the post's fire regulations.

Ireland's unique position in Britain's foreign relations made it a close to ideal subject on which to work while learning diplomacy by doing. Britain's first colony, Ireland was now an independent state as well as a member of what was then known as the European Economic Community. We had a complicated bilateral relationship to manage, as well as the business of co-ordinating our approach to European issues, notably the Common Agricultural Policy. But everything was overshadowed by the problem of Northern Ireland, and the search for a solution following the breakdown of the Sunningdale process* in 1974.

The foundations of good diplomacy are honest reporting and clear analysis. Our Embassy in Dublin sent back a stream of reports, by telegram and, twice weekly, in the diplomatic bags carried by the Queen's Messengers back and forth across the Irish Sea. The opening of the bag in London always brought a flood of letters from the Dublin Chancery (or political section), covering many different aspects of Irish politics, the Irish economy and Irish society. The Ambassador, Sir Robin Haydon, would send private letters, typed on blue Foreign Office airmail paper in the large typeface then reserved for ambassadors, reporting, often in amusing terms, his encounters with Irish ministers and senior officials. We read all the main Irish papers and magazines. I took the *Irish Times* each day, and came to love it. Once I was made a

---

* In December 1973 an agreement was signed at the conclusion of a conference at the Civil Service College at Sunningdale establishing a power-sharing executive for Northern Ireland and a cross-border Council of Ireland. The agreement collapsed in the face of Unionist opposition, culminating in a general strike in May 1974.

temporary Queen's Messenger, with a special passport on a folded sheet of vellum, and sent to Dublin with the diplomatic bag. I was so proud to be sitting at the front of the BA flight, beside me the white canvas mailbag, on which was stencilled in black the legend 'Her Britannic Majesty's Diplomatic Service'.

I made my first acquaintance with the world of secret intelligence. We received a steady flow of intelligence reports, of varying quality. Some were gold dust, real secrets, but many were little more than gossip, which we would sooner or later have picked up anyway. Others had more comedy than political value. One reported solemnly on a conversation between two IRA men, during which one managed to set himself on fire as they talked. The report's editor prissily inserted '[expletive deleted]' more than a dozen times, but we could guess what 'Seamus' had been saying. Another revealed that a senior Irish diplomat had visited Belfast disguised as a priest, to find out what was happening there.

Like every other British embassy, the Chancery in Dublin kept, and regularly updated, a folder of Leading Personality Reports on key figures in Irish life. Each individual entry was in a set format, with basic biographical information, followed by an account of the subject's career, and ending with comment and some more personal details. Later much of the juicy stuff was removed, after Mrs Thatcher, as prime minister, complained that Foreign Office LPRs were too gossipy. In 1977, however, it was still possible to record that one senior Irish minister had 'an unconventional method of mounting a horse'.

Another great advantage of being trained while working on Ireland was that the job involved dealing with much of Whitehall beyond the Foreign Office. The Home Office, for example, was concerned with the operation of the Common Travel Area. The Department of Energy was interested in talking to Ireland about oil and gas in the Irish Sea. The Department of the Environment was anxious to reassure Ireland about discharges from the Sellafield nuclear-waste processing plant in Cumbria. The Ministry of Agriculture had many exchanges on Irish farming issues, both bilaterally and in the context of the European Community. At that time the President of the British Friesian Cattle Society was an Irish priest.

A symptom of the intimate complexity of the relationship was the problem of desertions decades earlier by Irish citizens who had enlisted in the British Army. The Special Branch at Dover would run anti-terrorist checks on lorry drivers passing through the port. Almost every week, or so it seemed, their records would show that twenty or thirty years earlier Sean Higgins (or whoever it was) had deserted from one of the British Army's Irish regiments. Although an Irish citizen, as a deserter he was subject to British military law, and was immediately transferred to the custody of the Royal Military Police. With his lorry abandoned at Dover, a horrified middle-aged Irishman would then be taken to the depot of his parent regiment, often many miles away, formally to receive a dishonourable discharge. In the meantime, his firm or family would have alerted the Irish Consulate in London, who would ask me to find out what was going on. It was a small but painful hangover from history.

But in 1977 the government departments most concerned with Irish issues were the Northern Ireland Office and, to a lesser extent, the Ministry of Defence. Dealing with these two very different departments was an invaluable experience. The NIO had been formed only in 1972, when the Government in London had imposed direct rule on Northern Ireland. It was composed, in a hurry, of able and dedicated officials from across Whitehall, mainly from the Home Office, but also from the FCO and elsewhere. With bases in London and Belfast, the NIO's purpose was to work itself out of existence, by restoring devolved government to Ulster. The whole NIO was thus dedicated to the proposition that Northern Ireland needed a political solution, and that a security-only approach would never be enough. The failure of the Sunningdale process had been a huge setback. It had been launched by Ted Heath's Conservative Government in 1973, but had collapsed thanks largely to the new Labour Government's unwillingness to face down the Ulster Workers' Council strike the following year. But even then everyone knew that, as proved to be the case twenty years later, the eventual solution would be on the broad lines of Sunningdale: power-sharing in Northern Ireland, with an 'Irish dimension' – that is, recognition that Dublin should have a benign role in overseeing the governance of the six counties of Ulster. As the Social Democratic and

Labour Party MP Seamus Mallon was to remark in 1998, the Good Friday Agreement of that year was 'Sunningdale for slow learners'.

The NIO's officials – and most of its better ministers – never lost their humane and intelligent vision of how the conflict would, and did, end. And many of them came to love Ulster, and its rich landscapes and cultures. At the same time, they understood that the Nationalist minority's aspirations had to be accommodated politically in an all-Ireland arrangement which took account of the wish of the Protestant communities – the majority in Northern Ireland, a minority in the whole island of Ireland – to remain part of the United Kingdom.

The Ministry of Defence was rather different. A vast military–civil bureaucratic machine, it had a divided population. On the one hand, enthusiastic officers from all three armed services, socially and intellectually confident but taken temporarily from what they regarded as proper soldiering to 'drive a desk' in Whitehall, as a necessary stage of purgatory on the military cursus honorum. On the other hand, career MOD civil servants, generally better educated, at senior levels more intellectually gifted than their colleagues in the uniformed branch, but less well paid and less socially ostentatious. It was, and is, an uneasy union, that works, more or less, provided there is clear direction from the politicians at the top, and from the most senior civil servants who support them.

Working on Ireland also acquainted me with civil servants from shadowier parts of Whitehall: not just the smooth extroverts of MI6 (or Secret Intelligence Service, SIS), many of whom operated under Foreign Office cover, but also the quieter, somewhat more stolid (and probably therefore more reliable) operatives of MI5 (or the Security Service), as well as the frighteningly clever, and often rather geekish, introverts of Government Communications Headquarters (usually known as GCHQ). All three agencies ran courses to present their wares to new entrants to the Diplomatic Service. 'Six' came across as a bit too slick. 'Five' or 'Box 500' (after the PO Box they used) seemed more conservative: every one of our lecturers wore a military tie. They spoke, perfectly sensibly, about the threat from Communist espionage and from Irish terrorism. But there was also some alarmingly right-wing talk of the need to monitor the trade unions and keep an eye on industrial subversion. The 'West Country' course – GCHQ is based in Cheltenham – felt a bit like a seminar for prospective mathematics students.

In a separate – but not lower – league were the senior officers of the Metropolitan Police Special Branch. They came across as real Flash Harrys, who dressed and behaved like the stars of some cool television series. They took us, at police expense, to Italian restaurants, and ordered in what was meant to sound like Italian. They were a world away from Whitehall. But they knew what they were doing: the Special Branch had, after all, been created as the Special Irish Branch to deal with the threat of Fenian terrorism in the late nineteenth century.

Back in the Foreign Office, I learned how everything revolved around the Foreign Secretary, known in house as the Secretary of State. In 1977, only nine years after the Foreign and Commonwealth Offices had merged, there was still a rearguard action to remind everyone that the minister in charge was technically the Foreign and Commonwealth Secretary, and to describe him as such. But it was a battle finally lost when Sir Geoffrey Howe, on becoming secretary of state in 1983, said that he wanted to be known simply as the 'Foreign Secretary'. And there was a definite feeling that working on Commonwealth issues wasn't serious foreign policy: Trevor Mound had told me that, India apart, it was better to avoid being sent to a Commonwealth post – where our embassies were known as high commissions – if I could.

In August 1977, the Secretary of State was Dr David Owen, at thirty-seven the youngest Foreign Secretary since Eden. He had been promoted by the Prime Minister, Jim Callaghan, in April that year, when Tony Crosland had died, in the Radcliffe Infirmary in Oxford, of a heart attack after going to fetch the Sunday papers. I woke up one morning in Oxford to hear the terrible news, and regretted that I wouldn't be working for Crosland, if and when I joined the Foreign Office that autumn.

Owen was a man in a hurry, determined to make a difference, above all on the problem of Rhodesia. There the insurgency against Ian Smith's illegal minority regime was gathering pace. Owen spent much time on shuttle diplomacy with President Carter's envoy, the former Mayor of Atlanta, Andy Young. In the rush for results, Owen lost patience with Foreign Office procedures. He preferred to operate through the SIS network, sending messages on their channels, rather than using the Foreign Office's rather more stately telegraph system. Owen's apparent disdain for conventional diplomacy showed me how important it was to work in ways which satisfied the demands of politics.

Rumours filtered down of tensions between the Secretary of State and officials at the top of the Office. In one of his regular private messages to ambassadors abroad, the Permanent Under Secretary described the Foreign Secretary as tired and under strain, as a result of trying to do, and travel, too much.

All that only added to the sense of awe when I was asked occasionally to walk urgent papers down to the Foreign Secretary's office, or to retrieve them from there. The Private Office (as it was known) consisted of the Foreign Secretary's own magnificent office, with its views across Horse Guards and St James's Park, and, separated from the Secretary of State and from the corridor by great oak doors, the private secretaries' room. The walls of the latter were covered with small portraits, latterly photographs, of every previous holder of the office, including Tony Crosland and Jim Callaghan. Around the side of the room sat the four private secretaries at their great desks: in the far corner, with a bust of Pitt the Younger behind him, the Principal Private Secretary. The other occupants of the room were two bright mid-career diplomats as assistant private secretaries, and a diary secretary. The Principal Private Secretary seemed impossibly grand: I never dreamed that one day I would do his job.

'Walking a paper down' meant entering the private secretaries' room, and approaching the desk of the private secretary in question, always aware that at any time the great oak door might swing open and the Foreign Secretary himself emerge. The first time I went down, pretty terrified, I was pleasantly surprised that, in the middle of the maelstrom, the Assistant Private Secretary who dealt with Ireland, Kieran Prendergast, had time to ask me who I was and what I did. It turned out that he had known my Dutch journalist cousin during his last posting, in The Hague.

But the Foreign Secretary isn't the only minister in the Foreign Office. Usually, he is the department's sole representative in the Cabinet, but there are at least four other ministers, including a peer to cover Foreign Office business in the House of Lords. For Ireland, in 1977, our junior Minister was Frank Judd. Personable, able to take a brief and speak to it, Judd was all that officials wanted in a junior minister. He did the political and representational jobs the Foreign Secretary couldn't do, but without interfering unnecessarily in policy.

Ministers apart, the most intimidating aspect of starting in the Diplomatic Service is getting to know your way around a building that once housed four separate ministries: the Foreign, India, Colonial and Home Offices. Palmerston had asked for the present Italianate design, in place of Gilbert Scott's Gothic vision, which instead became St Pancras Station. In 1977, the hugely imaginative and expensive restoration programme for the Old Public Offices had not yet started. They were still in a state of post-war squalor. The glories of the Locarno rooms were concealed behind plywood partitions, erected to create more office space in wartime. The beautiful marble floor of the Durbar Court of the India Office was covered with Nissen huts, housing communications equipment, even though the Court was roofed over (rather leakily). Only ten years earlier, the building had still been heated by the coal fires which adorned most offices. The ashes of that era still seemed to cover everything in a fine film of dust. The Republic of Ireland Department was hidden away in the roof spaces of what had once been the Colonial Office. Only yards away was the old Colonial Office Library which still houses the stuffed anaconda, known fondly as Albert, brought back from distant parts who knows when or why. As gradually I found my way round the great building, I came to know and love the place where I was to spend much of the next three decades. I was immensely proud of its wonders, and its stories. Even then I used to invite friends in to show them the marvels of the India Office or of Sigismund Goetze's kitsch post-Great War murals – apparently detested by Lord Curzon when he was foreign secretary – which adorn the great landing at the top of the main staircase. Then, as now, I marvelled at the allegory of Britannia Pacificatrix, surrounded by her victorious allies at the end of the First World War: France in her revolutionary bonnet, Belgium and Serbia depicted as naked maidens, Africa represented by a small black boy with a bowl of fruit on his head. Or the hooded figure invoking 'Silence!' above the door into the Foreign Secretary's office. Best of all is Britannia Nutrix, breast-feeding her young colonies, just beside the Ambassadors' Waiting Room where the Foreign Secretary's visitors sit before they are summoned in. One of the best things the Foreign Office ever did was to institute guided tours of this magnificent labyrinth, at the heart of our imperial history.

From my first day in the Foreign Office, I knew that I was going to love the job. I was thrilled when, after six months, Philip Mallet told me that he quite liked my work, even though there was plenty of room for improvement. I had already noticed that he used bits of some of my drafts.

The weeks passed into months, and our group of new entrants began to wonder what next. We knew that the usual pattern was a year learning on the job in London, before language training and a first posting overseas. We called ourselves – and still do – the G77, borrowing the name of the UN developing countries' caucus. We met regularly for drinks and dinner, usually at Mon Plaisir in Monmouth Street, and compared notes. One of us had been sent straight abroad, as the annual reinforcement for the British mission to the UN in New York for the General Assembly session. We asked him what life was like overseas; the answer came back that it was even better than in London. Living abroad, working with foreigners, was just as rewarding as advertised: it was what we had joined the Diplomatic Service for. And the free accommodation, and allowances, would help pay off our debts.

When sitting the Qualifying Tests at Oxford, and again soon after joining the Diplomatic Service, we had been obliged to take a language-aptitude test. The test involved learning Kurdish in an afternoon. It examined every aspect of aptitude (or otherwise) for learning foreign languages: aural as well as oral ability, written expression, grasp of grammar and so on. Foolishly, I had a glass of wine at a picnic in the park with my aunt just before the second test, on the grounds that it would improve my fluency. I was quite wrong, but my average mark over both tests was just good enough to suggest that I might be capable of learning what the FCO Training Department called Class I languages: essentially, Arabic, Chinese or Japanese. It didn't take me long to choose. My poor ear for pitch meant that I could not hope, so I thought, to master a tonal language such as Chinese or Japanese. But what tipped the balance was that I knew very little about the Far East, and a bit more about the Middle East, based mainly on my study of ancient history. I opted for Arabic, and was told that I would start at the Foreign Office's famous Middle East Centre for Arab Studies, or MECAS, in the village of Shemlan, above Beirut, in September 1978.

Three other contemporaries were selected for Arabic training. Others went off to learn Chinese, Japanese, Korean and Russian. About half of the entry managed to avoid hard language training and instead brushed up their French, or acquired German or Spanish, for European postings.

We had taken our first steps on the perpetual treadmill of diplomatic life: with the average posting lasting three or so years, you are always either speculating about your next posting or preparing for it. The sense of continual anticipation of working somewhere on something, or with someone, more interesting than your present job is what keeps many diplomats going – and what makes life such a let-down when the wheel finally stops turning.

That summer of 1978 I met up with an Oxford friend who had failed the Foreign Office entrance exam, and asked him what he was now doing. He was working as a rep for Thomson Holidays, 'on the basis', he said, 'that the work will be much the same as in the Diplomatic Service'. As I soon discovered, he wasn't far wrong.

Chapter 2

School for Spies

'Where did you learn such good Arabic?' asked the man in the suq. 'In Lebanon, at Shemlan above Beirut' was my answer. 'Ah,' with a knowing look, came the reply, 'the British spy school.'

For a generation of British diplomats and spies, such were the first words of tens of thousands of encounters across the Middle East, as the graduates of the Foreign Office's Middle East Centre for Arab Studies engaged, in Arabic, with real Arabs.

MECAS was set up in Jerusalem in 1944, as the end of the war approached. Its job was to teach British diplomats, spies, officers and other officials Arabic, and about the Middle East. Its first Chief Instructor was Jewish: Major Aubrey Evan of the British Army, later, as Abba Eban, Israel's UN Ambassador and Foreign Minister. In 1948, when Britain pulled out of Palestine, the school moved to Lebanon, eventually to a purpose-built mini-campus in the Christian village of Shemlan, in the mainly Druze-populated mountains above Beirut. It was the Egyptian ruler, Gamal Abdul Nasser, Colonel Nasser, who in the run-up to the Suez crisis of 1956 had dubbed MECAS the 'British spy school'. The name stuck. For thirty years, anyone of any education in the Middle East, and many of no education, knew of the British spy school, thanks to the free air time Nasser had given the institution.

Despite Nasser's flattery, the school was probably never quite as good as its reputation. It turned out Arabists with a good grasp of basic grammar and political and economic vocabulary. They could communicate with each other in the curious self-referential dialect they learned and practised in the village cafés of Mount Lebanon, and in the bars and suqs of Beirut. But once sent out into the wider Middle East they

19

faced the barrier confronting every student of Arabic: that, while written Arabic is more or less standardised across the Arab world, the spoken language varies widely, from country to country, and sometimes from region to region. Converting the ingratiating wheedle of Lebanese colloquial into words that worked in Aleppo, or Baghdad, or Cairo, let alone in Abu Dhabi, or Jeddah, or Kuwait, or Sana'a, or Tripoli, was harder work, usually never fully accomplished. Opening one's mouth, however, and speaking something that sounded like Arabic, was a start at least, and showed willing.

But in the summer of 1978 all that was ahead of me. I was proud to have been selected for MECAS, to have been chosen as a prospective member of the Foreign Office's cadre of Arabists – the 'camel corps' much abused by some of the department's Zionist detractors – an elite within an elite. And I was relieved that it had been decided that MECAS would definitively reopen that September, having suffered since 1975 a series of temporary closures caused by the Lebanese Civil War.

After the austerity of months in the salt mines of London, preparing for an overseas posting felt a bit like the run-up to Christmas. Once the posting had been confirmed, a letter from the FCO's Personnel Services Department arrived, describing the allowances we would receive overseas, and the advances of such allowances we would be given even before we left the United Kingdom. For me, aged twenty-three, with an overdraft dating back to university, it was unbelievably exciting.

The full list of Foreign Office overseas allowances was breathtaking. As minister resident in the Mediterranean, Harold Macmillan once complained that the two very distinguished diplomats advising him, Harold Caccia and Roger Makins, seemed obsessed by allowances and car entitlements. 'Why do diplomats never discuss anything except houses, furniture, motorcars, food, wine and money?' he wrote.* Reading the list one could see why allowances mattered so much to members of the Diplomatic Service, and to their spouses.

First, and most important for someone whose main means of transport in 1978 was a Honda 50cc motorcycle, was the interest-free Car

---

* Harold Macmillan, *War Diaries: Politics and War in the Mediterranean, January 1943– May 1945*, London: Macmillan, 1984, p. 491.

Loan. Provided you bought British, you were entitled to order a car tax-free and at a discount for diplomats, usually 15 per cent, and to run it in Britain for six months before taking it abroad. A complication for those posted to the Middle East was that makes such as Ford were subject to the Arab boycott, on the grounds that they were sold in Israel. But I wanted something racier than the Hillman Avengers which most young British diplomats then posted to the Arab world seemed to run. I opted for what I thought of as a Mini Cooper, even though, as my brother woundingly pointed out, the British Leyland Mini 1275 GT of 1978 was far from the original Cooper creation. The only colour available in the time in which I needed my car was what the British Leyland catalogue described as 'Reynard Metallic' – a sort of liquid light brown. When eventually I arrived in Shemlan, the MECAS Director immediately and cruelly described my beloved first motor as 'diarrhoea colour'. I was glad when my Mini was covered in the dust and dirt of Middle Eastern motoring.

Also of interest was the Climatic Clothing Allowance. In those days, diplomats posted to especially hot or cold countries were entitled to extra clothing allowances. Based on his experience travelling up and down the Gulf, Michael Hodge of the Republic of Ireland Department had recommended that I buy a set of washable nylon suits that could be worn after a night on a hanger in a hotel bathroom. I thought that, as a fast-stream officer, I was entitled to something grander. I ordered a lightweight sand-coloured suit from the tropical outfitters Airey & Wheeler of Savile Row. The suit turned out to be an expensive sartorial folly. It showed every mark, and I soon learned that Arabs expect any serious Westerner to wear a dark suit. But sporting my Airey & Wheeler extravagance in England that rainy summer I thought I looked the part of the young diplomat en route to the Middle East.

Even more welcome for an ex-student with little more than a kettle and some chipped mugs in the way of household goods was money for equipping my future Middle Eastern residence for representational purposes. The list of favoured suppliers issued by the Overseas Allowances Section of the Personnel Services Department recommended Thomas Goode of South Audley Street, W1, as a shop (if that is the right word for such an emporium) which offered good discounts for diplomatic orders. So there I went, in search of glasses and china, and found that, even at discounted Thomas Goode prices, my budget stretched only to half a dozen crystal tumblers and a remaindered, and incomplete, dinner service. I would have been better off at Habitat. I went round London discovering that, as the Treasury must have known, the reality of what the allowances would buy was much less than the promise. I remembered Trevor Mound's cautionary tale, of the first grammar school boy to have joined the Foreign Service fast stream, just after the war. In order to keep up appearances, and encouraged by some who should have known better, he had almost ruined himself by ordering a Lagonda for his first posting, to Buenos Aires, only to arrive in Argentina and find that all the supposed toffs in the Chancery were running around in Ford Populars.

Most of the 'representational' stuff I acquired that summer went straight into storage, to await shipping to my first substantive posting, somewhere – I didn't yet know where – in the Middle East, once MECAS was over.

The next task was actually getting yourself to post. Until only a few years ago, Diplomatic Service Regulations offered those travelling out to or back from postings a choice between what was called the Approved Route, and one or more Optional Routes. In 1978, the Approved Route for MECAS was by Middle East Airlines to Beirut, with an allowance for taxis at both ends. The Optional Routes were more exciting, providing, incredibly even in 1978, for train and sea travel. With two friends and colleagues who were also starting at MECAS in September, I decided that it would be fun to drive from London to Beirut. We would make our own ways to Turkey, and rendezvous in late August on top of the ancient citadel of Pergamon – now Bergama – on the Aegean coast north of Smyrna – now Izmir. With my brother as co-driver, I would travel via Paris (where we would meet friends) down to the heel of Italy. From there we would take the ferry from Brindisi to Patras (reliving my schoolboy classicist's journey eight years earlier) and drive up through Greece, before crossing the Bosphorus at Istanbul.

The Mini needed some mechanical attention to equip it for Arabia. I had not realised that poor-quality fuel in much of the Middle East meant that the famous 1275cc engine would have to be converted from high to low compression, by boring out the cylinders, very expensively. At the insistence of my worried mother, the garage also fitted a massive sump guard, to protect the underside of the low-slung transverse engine against bumps in the road. More powerful shock absorbers were installed. The car now looked ready for the Middle East equivalent of the Monte Carlo rally. In reality, the super-heavy sump guard dragged the car even lower, making for jarring encounters with even relatively small obstacles of the kind then found on most roads east of Trieste.

The journey out to Pergamon went smoothly enough. As a condition of our driving to Beirut, the Foreign Office had insisted that we call in at each British embassy en route to check that the deteriorating situation in Lebanon had not become so bad as to oblige us to turn back. I therefore dropped in at our embassies in Paris, Rome and Athens, obtaining glimpses of a grandeur I was to encounter later in my career. But no problem was reported. Passing through Greece the short-wave radio I had installed in the Mini relayed the signature of the Camp David accords, bringing peace between Israel and Egypt, but not between Israel and the Palestinians or its other Arab neighbours. I little guessed how they would dominate much of my diplomatic career.

The three cars met at Pergamon, exactly as planned. From there, we raced across Asia Minor in convoy, full of excited anticipation. My brother flew back from Antalya. The rest of us crossed into Syria, and went straight to Damascus, our first encounter with one of the greatest of Middle Eastern metropolises. After checking with the Embassy there, we headed almost due west up over the hills to the Lebanese frontier. Entering and leaving Syria, and entering Lebanon, we used what seemed like relics of a bygone age of international motoring, the huge orange customs Carnets de Passage obtained from the AA in London, guaranteeing that our cars would be re-exported. Frontier formalities took ages, a succession of guichets and tickets and stamps and fees, all resulting in passports proudly adorned with more stamps (with postage stamps affixed) than they had gathered traversing the whole of western Europe.

Once over the border, in Lebanon, the atmosphere changed. The roads were lined with Syrian Army vehicles, Soviet Bloc equipment of every variety, wheeled and tracked, armed and unarmed, armoured and soft-skinned. Sitting and squatting in, on and under them were hordes of feckless Arab conscripts, the ballast of a Middle Eastern army, thirsty, hungry, bored and occasionally frightened. We remembered the advice of our Embassy in Damascus: never ever look Arab soldiers or policemen in the eye. Descending into the Beka'a Valley (the northern extension of the Great Rift Valley), and then climbing the winding road back up the eastern slopes of Mount Lebanon, we passed through checkpoint after checkpoint, manned by Syrian soldiers and military police, and, more sinisterly, the goons of Assad's intelligence service, the much feared *mukhabarat* in their trademark cheap safari suits.

And then, over the top of the mountains, with the Mediterranean glistening before us, and Beirut below, we swung left and south off the main road which led down to the city, and took the route along the ridge, through the little town of Suq al-Gharb (or 'market of the west') to the village of Shemlan. There, in the centre of the village, a great white sign proclaimed, in English and Arabic, 'Middle East Centre for Arab Studies'.

MECAS was neither a school nor a university, but it had elements of both. Its Director was one of the shyest, and cleverest, of Foreign Office Arabists, who would go on to become ambassador to Yemen and then to Qatar. Julian Walker's place in the history of the modern Middle East had already been assured by the part he had played, as a young assistant political agent in the Gulf, in marking out (in stones, it was said) the border between the Trucial States (later the United Arab Emirates) and Saudi Arabia. His Director of Studies was a more flamboyant character, a sort of Scottish intellectual commando whose academic expertise was the Tuareg dialects of Tunisia. Douglas Galloway came from St Andrews, but he was one of those universal Scotsmen who seem to pop up in all the most exotic corners of the globe, trading, teaching and generally flying the flag for their beloved homeland. He loved Arabic and the Arabs, and his enthusiasms were infectious. The only other Diplomatic Service officer on the MECAS staff was an administration officer. His day job, of administering the staff and pupils, and the buildings, seemed almost incidental to the fun he was having, starting mainly in the MECAS bar.

The other pupils on the Long Course (a year until the Intermediate Arabic exam, and then a further six months before the Higher) were a mixed bunch, in every sense. The core was made up of my fellow fast-stream Arabists and me. Back then, the idea of any of us ever actually becoming an ambassador seemed impossibly remote. But in time we all did, using our Arabic too, heading embassies in Amman (two of us), Baghdad, Beirut, Cairo, Kabul, Kuwait, Riyadh and Tel Aviv. One of us ended up as ambassador in Brasilia, another in Rome. One of our main-stream colleagues – and the best Arabist of our year – became Britain's last ambassador to Qadhafi's Libya.

Others on the course included a handful of young spies pretending to be diplomats. There was a group of main-stream members of the Diplomatic Service. They were rather older and more experienced than us, and had been selected for Hard Language Training as they approached mid-career. The FCO would extract real value from their Arabic, working them hard as consuls and vice consuls and commercial and management officers – the backbone of our posts across the Middle East – for the next two decades. Australia, New Zealand and Japan also sent students to MECAS, as did one or two of Britain's more inter-national banks. Partners – mostly women in those days – were encour-aged to join in the lessons and, if they paid, sit the exams. Mixed in background and ability we certainly were, but united in our eager antic-ipation of working lives to be spent in and on the Arab Middle East.

Our teachers were the most interesting element of the MECAS community. Some were Lebanese, some Palestinian, mostly they were Christians, from many of the different Churches which populate the Levant. The Palestinians in particular had known tough times, leaving homes and possessions behind in the disaster of 1948. The Lebanese had more recent tales of suffering. But few of our teachers let the bitter-ness of their personal experience of what Britain and the West had failed to do for the Arabs of the Middle East infuse their teaching. Instead, they each exuded real pride in their language and literature, and were eager for us to run linguistically almost before we could walk. Like all good teachers, they found fulfilment in the achievement of their pupils, for whom they showed genuine affection, and unlimited patience.

We struggled. First with the alphabet, then with the rules of an unfamiliar grammar and a strange new vocabulary unrelated to any language any of us already knew. For me, as a recently lapsed classicist, the elegance of Arabic grammar was a delight. It was learning and relearning lists of words that was such hard work. The effort to produce even half-elegant script reminded me of the humiliations of learning to write, some twenty years earlier. But two things gave us hope that we would one day master what in those early days seemed like an impossible language. First were the course materials, tried and tested on a generation of Foreign Office Arabists: the *MECAS Word List*, the *MECAS Grammar* and *The Way Prepared* – a set of fifty political texts of graduated difficulty, showing their age even in 1978, but giving us clues to how the West's relations with Arabia had evolved since, it seemed, the Balfour Declaration of 1917. The second comfort was the logical key to a Semitic language: the root system. We marvelled at how three consonants could be used to derive every noun, verb and adjective associated with a particular human activity. The root for 'writing' for example – *k, t, b* – enabled you to find the words for everything from a book to a library, and much else in between. The twelve forms of the verb made the active and passive voices of prep-school Latin seem lame: Arabic verbs could be engineered to operate reflexively, causatively, intensively, co-operatively, among other things. A further delight, half remembered from ancient Greek, was the number between singular and plural: the dual, usually denoted by the suffix *-ain*. Thus, the root for 'ruling', or 'possession', is *m, l, k*. To rule is *malik*, a king is the active participle *maalik*, and two kings are *maalikain*.

Being paid, much more than we had received in London, to study all this in a beautiful village in the mountains above Beirut made us all feel incredibly lucky. So did the expeditions we mounted at weekends, idling in the bookshops of Beirut, swimming in the ice-cold mountain river at Jisr al-Qadi, marvelling at the Ottoman delights of the summer palace at Beiteddin, relaxing with wonderful fresh food and Lebanese wine in the Palmyra Hotel at Ba'albek after visiting the massive temple of the Sun God.

But there was trouble in Paradise. As each of us was to see, at different times and in different places in our careers, little in the modern

Middle East is as delightful as it may at first seem. Beneath the sun-bleached surface lie deep wounds. Conflicts past are always present. The sand is too often stained with blood.

And so within days of our arrival the tensions between the parties to Lebanon's civil war started to rise again. After a few weeks, we were told that we could travel only in tightly restricted areas. In what was to become a wearily familiar ritual in later years, we found ourselves receiving a daily security briefing. We started to hear small-arms fire at night, distant at first, and then disturbingly close. The Syrian soldiers manning the checkpoint in the village snapped from sleepy insouciance to dangerous menace. They detained some of our students, briefly and for no real reason. Israeli aircraft began to buzz Beirut, breaking the sound barrier high above us, just to remind everyone north of the Litani River who was top dog, and top gun. Then the Syrian Katyusha multiple-launch rocket batteries (known as 'Stalin's Organs') in the valley behind the mountain started to fire over us, towards east Beirut. The huge oil tanks in the port caught fire, sending a fat column of thick black smoke high into the air.

Suddenly, the Foreign Office's judgement that it had been safe to reopen MECAS looked wildly over-optimistic. We worried not about our safety, but that we would be forced back to London. Absurdly, we petitioned Britain's impossibly elegant Ambassador in Beirut, Sir Peter Wakefield, saying we wanted to stick it out. But we were told we had to go. MECAS would close, without announcement, and re-form in London. Everyone, including the teachers, would be evacuated. We were bitterly disappointed, but the tide of violence rising rapidly around us had a compelling logic of its own.

And thus, almost five weeks to the day after we had driven up the mountain, we were driving down again, this time in a longer convoy, adorned with a Union flag (for safety, we said, but really for our morale), before racing up the Beka'a Valley to the northern crossing point into Syria. MECAS closed, with a whimper, never to reopen. Its spirit lingers on, in an alumni association and in the memories of a generation of British and allied Arabists. Somehow, our sudden surreptitious departure from Shemlan seemed a kind of metaphor in a minor key for the recessional in which we would play a part for the following thirty years.

We made it back to London in record time, and were soon regrouping in the ramshackle premises the Foreign Office found for us – Palace Chambers above Westminster tube station, already condemned for demolition to make way for the new Parliamentary building. It was there that over the next fifteen months we finished our formal Arabic training. It was there that we mounted a morale-raising Christmas pantomime only a month after our return. It was from there that some of us heard Airey Neave's* car explode as he drove up the ramp of the Commons car park in March 1979. And it was there that we wondered what difference Mrs Thatcher and her Government would make to our working lives, as she took office just five weeks later.

From Palace Chambers we were twice sent out on 'language breaks', to Syria. On arrival in Damascus, by British Airways Super VC10, we were each given £200 or so in dirty Syrian pounds, and told to go away for three weeks. The only conditions were that we were to keep away from each other, and to talk (and think) nothing but Arabic. Within Syria we could travel where we liked. How times have changed.

And that it is exactly what we did, from Bosra's black basalt rocks in the south to Palmyra's wonders in the eastern desert, down the Euphrates to Deir al-Zur not far from the Iraqi border, north from Damascus through Hama and Homs to Aleppo, west to the ultimate Crusader castle of Krak des Chevaliers and to the shabby port city of Lattakia. We saw the wonders of Syria – Greek, Roman, Nabatean, Persian, Arab and Ottoman. I at least learned the joys of solo travel. My dread of being lonely was quite unfounded: the problem was getting time to myself. We lived and ate and dreamed Arabic, replaying the formulae at the start of this chapter a hundred times. And, while the language was Arabic, the people we met were far from being only Arabs: we came across Armenians and Kurds, Circassians and Turks, and started to understand that since 1917 the only significant change to Ottoman imperial demography had been the establishment in Palestine of the Jewish state.

---

* Airey Neave MP was one of Mrs Thatcher's close advisers in Opposition. He was mortally wounded by an Irish terrorist bomb just before 3 p.m. on 30 March 1979.

My favourite memories are of long sessions in the suq in Aleppo discussing linguistics with an Armenian jeweller called John; and of a ride on the Hejaz railway south from the great terminus in Damascus, steam-hauled in the same rolling stock T. E. Lawrence would have attacked only sixty years earlier.

It was from Palace Chambers too that we went across St James's Park to sit, and pass, in the summer of 1979 the Foreign Office Intermediate Arabic Examination and then in the spring of 1980, with more of a struggle and less distinction, the Higher. We translated written Arabic into English, and English into Arabic; we drafted letters in Arabic; we were made to summarise news broadcasts in Arabic; we acted as interpreter for a fictional British minister. We didn't yet know how realistic, and relevant, those ordeals by examination would be.

And it was in Palace Chambers, just before Christmas 1979, that we were told to which Middle East post each of us was to be sent: Abu Dhabi, Khartoum, Kuwait and, for me, a spell of further study in Alexandria supposed to turn me into that year's 'super-Arabist', before starting in the Embassy in Cairo in the late summer of 1980. I could not have been happier, or more grateful.

And so, in March 1980, exams behind me, Heavy Baggage shipped, Unaccompanied Air Freight despatched, I set off again for the Middle East in my much loved Mini. Again, I travelled via Paris. Again, my long-suffering brother kindly acted as co-driver for most of the way. But this time, on reaching Italy, I turned left, to Venice, and took the ferry from there down the Adriatic and across the Mediterranean to Alexandria.

Arriving by sea in Egypt was an unforgettable experience. As I drove my car up the ramp out of the ferry's dark hold into the blazing noon-day sun and on to the quayside, it was as though I had crossed from the calm of the First World into the boiling chaos of the Third. As indeed I had. Never in my life had I seen so many varieties of *Homo sapiens* crowded together in a single space. The dockside was heaving with humanity. Policemen, customs officers, soldiers, sailors, businessmen, bedouin, hawkers and brokers, sellers of souvenirs and refreshments, Africans and Libyans, and, everywhere, hordes of Egyptian *fellaheen* (or peasants). And then there was the noise: hooting, shouting, spitting, yelling, in Arabic mainly, but also in other languages I couldn't recognise, let alone understand. It was complete chaos, or so it seemed.

After only a few yards, the press of people brought the car to a stop. I was utterly lost. I climbed out, and, blinking and fearful, looked around. And then, out of the crowd, appeared a balding Egyptian in an electric-blue safari suit, swinging a black plastic briefcase about him and sweating heavily. His cry of 'Mister Shiraard, Mister Shiraard' could just be heard. It was Magdi, the 'Management Assistant' from the British Consulate-General in Alexandria, come to rescue me and, more important, my car. Magdi was my first – but far from last – experience of a phenomenon found right across the Middle East and beyond: the 'fixer'. No career member of the Diplomatic Service ever asks what exactly Magdi and his kind do, or how they do it. The Bribery Act 2008 now bans Britons from buying the 'facilitation' services they provide. But in Alexandria in 1980 all that matters is that Magdi is there to do it. In return for small but significant 'administrative payments', always in cash, and often in dollars, permits are procured, licences issued, telephones connected, passports stamped, diplomatic bags despatched inviolate, and goods and people extracted undamaged from customs. Later Magdi even obtained an Egyptian driving licence for me, for five Egyptian pounds.

For the next three hours, I watched in wonder, as Magdi moved from desk to desk, hut to hut, acquiring the stamps and papers and permits which would in the end allow me to drive my car out of the port and into my future life. Rolled-up dollar bills slipped out of his hand as cards come down from a conjuror's cuff. After every port of call, he returned solicitously to where he had deposited me, on a shaded bench, to ply me with sweet tea and dirty tap water. Sometimes in Arabia it feels as though the Ottoman Empire's most significant, and baneful, modern legacy is the *jumruk* – the great racketeering enterprise which calls itself the Customs.

Eventually, we emerged. Following Magdi's battered car, which betrayed both its Russian design and its Egyptian manufacture, I rolled down the Corniche and up to the Cecil Hotel along one side of a seafront square. There I was to spend my first nights in Egypt. Before then, however, I had to introduce myself to the man who would be responsible for me – in modern jargon my line manager – during my four months of advanced language training: Her Britannic Majesty's Consul-General at Alexandria.

In 1980 the British Consulate-General in Alexandria was a shadow of its former self. And, in a continuing painful reminder of imperial retreat, that former self, the derelict shell of the original Consulate, a classical palace wrecked by an angry mob during the Six Day War in 1967, stood overlooking the square in which the Hotel Cecil lay. But the modern Consulate, on the higher ground of the pleasant inner suburb of Roushdi, had its own history too. For what had once been the residence of the Consul-General, with gardens to match, now contained homes and offices for him and his deputy, plus flats for the Ambassador and Naval Attaché from Cairo when they visited Egypt's second city and sometime summer capital.

The Consul-General, Jeffrey Greaves, and his wife Joyce could not have been kinder. They loved Alexandria, and Alexandria loved them. They had me to dinner many times in the next few months, and introduced me to a range of interesting Alexandrines. It was in seeing them in action that I realised how lucky the Diplomatic Service is to have in its ranks men and women who, in the past at least, joined straight from school, and put in long years of service in gruelling jobs and tough places. They may never be formally appointed ambassadors, but when, as with the Greaveses in Alexandria, they are called upon to represent Britain, they do so with quiet distinction, mixing with mayors and members of parliament, and academic worthies and whatever passes for local high society, in ways that reflect credit on them and their government. The Foreign Office never quite repays the compliment, but at least in places like Alexandria they are well housed and, overall, well rewarded, not least by the job itself.

It was through Jeffrey Greaves that I found the man who was to make my time in Alexandria: Ahmed al-Sheikh was a member of the English Department of the University of Alexandria. Greaves sent me to see Ahmed, to establish who in the university might be prepared to teach me. Ahmed said that he would do it himself. For the next four months, he and I travelled the byways of modern Egyptian literature. We read plays and poetry written in Egyptian colloquial. But we went further than that. Like most of his generation of Egyptian intellectuals, Ahmed was a Nasserite. He told me what he thought, of Sadat, of the Camp David accords, of Britain and America, and of Russia. Studying with him was a journey through a wonderland of unfamiliar ideas, and words. So too was the visit to the University Library. I had visions of the Great Library of Alexandria of antiquity, but instead found a dusty warehouse, with books shelved not by subject or author, but in order of acquisition.

And it was Ahmed who helped find the family with whom I was to lodge. After a few nights in the Cecil, I had decamped, several miles along the Corniche, to the Swiss Cottage Hotel, a cheap imitation of its namesake in north London, high on a cliff above Stanley Bay. But I told Ahmed and everyone I met that I really wanted to live with an Egyptian family, in order not only to convert my Levantine colloquial into something more Egyptian, but also to understand more of what, in the 1830s, Edward Lane had called the manners and customs of the modern Egyptians.* After a few days, Ahmed introduced me to the Abu Awad family.

Mr Abu Awad was in his late fifties, and, as he told me more than once, had married 'beneath' him. He and his much larger and rather younger wife and four children (two boys and two girls aged between fourteen and eight) were crammed into a tiny two-bedroom flat overlooking the east–west tramway which runs the length of Alexandria's fifteen-mile Corniche, a block or so in from the sea. Just up the street from them was what had once been one of the Middle East's finest educational institutions, Victoria College. Founded as a public school on the English model, staffed by schoolmasters from Britain, it had a proud history. King Hussein of Jordan had studied there, before going on to Harrow. So had Omar Sharif, and a generation of Arab leaders from across the Middle East. But, nationalised by Nasser, and renamed Victory ('Nasr' in Arabic) College, it too was a shadow of its former self.

But Victory/Victoria College was a world away from the Abu Awads. Mr Abu Awad spent most of the week in Port Said, where he worked in

---

* E. W. Lane, *An account of the manners and customs of the modern Egyptians*, London: Charles Knight, 1836.

the import and export of what he described as 'popular handkerchiefs'. He had learned some elementary English working as an interpreter for a Sergeant Macpherson of the Royal Military Police during Britain's occupation of the Canal Zone, which had finally ended in June 1956. The origins of his command of colloquial English became clear later. One day, pointing to his children pushing and shoving each other on the sofa on the other side of their small sitting room, Mr Abu Awad told me solemnly: 'Shiraard, I am very proud of my buggers.' It took me a few moments to work out that, as Mr Abu Awad had ridden round Ismailia in the Military Police jeep listening to Sergeant Macpherson speaking British military English, the only term he had heard for 'child' had been 'little bugger'. Mr Abu Awad would have been mortified if he had known the true meaning of the word.

Despite Mr Abu Awad's frequent absences in Port Said, the family were prepared to accept a young Christian bachelor lodging in the second of their two bedrooms, in exchange for what would be for them quite large sums of cash. I didn't realise, when I first met the family, that my presence would mean the parents plus the four children sleeping in one double bed in the second bedroom. I would have been more embarrassed if I hadn't done so much to help them.

There was plenty else I didn't realise when I agreed to move in with the Abu Awads. There were the little things, like managing for four months without lavatory paper,* or being obliged to spend most of my time in the flat wearing what the Abu Awads had concluded were my fashionably striped old English pyjamas. There was the constant noise. I soon discovered that, if I tried to shut the door of my bedroom, to have some quiet time on my own, a worried member of the family would come rushing in, to see what was the matter. The hours were difficult. I used to creep out of the flat soon after 9 a.m., leaving the rest of the family (unless Mr Abu Awad was home) asleep, for my lessons with Ahmed al-Sheikh. I would return at what I regarded as lunchtime, but we seldom ate before three. After a siesta, I would usually be required to drive Mrs Abu Awad, and several of her equally

---

* I had read that Arabs cleaned themselves with water or, in the desert, with a flat stone, but somehow hadn't realised this would apply in a Western-style flat in Alexandria.

large cousins, around town, making calls on innumerable friends and relations. The sight of us all squashed into my Mini would have caused amusement if any Westerner had caught sight of us. But, for lower-middle-class Egyptians in those days, to have the use of a car was too precious not to be exploited whenever possible. Such journeys round town, often stuck in traffic, with no air conditioning, took up most of the evening. Usually we would be back home by eleven. We would spend the next two hours watching the interminable soap operas and slushy feature films pumped out on Egyptian television. Dinner would come only when Egyptian TV closed down for the night, at 1 a.m. I would fall into bed at 2 a.m., utterly exhausted.

Although we ate meat only once a week, I found the food surprisingly good. I came to love *ful*, Egyptian beans. The only dish I could not stand was a greasy glutinous soup called *mulookhia*. As with everything else though, there was no escape from accepting a plateful and eating it: anything less would have been taken by the family as proof of mortal illness. Saying I did not like the viscous green slime in front of me was never an option. The other culinary ordeal came on Friday mornings. After Mr Abu Awad had been to the mosque, he and I would go to the market and buy a fish called *bolti* found in the fresh(ish) waters of the Delta. This was regarded as a great delicacy. As the permanent guest of honour, my standard weekly treat was to be invited, with the whole family watching, to suck the snot-like brain of the fish out of the back of its severed head.

I learned more that spring and summer in Alexandria than I can ever record. My classical training, my student struggles with Lawrence Durrell's *Alexandria Quartet*, my acquaintance through Durrell with his 'old poet', the modern Greek C. P. Cavafy, the knowledge that E. M. Forster had spent much of the First War in Alexandria, as a Red Cross volunteer, trying to seduce the conductor on the tram to Montazah, while writing the best of all guides* to the ancient metropolis – all these added to the interest and attraction of the great city on the sea. When I could, at weekends, I would get away from the Abu Awads. I made contact with a handful of other British students of Arabic. With them,

---

* E. M. Forster, *Alexandria: A History and a Guide*, London: Haag, 1982.

I visited Alexandria's gem of an archaeological museum, full of Greco-Roman treasures. We went down the catacombs, and east along the coast to King Farouk's fantastic palace at Montazah and beyond to the fish restaurants on the beach at Abu Kir, overlooking the bay where Napoleon's eastern adventure had come to grief at Nelson's hands. We went west to El Alamein, walking the well-kept lawns of the Commonwealth War Cemetery. We marvelled at the Italian ossuary and the cemetery in the style of a schloss in which the Afrika Korps were buried. We ate calamari and drank Egyptian Stella beer in the Spitfire Bar, where the Eighth Army had been only just over thirty years earlier. We met the waiter in the Union Club who claimed to have served Monty, and who told us about Mary's House, out of bounds to other ranks. We found, in the Greek Consulate-General, Cavafy's death mask, and in a café near by met some Greeks who had known him. We persuaded the ancient custodian of the great deserted synagogue, whose Torah scrolls had been sent to Oxford, to let us look inside. We stood where the great Pharos (or lighthouse) had once stood, a Wonder of its World. Outside the little Anglican church at Stanley Bay on Sunday, we discussed the news of President Carter's disastrous effort to rescue the American Embassy hostages from Tehran, and of the SAS's successful raid on the Iranian Embassy in London.

Alexandria was – is – a palimpsest, one of those ancient manuscripts used and reused by civilisation after civilisation, in script after script. A city of all religions and of none, it had known great wealth, most recently when cotton was king, but was now crowded, busy and poor.

Unconsciously, the varieties of the religious experience in the Abu Awad household caught Alexandria's essence. Mr Abu Awad was a devout and observant Muslim, as the *zabeeb*, or raisin, where his fore-head hit the ground was meant to tell the world, and me. He prayed, ostentatiously, five times a day, taking up much of the tiny sitting room to do so. He had been to Mecca and Medina on the Hajj.

Naturally the rest of the family were respectable Muslims too. But, unknown to her husband, once a week Mrs Abu Awad asked me to take her and a cousin to one of Alexandria's many Catholic churches, St Rita's, Alexandria. Neither Mrs Abu Awad nor I knew that Catholics regard St Rita as the patron saint of hopeless causes. So that wasn't why

Mrs Abu Awad lit several candles on each weekly visit to the shrine, before kneeling in silence, and presumably praying.

But the other religious practice in the Abu Awad household was more unexpected. One day, on my return from my Arabic lessons, I found in the poky little kitchen of the flat three cardboard boxes, containing, respectively, two live pigeons, two live rabbits and two live chickens. I assumed that we were preparing a celebratory meal of some kind. But then Mr Abu Awad insisted that I went with him to a tea house near by, for no apparent reason. We sat there, for an hour, and then for another hour, with nothing much to say to each other. Eventually, Mr Abu Awad said it was time to go home. And then I discovered why he had wanted me out of the way. The livestock I had encountered earlier were now all dead, with their throats cut. An old man in a skull cap was presiding over some interminable ceremony, in which the blood of the dead birds and rabbits was sprinkled over the threshold of the flat, and smeared over Mrs Abu Awad's ample chest. Much to her husband's embarrassment, I was witnessing the last stages of a pre-Christian, pre-Muslim *zarr*, or exorcism, designed to expel from the flat the evil spirits held responsible for some unnamed malady from which Mrs Abu Awad suffered.

For me, those three varieties of religious experience – Muslim, Christian and animist – in a single Arab household captured my Alexandria. It was the best of introductions to the modern Middle East.

Chapter 3

Death on the Nile

I knew I shouldn't have been watching television. As so often, I had promised myself I would be good, and work, but not quite yet. I wanted to see the big parade, to spot the tanks and guns and rockets and trucks in Egypt's armoury. I wanted to see who was on the saluting base with President Sadat, as he and his ministers and generals celebrated the eighth anniversary of his great and only – the Arabs' great and only – military victory over Israel, the Yom Kippur or Ramadan War of October 1973.

I couldn't go in person, but the Ambassador was there, and so were the three defence attachés – military, naval and air – in tropical uniform. As the Embassy press officer, I had, however, been allowed the only television inside the secure area of the Cairo Chancery, and so I could watch the great day unfolding in grainy black-and-white, from the privacy of my office. It was better than redrafting yet again the Embassy's Leading Personality Reports for Egypt. Or updating the Calendar of (past) Events every British Embassy was obliged to send to London each January, but which few in the FCO ever read.

It was 6 October 1981. The television showed lines of lumbering Soviet 6x6 trucks, with rows of soldiers sitting upright in the back, moving past the saluting base. Suddenly, the camera lurched and dipped away. The sound, of bands and truck engines and aircraft overhead, went dead. For twenty seconds or so, though it seemed much longer, the only image was a silent still of the ground beneath the cameraman's feet. Then the Egyptian equivalent of the test card came up, followed five minutes later by archival propaganda footage of Egypt's past military triumphs, with patriotic music to match.

I knew something was wrong, but not how wrong. It could just have been the usual technical difficulties which seemed to plague any outside broadcast in Egypt thirty years ago. But it could have been something more. There was no way of finding out quickly. Mobile phones hardly existed. Landlines were poor. In any case, whom would I call? I wandered along the Chancery corridor, and told one of the other young diplomats what I had seen – or, rather, not seen.

Then I struck lucky. The ancient telephone in my little office jumped, and its bell rang. The veteran Embassy switchboard operator said a Mr Wright wanted to speak to me, urgently. It was Jonathan Wright, of Reuters. Jonathan had been at the parade, but was phoning from a building near by. All he knew was that there had been an attack on the Presidential reviewing stand, by a group of soldiers. They had jumped off one of the trucks, before charging the saluting base, heading straight for the President and those around him. Several people had been killed and injured. Sadat had been wounded, possibly quite badly. Others too had been hit. All was now chaos. Jonathan assumed that the Ambassador and his three defence attachés were on their way back to the Embassy.

I thanked Jonathan for what turned out to be the scoop of my diplomatic career. I rushed straight to the office of the Embassy's number two, Tony Reeve, and told him what I knew. He said at once that we needed to warn London, pending the Ambassador's return. For the first, and last, time in my diplomatic career, I drafted a FLASH telegram: 'Sadat wounded at October War parade. Ambassador believed safe. Further reporting to follow.' Tony approved it, and it was rushed upstairs, for encryption and then transmission by the Embassy communicators. A FLASH telegram took precedence over all other cable traffic, and was supposed to be delivered instantly, at whatever time of day or night it arrived. On a Tuesday afternoon, our cable took a sleepy London by complete surprise.

Within an hour or so, the Ambassador and the three attachés had arrived back at the office, hot, tired and still in shock. We gathered in the Ambassador's office. Everyone was on edge. Without warning, a heavy metal roller shutter dropped down, with a loud bang. Not hesitating for a second, the Air Attaché dived under the Ambassador's conference table, yelling, 'Get down! Take cover!', only to crawl shamefacedly back out a couple of minutes later when he realised what had caused the noise.

The Ambassador described what he had seen at the parade. The soldiers leaping off the truck, and charging at the main stand, emptying their Kalashnikovs as they ran. Sadat had been hit: of that there could be no doubt. John Woods, the First Secretary at the Australian Embassy, whom many of us knew well, had been badly wounded. The Israeli Ambassador, Moshe Sasson, had been pushed to the ground so hard by his bodyguards that they had – it later emerged – broken several of his ribs.

We soon established that the President had been flown by helicopter to the Military Hospital south of Cairo, with Madame Sadat at his side. The US Ambassador rang ours to say that the Americans believed that Sadat was badly wounded but stable. We reported this to an increasingly worried London, now starting to react to reports on the agency tapes.

But the Americans were wrong. Sadat was already dead, and had probably been so since the first moments of the attack. He had had over thirty AK-47 rounds pumped into him. His Vice President, Hosni Mubarak, had survived, and so had the rest of the senior leadership. Later that evening, Egyptian television carried a formal statement, announcing Sadat's death, and that Mubarak had taken over as acting president.

In 1981 Egypt was still basking in the warm afterglow of the Camp David accords of 1978, and the American-orchestrated Western approval that had accompanied Egypt's one-sided peace with Israel. In 1977 Sadat had broken the mould of the Arab–Israel dispute by flying to Jerusalem. He had become the first Arab leader to make peace with the Zionist enemy. But he had taken the biggest threat to Israel out of the fight without securing anything for the Palestinians other than continuing talks on autonomy. Three years later, American, Arab and Israeli negotiators were struggling to turn those words into reality – as they still are, more than three decades on.

Deep down, many of us thought that through his violent death Sadat had paid the price for that peace and, at least as important, for the love affair with America, and with American and Western ways, which had accompanied his accommodation with Israel. There had been many examples of increasingly pharaonic, not to say eccentric, behaviour as Egypt's leader lost touch with his long-suffering people. For me, and probably for millions of desperately poor Egyptians, the low point had been Frank Sinatra singing at a fashion show for the President's wife, before the floodlit Pyramids. Another symptom of Sadat's grandiose style had been the live broadcast, on prime-time television, of three wretched Egyptian professors of English literature examining Madame Sadat on her recently submitted doctoral thesis on Shelley. What the *fellaheen* made of it I never found out; but the Cairo intelligentsia had plenty to say about the very high mark her treatise had received. Sadat's decision to offer the Shah of Iran refuge in Cairo when he fled Tehran in 1979 was a gesture of quixotic kindness that did him no good at all with ordinary Egyptian Muslims. Today there are roughly twice as many Egyptians as when I served in Cairo thirty years ago. But then, as now, after a second Egyptian revolution, their priorities are the same: work, security and the dignity of being able to choose how they are governed and how they express their faith.

Sadat's funeral was not, however, the time for negative reflections. Solidarity had to be shown. Western politicians were falling over each other to attend an event boycotted by almost the whole of the rest of Arab world.

I was plunged into making arrangements for the first of four funerals for Arab heads of state I was to witness in my diplomatic career.* The British delegation selected itself: the Prince of Wales, who had visited Egypt on honeymoon only a few weeks earlier; the Foreign Secretary, Lord Carrington; and, to represent the Opposition, the former Prime Minister and Foreign Secretary Jim Callaghan, himself a recent visitor to Egypt.

But, as always in the modern Middle East, we were outgunned by the Americans: three US presidents – Nixon, Ford and Carter – led an American delegation hundreds strong, in which President Reagan's first Secretary of State, General Alexander Haig, cut a relatively minor figure.

---

* Anwar Sadat of Egypt, October 1981; King Hassan of Morocco, July 1999; President Hafez al-Assad of Syria, June 2000; King Fahd of Saudi Arabia, August 2005.

Not to be outdone, the Israelis sent their Prime Minister, Menachem Begin, and many other senior Israeli admirers of the late President. Typically, Begin's attendance was complicated by the fact that, as the funeral took place on the Jewish Sabbath, his religious views meant that he could use no mechanical device, including cars. He had to walk everywhere, creating nightmare difficulties for those charged with keeping the hated Israeli leader safe.

Our delegation had arrived in an RAF VC10 the evening before. They had their own minor dramas. Sadat had awarded both the Prince and the Princess of Wales the Order of the Nile, First Class, when they had visited Egypt on their honeymoon in August 1981. Sadat's funeral would be just the occasion to wear this decoration, out of respect for the late President. But Prince Charles found that his valet had packed the Princess's insignia, not his. Worse still, the valet had forgotten to bring a ceremonial sword to go with HRH's naval tropical-dress uniform. Our Naval Attaché spent the evening frantically buffing up his own long-neglected sword. The next day, no one important seemed to notice when the heir to the British throne appeared at the funeral wearing the insignia of the equivalent of a Dame Commander of the Order of the Nile.

The funeral was chaos, but satisfactory chaos, as most big Arab funerals need to be: somehow the pushing and shoving, and sweating and waiting, are all part of the liturgy of respect for the departed. Lesser men do not have a press of hundreds or thousands at their obsequies.

Our Ambassador decided that the Death of Sadat was worthy of a formal despatch to London, to be printed and circulated, on special blue paper, around all Foreign Office posts and departments, and across Whitehall too. Flatteringly, he asked me to have a go at the first draft, which I did, with relish. I cannot now remember how much of my effort survived. But I can take credit for the pretentious final line, from Lucretius: 'Tantum religio potuit suadere malorum' (Such is the evil that can be brought about by religion), applied by the Roman poet to the sacrifice of Iphigenia, which was supposed to appease the gods and allow the Greek fleet to sail for Troy. The previous Foreign Secretary, David Owen, had banned the use of foreign languages in diplomatic reporting, as pompous and old fashioned (he was right, of course). But we broke the rule for Sadat. Paradoxically, the Foreign Secretary, Lord Carrington, later confessed to the Ambassador that an expensive education hadn't equipped him to decrypt the vital phrase, and that he had had to ask for help from private secretaries who had been more diligent students of dead languages.

At about the same time, the Ambassador sent a telegram offering a pen portrait of Hosni Mubarak, and an assessment of the prospects for his Presidency. We reported that Mubarak had been a loyal and competent deputy to his larger-than-life leader. We recorded the nicknames Egyptians gave him – 'Tefal', because something (we didn't know what) didn't stick, and 'La Vache Qui Rit', based on a popular TV ad for the cheese, featuring a yes-man to whom Egyptians compared Sadat's loyal Vice President. The Ambassador concluded that Mubarak's limited political and other abilities meant that he was unlikely to last more than six months as president. He would be a transitional figure, before a new strong man emerged.

I had started my job in Cairo, just over a year earlier, in late July 1980. It was soon Ramadan, and many people, including the Ambassador, were away. The quiet heat of summer gave me time to settle in. My first priority was to find a flat. I quickly did, in the once smart district of Zamalek, which occupied much of the island of Gezira (meaning 'island') in the Nile. The flat was on the first floor of a grimy block built in Cairo's modern prime, in the 1930s. It was not slick, but it did the job that I, as a bachelor, wanted it to do: to provide good spaces for entertaining my guests, and for having visitors from London to stay. The furniture was reproduction Empire, what we called Louis Farouk. There were ceiling fans in the main rooms, plus loud and noisy wall-mounted air conditioners there and in every bedroom – this soon became the subject of comment among the Embassy wives, as at that time third secretaries were supposed to have only one air conditioner, in the main bedroom, and one other in the guest room, and no others. Everything was covered in dust and, at times, sand. A balcony gave a sideways-on view of the Nile.

I was delighted, and even more so when, aged twenty-five, I found myself looked after by an elderly cook cum houseboy (known in Egypt as a *suffragi*) and an almost equally ancient maid. The former, known as Abdul since his days with the Eighth Army, was a Nubian, and carried a faded photograph of Mr Churchill in the breast pocket of his *galabia*. Like Mr Abu Awad, Abdul could speak a few unprintable words of British military English. At 7 a.m. every day except Friday he produced porridge, and a full cooked breakfast. Lunch, served when I returned from the Embassy at 2.30 p.m., was always three courses: a heavy soup, meat or fish and fried or boiled vegetables, and then pudding, usually with custard. I began rapidly to put on weight, something corrected only when I married the next year. Abdul could also do a good dinner party, even, as one Embassy wag suggested, ordering up the guests. But his fondness for the dregs of the wine bottles made his performance, and that of his Sudanese friends drafted in for such occasions, increasingly erratic as the evening progressed. Once, when the Embassy got rid of its emergency stock of British Army 'compo' rations, Abdul asked me to bring him a ten-man pack: all he wanted was the British military Spam, remembered fondly from forty years earlier. Poor Abdul, and all the other *suffragis* in the building, lived in windowless rooms off the garage underneath the apartment block. They travelled back to Sudan to see their families only once a year, by train, and then by boat across Lake Nasser.

Um Nasr was different. She was Egyptian, from the Delta, and had no English whatsoever. She kept the flat reasonably clean, and washed my clothes. But they were ironed by an ancient *makwagi*, or ironing man, in his open shop across the street: from the front balcony I could see him heating up his flat iron on a venerable coal stove, and then spitting on the clothes to wet them before they were subjected to a pounding from his iron. Shirts from Jermyn Street did not long survive such brutal assault.

In 1980, despite the pretensions of the British Embassy in Jeddah (then headed by our most distinguished Arabist, Sir James Craig), the British Embassy in Cairo was still our largest in the Arab world. It was, it seemed to me, a proper embassy, headed by a proper ambassador. Sir Michael Weir had read classics at Balliol before joining the Foreign Service. After MECAS, he had spent most of his career working in and on the Middle East. He had started as an assistant political agent in what were then the Trucial States, manumitting slaves by allowing them to touch the flagpole of the British Government compound. He had gone on to key Middle East policy jobs in London, Washington and New York. But Michael was certainly not an ambassador out of central casting. He had gone to Oxford after service in RAF intelligence and from a Scottish grammar school, and spoke with a hint of a Scots accent. Highly intelligent, with excellent judgement (despite the miscall over Mubarak's prospects), he was neither pompous nor censorious. He had a wry sense of humour. And he had four amusing children, of roughly my age, who came out for holidays and were at the centre of young expatriate Cairo: one of them, Arabella, became a successful actress and author, rising from playing an anonymous rustic wench in *The French Lieutenant's Woman* to starring in *The Fast Show*. Michael's second wife, Hilary, with whom he had two younger sons, had also been a member of the Diplomatic Service. Again, appearances were deceptive. Hilary Weir had been educated at Benenden and Lady Margaret Hall, Oxford, and had all the confidence and poise of the upper-middle-class milieu from which she came. Hilary's family and mine lived close to each other in Kent, and she had had the same riding teacher as my brothers. Whereas Michael was relatively short and quiet, Hilary was tall and could be loud. But all that was superficial: what mattered to us in the Cairo Embassy in the early 1980s was that Michael and Hilary Weir operated as a true team. In their love of their work, of Egypt and – it has to be said – of each other, they showed what a powerful tool for promoting national interests and influence a committed diplomatic couple can be. Together, they entertained, and were entertained, not just in the usual society circles in which diplomats move in most capitals, but far beyond, among Egyptian architects and archaeologists, painters and poets, Nasserite intellectuals sceptical of what Sadat was about, and orchard-owning horse breeders who wanted nothing to do with politics. They shared a sceptical left-of-centre view of the world, born of wide experience and high intelligence. In my first post, I felt lucky to be working with and for such a talented couple. More than twenty years later, in September 2006, I was honoured to be asked by Hilary to give an address at Michael's memorial service. Two years later, I proudly entertained Hilary in Kabul, which she was visiting in order to see what the Brooke Trust (which she chaired) could do to help the working animals of Afghanistan. Within weeks, she was dead, of a cruel and unexpected cancer. I still mourn them both.

But a real embassy is much more than an ambassador. In 1980, Her Britannic Majesty's Embassy in Cairo had everything a proper embassy should have: its staff list covered a full page of the 'White Book', the list of staff in Diplomatic Service Posts Overseas, published twice a year by the Foreign Office.

Below the Ambassador came the Deputy Head of Mission, who stood in as chargé d'affaires whenever the Ambassador was away. He was also the Political Counsellor, or senior political officer in the Embassy. For my first eighteen months or so, the job was done with great flair by Nicholas Barrington, a bachelor-diplomat of great gifts who knew all about social networking long before it had been invented. His successor was the altogether more modest Tony Reeve, whose dry appreciation of the ridiculous and insightful intelligence more than compensated for a social diffidence that I suspected was more affected than real. Using a pseudonym, Tony already had two novels about diplomatic life under his belt. In their very different ways, both Nicholas and Tony were supremely talented diplomats, who went on to the highest levels of the Diplomatic Service, retiring, respectively, as high commissioners to Pakistan and to South Africa. It was a measure of Cairo's importance in those days that the post of deputy to the Ambassador was filled by officers of such obvious quality.

Alongside the Political Counsellor, but slightly more junior, was the Commercial Counsellor, in charge of the Embassy's trade promotion team. Below them both, right at the centre of the Embassy, was the key figure of the Head of Chancery: effectively the Embassy's chief operating officer, in charge of its political work, but also of its administration and daily functioning. The Administration Officer, responsible for managing the Embassy's people, property and money, reported to him. So did HM Consul, in charge of the Visa Section and of a small consular team looking after British nationals living in Egypt or, increasingly, visiting as tourists. I have already mentioned the Defence Section, headed by three attachés (officers of roughly colonel rank), often enjoying a diplomatic posting as the final job in a career which had taken them far and wide, but not as high as some of their contemporaries. Of the Embassy, but not quite in it, was the Cultural Attaché, in charge of the British Council's work in Egypt, promoting British culture, but also increasingly involved in development work and English language teaching. In 1980, the British Council Representative in Cairo, Malcolm Dalziel, was a rather grand figure, and a far cry from the cross-cultural communications experts the Council sends abroad today. With his elegant beard and double-breasted suits, he came across as something between a regius professor and a director of one of our racier merchant banks. He really was Britain's cultural ambassador to Egypt. The Embassy also had a first secretary (aid), in charge of a small but growing development programme, sponsored by what was then called the Overseas Development Administration, part of the Foreign Office, but which became the independent Department for International Development in 1997.

In theory, my post, initially as third secretary (Chancery) (before I was promoted to second secretary), in this mission of some fifty British public servants, and at least twice that number of locally engaged staff, mostly Egyptian, put me at or near the bottom of the pile. But the practice was different: as one of only a handful of London-based staff who spoke Arabic, and with my Arabic fresh from my time in Alexandria, I had an advantage over others. More than that, I belonged to the small political team at the heart of the Embassy. Rather like the young Army officer newly posted to his regiment, as a member of the Diplomatic Service fast stream I was treated by some of the mainstream officers in the Embassy with a respect I didn't deserve and certainly hadn't yet earned. All this created expectations I had to live up to: I had to know more about Egypt, report more, do more, draft more quickly, than other members of the team. It was a daunting prospect.

I was helped by the fact that, as in the embassies of almost all major powers, other members of staff were in fact spies in disguise. In those days, insiders could tell a real diplomat from a fake one: one give-away was that intelligence officers knew how to type (in order to operate their communications equipment on their own), whereas few 'straight' diplomats could. Other clues were time before joining the 'Foreign Office' in the Army or – back then – a colonial police force: the Royal

Hong Kong Police was a favourite; or a better sporting but patchier academic record than weedier true fast-streamers tended to have. Paradoxically for a secret service, intelligence officers tended – and still tend – to be more colourful, or eccentric, than their rather more boring 'straight' Foreign Office colleagues. In Egypt at the time, linen suits and silk handkerchiefs tucked carefully in the cuff, plus sojourns with the desert bedouin and a carefully calibrated gentleman's degree, were among the tell-tale signs. But to outsiders, and to many Embassy staff, it wasn't, or shouldn't have been, apparent who was a real diplomat and who was really an intelligence officer operating under diplomatic cover.

On one occasion an intelligence officer went native, to the extent of having a tailor run up for him a natty, even naff, Egyptian equivalent of the Mao suit then worn by almost all Nasserite apparatchiks: Michael Weir's predecessor had sent him a rather pompous note telling him that 'native dress was not to be worn in the Chancery'.

Intelligence officers operating under a false diplomatic flag had to live their cover, and often found doing two jobs hard pounding. Inevitably, their diplomatic cover work suffered. At a time when the US television series *Dallas* ruled the world, one such officer charged with summarising the daily Arabic papers solemnly told the Chancery morning meeting that Sadat had announced the previous day that the *Dallas* approach had no place in the politics of the modern Middle East. Puzzled, we consulted the papers: Sadat had been referring to President Eisenhower's somewhat dictatorial Secretary of State John Foster Dulles. Without vowels, Arabic made no distinction between the two. On another occasion, an intelligence officer masquerading as a 'straight' diplomat struggled at a dinner in his flat to remember the assumed names of the colleagues from London he was hosting. At least his discomfort should have entertained those on the other end of the microphones infesting the great chandelier swinging over us.

And there were microphones everywhere. In 1980, it was only a few years since Sadat had turned westwards, kicking all the Soviet Bloc advisers out of Egypt. But the Communist influence remained, particularly in his security services. A few years earlier our Head of Chancery in Cairo had switched on the radio at home in Zamalek only to pick up what sounded like a live broadcast from the drawing room of the

British Defence Attaché a few doors up the street. He rushed round, and soon confirmed what his ears had told him. It *was* a live broadcast: a poorly tuned radio microphone installed in the Defence Attaché's house by, presumably, Egyptian intelligence had been broadcasting on the frequency on which you normally expected to pick up the BBC World Service. On another occasion, the most senior British intelligence officer in Egypt had been surprised to meet the Embassy's chief switchboard operator emerging from the headquarters of the Egyptian intelligence service – presumably after a regular debriefing. But in those Cold War days, and for another nine years, the main target was 'Sov Bloc' – hence the enthusiasm of intelligence officers for invitations to diplomatic receptions discarded by more senior or more genuine officers: all too often, bending over the buffet at the Czech Embassy, or pushing my way through the crowd at the Polish national-day party, I would encounter a colleague from a Western embassy, his card inscribed 'First Secretary (Regional Affairs)', cruising for passing Communist trade, in the diplomatic equivalent of creeping among the bushes on Clapham Common. Equally amusing was intelligence colleagues' passion for joining or setting up social clubs for young foreign diplomats in Cairo. You had to admire the persistence with which intelligence officers worked at finding individuals who could, by carrot or stick, be persuaded to betray their governments for the sake of the British Crown. When the Falklands War broke out in 1982, an intelligence officer sidled up to me to ask whether I could persuade a distant cousin's husband, who worked on the trade side of the Argentine Diplomatic Service, to become a British agent: I said simply that I would never even consider suggesting that he should betray his country.

Another reason why Cairo seemed like a proper embassy was that the Ambassador was driven round in a Rolls-Royce. Keeping the ancient machine going in Egypt was hard work. Egyptian gasoline was far too coarse for the refined taste of the Rolls-Royce, so, in an immensely dangerous operation performed by the Ambassador's chauffeur, it had to be diluted with aviation fuel. The Roller often broke down, including, memorably, en route to the opening of a Rolls-Royce gas-turbine power station (manufactured by the other R-R) in the Delta. Riding in the car with the Ambassador, with the special Union flag flown by ambassadors fluttering over the bonnet, gave me a frisson of pride. The use of the Rolls-Royce seemed the best perk of being chargé d'affaires.

In the summer of 1980, the irrepressibly energetic Chargé d'Affaires, Nicholas Barrington, used the Rolls-Royce to take his guests down to the centre of old Cairo, after *iftar* (the evening meal with which Muslims break the daily Ramadan fast) in his historic house in Zamalek. Ramadan in Cairo was pure magic. In Cairo's ancient heart, we saw and heard jugglers and musicians mingling with the crowds celebrating what is for Muslims a month of Christmases. Everywhere there was light and noise and jubilation. I watched entranced as a magician levitated a man, having first passed an iron hoop around his body to prove the absence of wires.

The Cairo Embassy lay in the shadow of the tangled history of Britain's engagement with Egypt since the late nineteenth century, when Sir Evelyn Baring, later Lord Cromer, had been Britain's consul-general in Egypt, with a modest title which belied great powers. The Residence itself, on the banks of the Nile in Garden City, had been built by Lord Kitchener, and its ballroom (in 1980 housing the Embassy Visa Section, but now restored to its original state) had had the only sprung dance floor in Africa.

The most notorious of Sir Michael Weir's predecessors was Sir Miles Lampson, who had been ambassador to Egypt throughout the Second World War. Immensely grand, he had referred to King Farouk as 'the boy'. But what Egyptians really remembered – and resented – about him was the action he had taken in February 1942 when Farouk had persisted in appointing a pro-Axis prime minister. When the King had refused to back down, Lampson had had the Abdin Palace in Cairo surrounded by tanks. A prime minister more sympathetic to the Allied cause was soon appointed. This was still known to Egyptians as the '4 February incident'. In blissful ignorance of the date's sensitivity, the BBC planned one 4 February to hold a party in Cairo to promote its Arabic Service: the Embassy intervened just in time.

Another story about Lampson was more personal, and was told me by John Keith, a City solicitor who had served during the Second World

War as Lampson's military ADC. Halfway through the war, Churchill had decided that the somewhat pompous Lampson should be ennobled, as Lord Killearn. Shortly afterwards, the exuberant Shakespearean actor Sir Donald Wolfit had visited Cairo with his troupe of players. As the Ambassador's lunch for the visiting thespians drew to a close, Sir Donald chinked on his glass. He wanted 'to say a few words' to thank the Ambassador for his hospitality. As he sat down, he added, with a flourish, that it had been 'particularly nice to have been entertained by you, Lord Killearn, as we have heard such terrible reports of your predecessor, Sir Miles Lampson'. John Keith said that the ensuing silence was long and painful.*

But what did an embassy like this actually do? First, we provided the Foreign Office in London, and many other parts of Whitehall, as well as other British diplomatic posts in, or interested in, the Middle East, with a pretty comprehensive political intelligence service. We reported to London by telegram and letter – not in those days by telephone – sending back vast quantities of the reporting and analysis that made Britain's Foreign Office the best informed in the world. What it was all for none of us asked.

We kept a close eye on what we called 'Egypt Internal' – the political state of the nation behind the façade of the Sadat regime, and of a National Democratic Party that was neither national nor democratic nor a real political party, but still won well over 90 per cent of the votes in national elections. For one of those elections, we spread out over the country to monitor exactly how Egyptian democracy worked in the early 1980s – long before such exercises had become commonplace. The results were not encouraging. At a deserted polling station in a village on the edge of the Delta, we found two police officers desperately putting crosses on ballot papers and stuffing them into the ballot boxes, worried that they wouldn't have filled their quota before the regional police commander did his evening round, to check on the state of the polls.

---

* Almost as formidable as Killearn is his widow, his second and much younger wife Jacqueline. She was still remembered by certain elderly Cairenes in 1980, and came to stay with us in Washington DC in 1987. In 2012, she was 102.

More interestingly, without offending a regime with whom Britain had good political relations, we tried to find out what we could about the sources of opposition to Sadat's increasingly autocratic and eccentric rule. Improbably, impossibly, one of the main sources of that opposition sat in a crumbling palatial villa only a few hundred yards from the Embassy, in Garden City beside the Nile. This was the home of Fuad Serageddin Pasha, a larger than life *ancien régime* figure, who, as King Farouk's interior minister, had dealt with the anti-British riots of January 1952 that had precipitated the Free Officers' Revolution of July that year. He led the Wafd Party, which took its name from the *wafd* or delegation which had tried to travel to London in 1918 demanding freedom for Egypt from British imperial rule. Serageddin used his Turkish title of pasha with some style. He used regularly to receive me in his palace, embracing me with a bear hug, a slobbering kiss and a fat cigar. He came from a different era. For all the Pasha's talk of democracy and reform, in those and later days there seemed to be less to the Wafd than met the eye.

The same could not be said of the Islamists with whom we struggled to make contact. Even before Sadat's assassination, we knew that, despite or perhaps because of the efforts of one of the most effective police states in the Arab world, tens of thousands of Egyptians were devout conservative Muslims, strongly opposed to the one-sided peace Sadat had made with Israel and to many of the more worldly aspects of his rule. The Muslim Brotherhood had been banned in Egypt since 1954, but, in many ways, it was less interesting and less effective that the more extreme fundamentalist groups which had given birth to the plot to kill the President. The much feared Egyptian internal state security service, the Mubahith Amn al-Dawla, kept many thousands of citizens under surveillance – when they were not behind bars.

At the other end of the spectrum were the Marxists and Nasserites of the old Egyptian intellectual left. They shared the Islamists' opposition to the Camp David accords and to the close alliance with America, but they favoured a secular society. Many of them had been educated or trained in the Soviet Union, and, as with the Afghan former Communists I was to meet a quarter of a century later, they had acquired there a fondness for vodka which made them less than perfect Muslims.

One reason why the Foreign Office at that time put so much emphasis on political reporting was that we had utterly failed to foresee the Iranian Revolution of 1979. The internal FCO inquiry, conducted by a bright young diplomat called Nick Browne,* had concluded that the Embassy in Iran had been too preoccupied with selling tanks and tractors to the Shah to notice what was happening in the bazaars of south Tehran. We needed to be on the lookout for similar earthquakes elsewhere in the Muslim world. At the time, I accepted this verdict. Later, however, I came to see that the comment made by the Ambassador in Tehran at the time, Sir Anthony Parsons, when he exercised his right of reply, was probably closer to the mark: our failure to foresee the fall of the Shah was, he wrote, due not to a shortage of intelligence or information, but to a failure of imagination. We simply could not conceive of Iran without the Shah. Just as later we found it difficult to imagine Egypt without Mubarak, or Libya without Qadhafi.

Despite this, the conventional wisdom in the Cairo Chancery in 1980 was that opposition to Sadat was growing, but did not threaten the regime. The murder of the Pharaoh – which we totally failed to foresee – did not change that view. That was not, however, the judgement – or wish – of the American and other Western media, who poured into Cairo in the days after Sadat's death looking for harbingers of a revolution that was not to come for another thirty years. Out of desperation, they ended up interviewing each other. One crestfallen US network decided to justify the expense of having sent a camera crew to Cairo to cover the revolution by instructing them to make a documentary entitled, rather lamely, *Why Was Cairo Calm?* None of that stopped a famous British foreign correspondent known for colourful prose connected only loosely to the truth from filing from Upper Egypt a piece suggesting that Egypt was on the edge of an abyss.

The firm grip which the Egyptian regime had on power did not mean that occasional demonstrations weren't allowed. We would go along to watch. Cruelly, I once persuaded a gullible friend from London, keen to accompany us to such a demonstration, that diplomats did so

---

* Father of an FCO minister in the 2010 Coalition Government, Jeremy Browne.

in disguise. With great enthusiasm, he donned the 'Arab sheikh' outfit he had bought at a tourist stall by the Pyramids. Imagining himself a latterday T. E. Lawrence, he turned up, with his black brogues protruding from beneath his *galabia*, looking more like Thomson or Thompson in a Tintin story. The languidly linen-suited diplomat who was going to lead us to the demonstration observed, witheringly: 'I think that's rather overdoing it, don't you?'

But, with the Government struggling even then to provide Egypt's teeming masses with the cheap food and decent jobs to which Nasser had told them they were entitled, it was a question not of whether there would be another revolution, but when: we would never have thought it would take another three decades.

Another area to which we paid close attention was the position of the Coptic Christian minority in Egypt. The Copts make up about 10 per cent of the population, and can justifiably claim to be the original Egyptians – 'gypt' is the same root as Copt. In 1980, the Coptic Pope, Shenouda III, had just been sent into internal exile by Sadat for criticising his rule. He died as I was writing this chapter, in March 2012, having performed a skilful balancing act over many decades, protecting his people, while maintaining relations with successive Egyptian regimes, including, latterly, the Supreme Council of the Armed Forces.

Sadly, in 1980 there were very few Jews left in Egypt from a community that had once numbered many thousands and had made an immeasurable contribution to the country's commercial and cultural life. But the great synagogues in Cairo and Alexandria were still there, looked after by aged custodians, and visited by some of the Jewish tourists then arriving in Egypt in great numbers. The ancient synagogue in Old Cairo was of particular interest, as it had hosted the priceless deposit of papers known as the Geniza, and now lodged mostly in the Cambridge University Library. This was essentially a large waste-paper dump, as Jews were not allowed to destroy papers on which the word of God had been inscribed. Incredibly, the ancient tailor recommended to me by rather dress-conscious colleagues in Cairo turned out to be Jewish, though he kept very quiet about it. Sadly, his age meant he was no Montague Burton: the buttons soon flew off his suits, none of which survived my return to London.

One of the most bizarre tasks I was given as the junior Chancery officer was to take an inflatable rubber cushion up to an ancient British lady known as Omm Sety. She lived, with dozens of cats, in a hut amid the ruins of the ancient city of Abydos in Upper Egypt. Born and raised in Blackheath, after falling downstairs and suffering a severe concussion aged three and then a trip to the British Museum, she had believed herself to be the reincarnation of the nanny of Seti I, a pharaoh of the Nineteenth Dynasty. She went on to study Egyptology, marry an Egyptian and work for the Egyptian Antiquities Department. Highly detailed dreams informed a remarkable 'recall' of life in the Pharaoh's palace. The Embassy regarded itself as having consular responsibility for her.

But we didn't look just at what was happening inside Egypt. As a Permanent Member of the United Nations Security Council, and a prominent member of the European Economic Community and of NATO, as well as the former colonial power across much of the Middle East, in the 1980s, as today, Britain still regarded itself as a significant player in Middle Eastern affairs. In fact, Britain's moment in the Middle East had long passed, probably with our precipitate scuttle from Palestine in May 1948, but certainly with the Suez debacle of 1956 and then, more recently and painfully, our humiliating early departure from Aden and South Arabia in November 1967. Anyone who had suggested back then that, thirty years later, we would be joining the Americans in not one but two ill-fated invasions of Muslim lands would have been dismissed as a fantasist.

In the 1980s, as now, much of our sense of diplomatic self-importance was based on unhealthy doses of nostalgia and of wishful thinking. Yet the irony was that, like many other people in the Third World, the Arabs then – and still today – attribute to Britain more power than it actually has. Perhaps more justifiably, they believed – or often told us that they believed – that Britons in general, and British diplomats and spies in particular, understood the Arabs better than the Americans. We would lie back proudly and think of MECAS. It probably was true, however, that Britain's diplomats spoke more Arabic less badly than those of any other power, except perhaps the smooth operators of the KGB.

In 1980, as in every year since 1948 until the present, top of the Middle East agenda was the dispute between Israel and its Arab neighbours over Palestine. The familiar theme was of European dismay at American reluctance to do much to promote real peace: at the time the excuse for US inactivity was a visceral refusal to acknowledge that the Palestinians were entitled to a state of their own, and a total boycott of the Palestine Liberation Organisation. At their summit in Venice in June 1980, the nine member states of the EEC had issued a declaration acknowledging the Palestinians' right to self-determination, and the PLO's right to be involved in peace negotiations, based on the famous Security Council Resolutions 242 and 338, passed in the wake of respectively the 1967 and 1973 wars. These days those European pronouncements look like little more than common sense or natural justice, but in 1980 this was revolutionary language, putting clear blue water between America and Europe on the Middle East.

So it was not surprising that much of the debate in the Middle East over the next few years was over whether we could expect a European initiative, with Britain and France in its van, to break the logjam. But such talk came up against two iron laws of Israel–Palestine diplomacy: first, that, for all sorts of reasons, America is essential (if not always enough) for progress, and, second, that no one can dance unless the all too imperfect Israeli democracy can be persuaded to come on to the floor. On this, as on so many other issues, the Europeans excelled themselves at producing towering clouds of puffery, but little or no significant action. They couldn't accept they had no real leverage over Israel. It was all too reminiscent of one perceptive journal editor's verdict on something I once submitted to him: 'Like much that comes out of King Charles Street, my dear Sherard, this is elegantly drafted – and utterly irrelevant.'

But inability to make a real difference was never an obstacle to diplomatic activity. And so throughout my three years in Cairo, the Arab–Israel dispute was Britain's main preoccupation in the Middle East. We in the Cairo Embassy spent much of our time talking to the Egyptians, still locked in the embarrassingly unproductive, US-brokered talks with the Israelis on the Palestinian autonomy that had been the other half of the Camp David accords. And we would cajole the American Embassy, from the Ambassador down, into telling their trusted friends, the Brits, what was really happening. At the time the officer in the US Embassy Political Section handling the 'peace process' was Dan Kurtzer, a devout Jew who spoke fluent Arabic and Hebrew, and who has dedicated his life to the cause of Middle East peace. It was a delight to come across Dan again in 2001 as my US colleague in Tel Aviv, after he had had a tough tour as ambassador to Egypt. All the information the Embassy picked up was distilled into thousands of 'groups' (the unit in which telegram traffic was then measured) telegraphed back to London, and into hundreds of letters, sent by the diplomatic bag, giving more context. British ministers toured the Middle East, talking privately and publicly, giving interview after interview, but never making any real progress: Lord Carrington came (and managed to fit in a Nile cruise) and so did his successor as foreign secretary, Francis Pym (but without the cruise). The Foreign Office Minister of State for the Middle East, Douglas Hurd, included Cairo in one of his regional tours. Arranging such visits, and reporting on them, gave the young diplomats in the Cairo Chancery plenty to do. We loved it.

But Egypt wasn't just an Arab state at the heart of the peace process. As Sadat and his Foreign Ministry used to remind anyone who would listen, it was also a Muslim state, and an African one. The Arab, Islamic and African circles of Egyptian diplomacy, plus the hangover from its role in the Non-Aligned Movement of the 1950s and 1960s, meant that Cairo was still a crossroads of international diplomacy. Following the Camp David accords, most Arab states had either closed their embassies in Cairo or reduced them to 'chargé d'affaires' status. The Arab League had left its purpose-built headquarters overlooking Tahrir Square and moved to Tunis. In its place, Sadat had set up a Potemkin 'League of Arab and Islamic Peoples': a formal call on its Secretary General by our Political Counsellor, Tony Reeve, and me ended in us both collapsing into helpless giggles at the absurdities of what we were being told. Despite the Arab boycott, there was plenty going on in Cairo with which to fill our reports to London. When I started work, I was told by Tony's predecessor, the meticulous Nicholas Barrington, that my first task was to report on Egypt granting political asylum to the son of Zog, former King of the Albanians. A month later, I was struggling to draft, on Nicholas's instructions, talking points for Denis Thatcher to use with Madame Suzanne Mubarak, during the official visit which Vice President Mubarak was to pay to London in September 1980.

Two Palestinian *intifadas* (or uprisings) and hundreds of thousands of Israelis settled in the Occupied Territories later, it is not easy now to recall the heady days of Egyptian–Israeli rapprochement of 1979–81. In those days, the hotels of Cairo were full of Jewish tourists, mainly from America, combining a week in Egypt with a week in Israel. Two young Army-officer friends of mine, one of whom was to rise to the top of the military establishment, were stationed in Cyprus with their regiment, the Green Howards. They decided to come over for a 'pulling expedition' up the Nile on one of the cruise boats then plying between Luxor and Aswan. They equipped themselves with panama hats, slick tropical clothes and a case of the Embassy's gin. A week later, they returned, crestfallen: they had been the youngest passengers on the cruise by about forty years, and had spent the week playing bridge with ancient widows and divorcees from Florida and New York.

In those days, the *Jerusalem Post* (then a much more balanced paper than it was later to become) was sold openly in the main newsagents of central Cairo. Israeli experts were helping install drip-feed irrigation systems in the agricultural schemes on the margins of the desert and the Delta. And, most convenient of all, there were regular long-distance bus services across the Sinai, between Cairo and Tel Aviv.

As foreign secretary in 1974–6, Jim Callaghan had ruled that all Foreign Office Arabists, fresh out of MECAS, had to go on a familiarisation visit to Israel before or during their first posting in the Arab world. When in 1982 my turn came, I was able to take the bus from Cairo to Tel Aviv, and begin a fascination with, and affection for, the Jewish state that has never left me. But the law of unintended consequences kicked in: what was meant by Callaghan as an effort to recalibrate the camel corps had the opposite effect. The uncompromising line taken by the Israeli briefers, the determination with which the early settlements around Jerusalem and across the Green Line* were then

---

* The 1948 Armistice line, separating Israel from the areas held by the Arabs, which Israel was to invade and occupy in 1967.

being established, and the obvious plight of the wretched Palestinians, particularly in Gaza, all served only to reinforce the conviction of the young diplomats sent on the course that a grave injustice had been done, and was being still being done, to the Arab inhabitants of historic Palestine.

As so often in the Middle East, the peace turned out to be too good to be true. In early June 1981 Israeli aircraft bombed the Osirak nuclear reactor south of Baghdad, and all hell broke loose. Years before the neocons had developed the doctrine of pre-emptive defence, the international condemnation was universal. Even the United States criticised the Israeli action, while blocking serious punitive action in the Security Council. Sadat reacted with fury at what he saw as a betrayal by his Israeli partner, Begin. The rapid cooling in Egyptian–Israeli relations that followed was unavoidable. And those relations were never as good again.

Alongside covering Egypt's internal politics and its external relations, my third area of work in the Cairo Embassy was as press attaché. In this, I faced in two directions: towards the Egyptian media, and towards the corps of impressive Western correspondents then based in Cairo. My daily routine involved repackaging for the Egyptian media a constant stream of good news stories about Britain (in reality, charmingly amateurish propaganda) sent out by the Central Office of Information. These ranged from texts of speeches by the Prime Minister to pieces puffing British products. I remember trying to place articles praising the merits of the new Austin Mini Metro, then rolling off the British Leyland line at Longbridge. Once a month, I would call on the head of Egyptian State Television and offer her a selection of news and feature clips from Britain to help fill the schedules. None of this was quite as absurd as it now seems: the state-controlled Egyptian media were hungry for material, and not too fussy about where it came from. If it helped promote the interests or exports of a country regarded as an ally, so much the better.

My propaganda work assumed a bit more importance during the Falklands War of April–June 1982, as Britain sought to build political and diplomatic support round the world for its claim to sovereignty over the islands the Argentines called the Malvinas. To my surprise, I did manage to secure some sympathetic coverage in the instinctively anti-colonialist Egyptian media, mainly because I could offer better images than the opposition. But the *Newsweek* cover of HMS *Hermes* and the task force steaming south, bearing the caption 'The Empire Strikes Back', was more help than all my efforts: the world needed to know that Britain meant what it said, and the victory which followed earned us grudging respect in Egypt and indeed across the Middle East.

In those days, there were three main daily Egyptian papers in Arabic, *Al Ahram*, *Al Akhbar* and *Al Gomhuria*, two in English, the *Egyptian Gazette* and the *Egyptian Mail*, and, perhaps surprisingly, one in French, *Le Progrès Egyptien*, whose origins lay with Napoleon's expedition to Egypt in 1798. Of these, the one that mattered most, and was least easy to influence, was *Al Ahram* (or 'Pyramids'). Gone were its glory days under Nasser, when its brilliant editor, Mohammed Hassanain Heikal, had been the voice of the Arabs. It was now the voice of the Government and the party. But that did not mean that some talented individuals didn't work for it, particularly the nest of Nasserites in the Al Ahram Centre for Strategic Studies, or that it wasn't worth engaging with them. The paper's name did occasionally cause confusion: I remember taking the former British Prime Minister, Edward Heath, to call on the editor, only to find that we were approaching the Sphinx on the edge of the desert west of Cairo: the driver had confused the paper with one of the greater glories of Pharaonic Egypt.

By contrast, the *Egyptian Gazette* was a rather run-down affair, obviously produced on an ancient press, full of mistakes and misprints. On the day the Israelis withdrew from Sinai, the *Gazette* managed to mark the event by printing on the top of its front page an upside-down map of the peninsula. Its staff usually included one or two young British interns, brushing up their Arabic and having fun at the same time.

The other side of being press attaché was liaising with the foreign journalists in Cairo. This was useful and important, as well as enjoyable. Cairo in the early 1980s was the place from which the Western media covered the Middle East. The BBC, Reuters, AP and UPI had big bureaux there. CNN was just getting going. All the major British papers had Cairo correspondents, many of them full time, as did the *New York Times*, the *Washington Post* and the *Los Angeles Times*. Meeting the range of talent and experience they deployed was a big privilege for a young diplomat – and I learned much from them, including some of the old ways of the Street of Shame. The hacks worked hard, but also played hard. After one memorable party, given by the correspondent of a British Sunday broadsheet, the host had to ring round all his guests to apologise for the way things had got out of hand the night before. A visiting correspondent regaled us with stories of his conquests on the night train to Aswan. For the British Embassy, the dean of the corps was the BBC bureau chief, Bob Jobbins, a reporter of scholarship and flair. One of the MI6 team in Cairo said we should treat Jobbins as 'cleared up to confidential', on the basis that he could be trusted with sensitive information, and that we could learn as much from him as he could from us. But the journalist of whom I saw most was a university friend, Charles Richards, who graduated from sub-editing the *Egyptian Gazette* to writing for the *Financial Times* and, later, the *Independent*. He knew the real Egypt better than any of us.

I also learned – the hard way – the importance of setting the ground rules before saying anything significant to a working journalist, even in a social setting. After a particularly gruelling visit to Egypt by the Duke of Edinburgh, I relaxed over supper with the *Guardian* correspondent and his wife – a member of one of Britain's most famous families, who worked part time as a stringer for the *Daily Express*. At dinner, I explained how almost everything that could have gone wrong with the visit had gone wrong. Fog had meant that we had had to cancel a visit to Sinai by Prince Philip, who was in Egypt in his capacity as president of the World Wildlife Fund. Instead, we had tried to take him to the wetlands of Lake Fayoum. Almost incredibly, crossing a desert with only two roads, the Egyptian police escort had lost their way. The convoy juddered to a halt. An unfortunate police major tried desperately to explain to the Duke what had happened. 'Your Highness, the road has been washed away' was the best he could do. 'I don't believe a word of it!' snapped Prince Philip, who strode off into the desert. On our return to Cairo, I had arranged for the Duke to brief the Egyptian press, expecting no difficulties from them. But Prince Philip was in no mood for flannel, telling them that the problem with their country was that 'you Egyptians breed like rabbits'. Asked at the end whether he planned to come back, he retorted, 'You must be joking.' Without warning me, my hostess put some – but luckily not all – of this on the front page of the *Daily Express*.

But the royal visit which caused us most difficulty was the honeymoon of the Prince and Princess of Wales in August 1981. Out of the blue the Ambassador called me in one morning to read a long personal 'DEYOU' (meaning it could be decrypted only with the Ambassador present) telegram from the head of the Foreign Office in London. It explained that the Top Secret plan was for the Prince and Princess of Wales, embarked on the Royal Yacht *Britannia*, to pass down the Suez Canal at the end of their honeymoon cruise through the Mediterranean from Gibraltar. On the assumption that they would have avoided the world's media during the cruise, the first 'press availability' would be at Port Said at the northern entrance to the Canal. The Ambassador's instructions were to plan for this, but to tell no one, certainly no Egyptian. In desperation, the Ambassador asked the Naval Attaché and me to help.

The first task was the most dangerous. Once *Britannia* had passed through the Canal, the idea was that Their Royal Highnesses would picnic on a beach on one of the deserted coral islands at the northern end of the Red Sea. The Ambassador was instructed by the Flag Officer, Royal Yachts (FORY) to find a 'mine-free, shark-free' beach. There was nothing we could do about the sharks, and the only way we could establish whether a beach was mine-free was for the Naval Attaché, complaining furiously, to be sent there in great secrecy and walk up and down it.

Somehow *Britannia* did elude the press as she made her way east through the Mediterranean, although there were one or two close calls. The Suez Canal Authority reserved a berth for *Britannia* alongside their majestic building in Port Said. Telling the Canal administrators meant that we also had to tell the President. To the fury of the Austrian Government, Sadat promptly cancelled, at about a week's notice, a state visit to Vienna, citing 'security reasons', in order to have dinner with the Prince and Princess of Wales when they arrived in Port Said. As *Britannia* steamed closer, the signals flew back and forth between the Rear Admiral in command and the Ambassador. One memorable exchange read something like: 'FORY to HMA: at dinner HRH will be wearing Royal Yacht Squadron rig' (none of us knew exactly what Royal Yacht Squadron rig was, but we guessed it involved a black bow tie); 'HMA to FORY: dinner jackets have not been worn in Egypt since the Revolution'.

Eventually, *Britannia* tied up in Port Said. The world's press, whom I had assembled on the roof of the Suez Canal Authority building, went mad. They couldn't see the Prince or the Princess, but they did now know where they were. Suddenly, I got a laconic message from my friend and Diplomatic Service colleague Francis Cornish, who was on *Britannia*, working as assistant private secretary to the Prince of Wales. 'Their Royal Highnesses are thinking of taking a private stroll on deck before dinner, and do not want to be observed. Please clear the press from the building.' And that was it. I had 200 baying journalists, scribbling, filming, photographing, recording, and had been told to prevent them covering the royal story of the year. The Egyptian police refused to help. After about thirty minutes of pushing and shoving, I managed to get them all down the stairs, and out of sight of the Yacht. Last to go were the BBC's Kate Adie and an aggressive leather-clad German news-agency photographer. 'All clear,' I signalled to Francis. 'Sorry,' came the reply, 'TRH have changed their minds: no stroll on deck this evening.' I could have throttled him.

Dinner over, press availability done, *Britannia* steamed south through the Canal, bearing her precious cargo. Passing Ismailia, half-way down the Canal (Francis told me later), the Officer of the Watch observed a scruffy little boat, rowed by two Egyptians, making for *Britannia*. Getting out a megaphone, and using their fruitiest language, the officers of the Royal Yacht instructed the Egyptian rowing boat to stay clear. But it just kept on coming. Somebody spotted several wooden crates in it. In later years, the Royal Marines would have opened fire. But in those innocent days the Suez Canal Authority pilot was allowed to ask the two oarsmen what their business was. 'On behalf of President of Egypt,' they replied, 'we bring boxes of mangoes for Highness Diana.' At dinner a day earlier, the Princess of Wales had confessed to Sadat her love for Egypt's favourite fruit. The President had his priorities.

Eventually, *Britannia* made landfall, at the Egyptian Red Sea resort port of Hurghada, where a VC10 of the Royal Air Force was waiting to take the honeymoon couple back to England. Sadat sent his Republican Guard to give the royal visitors a proper send-off. The world's press were too busy photographing and filming the newlyweds to notice the coal-scuttle helmets, field-grey uniforms and jackboots of a military formation that betrayed only too obviously Sadat's wartime sympathies.*

The other major royal visitor during my time in Cairo was Prince Andrew, then aged twenty. His Royal Highness had just won his helicopter wings – a qualification which, within a year, he would be using in war. But in 1981 as a reward for his success the Queen treated her second son to a Nile cruise. As the Chancery bachelor, I was detailed to accompany the young Prince. All I can say is that neither the Prince nor the Third Secretary did full justice to the distinguished professors of Egyptology whom the Egyptian Government deployed at every one of the great Pharaonic temples between Luxor and Aswan. But fun was had, not least during the last leg of the holiday in Cairo, during which Hilary Weir arranged for the young Prince to go riding in the desert and for a poolside barbecue (which became a bit more exuberant than she had intended).

As a result of this, Prince Andrew was kind enough to invite me to his twenty-first birthday party at Windsor Castle. About a thousand people were there, ranging from the Prime Minister and Mr Thatcher through to younger friends of the Prince. I found myself sitting next to one of them – a dashing American blonde – when, halfway through the evening, we moved into the Waterloo Chamber (I think it was) for a concert. A man in cap and spectacles strode on to the stage, sat down at the piano and started singing. I had no idea who he was, and turned to my neighbour to ask. 'You caaan't be serious,' she drawled, 'you are sooo sad. Don't you recognise Elton John? I flew over with him on Concorde two days ago.'

None of us had dreamed that one of the guests at the poolside party in Cairo a few months earlier would achieve fame, for a sadder reason. In helping Lady Weir draw up the guest list, I had suggested that we

---

* Sadat had been arrested at least once during the Second World War for espionage on behalf of the Axis.

include a young Egyptian diplomat, Rifa'at al-Ansary, who had just returned from a posting to London and was going places in the Egyptian Foreign Ministry. He duly came, and delighted the girls at least with a bravura display of disco dancing. Soon afterwards, he was transferred to what was then a front-line post for Egypt – the Embassy in Tel Aviv. The next time I heard of him he was on the front pages of the British press, dubbed by the tabloids the 'Cairo Casanova'. In Israel, it turned out, he had reconnected with a British diplomat, Rhona Ritchie, whom he had met during his posting to London. During what was by all accounts a passionate love affair, she had allegedly shown al-Ansary British diplomatic telegrams. Observing this, the Israeli security service, the Shin Bet, had tipped off Britain's Security Service. Apparently without the Foreign Office being properly briefed on what was happening, Ritchie was called back to London on a pretext and then arrested by the Special Branch at Heathrow, before being tried for espionage. In my view, and that of many of Rhona Ritchie's Diplomatic Service colleagues, it was a ridiculous overreaction to a serious lapse of judgement – to which the right response would have been dismissal, not imprisonment. When my Ambassador in Cairo, Michael Weir, was told that Rhona Ritchie's crime was to have shown al-Ansary British diplomatic telegrams, his response was that he did that all the time with the American Ambassador – with no authority, although admittedly America was a much closer ally than Egypt. Trading information is the core business of diplomacy: no successful diplomat can ever get it exactly right. Rhona Ritchie wasn't the first or the last to have got it seriously wrong, but she was unwise enough to have done it under the eyes of the world's most unforgiving security agency.

Some visitors to Cairo weren't royal, but expected to be treated as such. One of these was the Lord Mayor of London, in those days without any rival at City Hall, and conducting himself during his year in office with pomp and ceremony that have since – wisely – been greatly reduced. The guidance from the Mansion House told us that the Lord Mayor enjoyed a status equivalent to that of a Cabinet minister, although few Cabinet ministers travelled with a sword bearer and someone who described himself as the Chief Commoner of the City of London. As press attaché, my job was to ensure maximum favourable publicity for what was primarily a commercial visit. With this in mind, I arranged a showing in my flat of a Central Office of Information film about the job of Lord Mayor. But I fear this ancient newsreel-style production left my Egyptian guests more confused than enlightened. The film had opened with the Lord Mayor riding through London in his gilded coach, surrounded by the pikemen of the Honourable Artillery Company: that was what most Egyptians thought a Lord Mayor was. But then, presumably in order to show that the Lord Mayor was human, we cut to a scene of the same man, dressed in very English weekend-shabby clothes, digging potatoes and passing a trug full of the produce of his vegetable garden through the kitchen window to a grateful wife. Egypt grew some of the finest spring potatoes in the world, but her journalists thought that only peasants dug them. They couldn't work out what was going on with the Lord Mayor.

Nor did the Embassy press release announcing the imminent arrival of the Lord Mayor help much. There is in Arabic no exact equivalent for mayor. 'Governor' is not right; nor is 'head' or 'president'. So we opted for *umda*, the village headman of London. Translating 'Chief Commoner' into Arabic was even more difficult: we ended up with *rais al-fellaheen*, head of the peasants of London.

But these royal visitors and the Lord Mayor were only the most prominent of a constant flow of official visitors to Cairo in those days. The cynics in the Embassy couldn't help noticing how the numbers fell away in the hotter months of summer, and how many of our visitors managed to combine a day or two in Cairo with a fact-finding visit, official or unofficial, to Upper Egypt. Once again, I remembered my university friend who, on failing to get into the Diplomatic Service, had joined Thomson Holidays.

Away from the Embassy, there was plenty of fun to be had in Cairo in the early 1980s. Both there and in Alexandria, the heady days of the Second World War were not such a distant memory. Groppi's tea house was still there, as was Shepheard's Hotel, although it had been moved and rebuilt, hideously. There were still plenty of older Egyptians who remembered what the Eighth Army had called Groppi's Light Horse and Shepheard's Short Range Group – the men and women of General Headquarters Middle East.

In the villas and grander pre-war apartment blocks of Garden City, Zamalek and Heliopolis could still be found Egyptians who mourned the pre-revolutionary cosmopolitan days, which some hoped that Sadat's *infitah*, or opening, would bring back. Sitting next to an ancient hostess at a lunch – she would have said luncheon – party in Garden City, I was asked, seriously, whether we still danced the Charleston. She then recalled that, in her family, which was a branch of Egypt's former royal family, they spoke four languages: English for business, French in society, Turkish within the family and Arabic to the servants.*

There was also an Eighth Army dimension to the way I used to spend some winter weekends: staying with the settled bedu of Wadi Natrun, halfway along the desert road between Cairo and Alexandria, trying to shoot duck and occasionally snipe. We never killed anything much, but Nick Kittoe, the friend with whom I organised this, and I had huge fun. The night before the duck shoot we would stay with the sheikh of the local tribe, Abdul Gader, before rising at dawn to wait for the duck to come in. We built hides, and paid Abdul Gader to put down food for the ducks. But mostly we talked. Abdul Gader had spent the war working in the Wadi Natrun NAAFI canteen. Using his few words of British military English, he would mimic the way he had been taught to answer the telephone: 'Wadi Natrun 234 Hello'. He was proud of his four wives: we would see them all, unveiled and unashamed in the way bedouin women are, feeding their babies in line along the wall of the majlis (or sitting area) in his breezeblock hut.

Fun too, though also terrifying for a hopeless non-horseman like me, were hours spent riding in the desert around the Pyramids. Sadly, Frank Gardner's memory, in his book *Blood and Sand*,† of me as a fine horseman galloping across the desert is a mirage. But gazing at the view of the Pyramids, over a glass of Stella beer, from one of the rest houses of Sahara City (later demolished by Sadat) was one of the great pleasures of that time in Cairo.

---

* Reminiscent of the Emperor Charles V's comment: 'To God I speak Spanish, to women Italian, to men French and to my horse German.'
† London: Bantam, 2006.

It was the combination of Arabic (which she had studied at the School of Oriental and African Studies in London) and horses which had brought my future wife, Bridget, to Egypt. After a holiday there, she and her sister (who taught ballet) and a girlfriend (who taught English) had decided to spend more time in Cairo, renting a flat by the Pyramids and spending much of their time riding. About the only things they brought with them from England were three English saddles. As the Embassy bachelor, I was introduced to the three girls by the *Economist* correspondent in Cairo, Alan Mackie, in February 1981. Bridget and I married, in London, the following January. Our eldest son, Harry, was born in Cairo in November 1982, at a hospital on Roda Island in the Nile – just near where Moses was supposed to have been found in a basket among the rushes. Witnessing a birth in an Egyptian hospital was not easy. Bridget was given, quite unnecessarily and perhaps dangerously, a general anaesthetic, Harry was extracted with a pair of forceps that I could have sworn were rusty, and, immediately after his arrival, I, as the lucky father, was expected to give a thank-offering, in dirty Egyptian pound notes, to each of the delivery room staff. In the end, however, all was well: thanks in part to Um Nasr's attention, Harry thrived in Egypt, and I was for ever after known to Arabs as Abu Heneri – the father of Henry.

Three and a half years in Egypt passed quickly. Soon it was time to return to a job in the Foreign Office in London. Before I did, I had to hand over to my successor. Michael Crawford had joined the Foreign Office after doing research at Oxford on the Wahhabis of Saudi Arabia and after qualifying as a barrister, so he was a bit older, and much wiser, than me. He also had better Arabic. So, full of enthusiasm, I showed him the business card (reproduced in the endpaper of this book) which I had had printed locally, with English on one side and Arabic the other. 'You must have one of these,' I gushed. With the quizzically dry manner for which he was later to become well known, my successor examined both sides of the card. 'Sherard,' he said, 'there is something wrong here. The English describes you as "Second Secretary (Information)", but the Arabic gives your title as "Second Secretary (Flags)". I grabbed the card back, and my heart fell: a misplaced accent had changed the Arabic for 'information' to 'flags'. What a humiliation! But, just as I hadn't noticed, nor over three years had any Egyptian. Perhaps they had been just too polite to say anything, or perhaps they had thought that the British Embassy really did have a junior official with the quaintly antique title of 'Second Secretary (Flags)'.

That mistake in Arabic had been a blow to my pride, but not potentially fatal. The Political Counsellor in the Embassy, Tony Reeve, had, however, had a rather closer call. One Monday morning he asked me breezily to remind him what the Arabic for 'mines' as in land mines was. I told him: *alghaam*. He turned white. He had spent the weekend with his family on the Red Sea coast. Like the Prince and Princess of Wales, he had wanted to find a mine-free beach from which the family could swim. He had asked a feckless Egyptian sentry if there were any mines on the beach they had chosen. None, the sentry, had replied. But Tony now realised that, from his dimly remembered MECAS *Word List*, he had retrieved the word for mineral mines (*managim*), not that for land mines. He was hugely relieved, the more so when a few weeks later we heard that two Norwegians had chosen the same beach for a swim. They had stepped on a mine, and left nothing but their shoes.

In late July 1983, Bridget, Harry and I left Cairo by Land Rover. We crossed the northern Sinai Peninsula, taking the coast road past the Israeli settlements which had been demolished when Israel had finally withdrawn from Sinai in April 1982. On the Egyptian side, the border post was a fly-blown affair, with a hut, a guard and an ancient field telephone. We were looking forward to relaxing in Jerusalem with the friends with whom we planned to stay. But not so fast. The border guard announced that nine-month-old Harry could not leave Egypt. He had an exit visa, to be sure, but no entry visa. As patiently as I could, I pointed out that he had been born in Cairo, and could not therefore have an entry visa in a passport issued by the British Embassy there. The border guard insisted. I got him to try to raise Cairo on his field telephone. After cranking the handset for what seemed like an age, he announced that there was no reply. But then our secret weapon kicked in: Harry started to cry, very loudly. Egyptians are kindly people, and none can resist the sound of a bawling child. The border guard offered a compromise: Harry (and his mother) could leave Egypt on the exit visa, go round the hut, re-enter on an entry visa the guard would provide for a fee, and then leave again. It was a neat solution to a problem that should never have been: the Egyptian Arabic for red tape is *al Ruteen*.

We crossed the frontier, to be greeted by striking Israeli women border guards, flaunting Uzi sub-machine guns. But appearances were deceptive: courtesy was not a quality they shared with the Arabs on the other side of the fence. We raced on, through the pine groves of the Gaza Strip. Three happy days in Jerusalem followed, and then we set off for the port city of Haifa and the ferry back to Piraeus, via Cyprus and Rhodes. Our fake Egyptian diplomatic number plates (which the Embassy garage had run up for me, after the originals had had to be returned to the Foreign Ministry) attracted surprisingly friendly attention within Green Line Israel but hostile stares in the Occupied Territories. We soon worked out why: Israel had opened its border with Lebanon to its Maronite allies in the South Lebanon Army, and Arabic number plates from Christian Lebanon were not an uncommon sight in Israel. Nothing in the Middle East was simple.

As we sailed from Haifa, with all its memories of the British Mandate over Palestine, I little dreamed that, in eighteen years' time, I would sail back into the great harbour as British ambassador to the State of Israel.

Chapter 4

Immortal Junior Typist

In 1983, I took the Optional Route for my return from the Middle East, just as I had on the way out in 1978 and again in 1980. Wisely, the Foreign Office still allowed its diplomats and their dependants travelling to and from the region to go by car, train or ferry, and would meet the costs, up to the price of an air fare for each of the travellers. And so, as our Land Rover rolled off the ferry at Piraeus, and we started the long haul north and west, we knew that most of what we spent on travel could be reclaimed on arrival in London. But the Office's apparent generosity wasn't disinterested: giving young diplomats time to explore and learn made good operational sense. It was an idyllic journey, up from Greece's coastal plain, through the mountains of Macedonia and along the valleys of the Sava and Drava rivers, through mountains and forests of extraordinary beauty at rest in the August heat. Everywhere was hot and still, and surprisingly green. After the parched hills of Palestine, it was good to be back in the verdant lands of the north. Mostly, we camped, or stayed in cheap hotels. But in Belgrade we caught up with friends in the Embassy and saw something of the magnificence of the city. We paid our respects at Tito's tomb. In the open-air privacy of the fields around the dacha our friends were renting on the Danube, we heard about the rigorous tradecraft and suffocating loneliness of operating as an intelligence officer. In Old Belgrade, there was that elegiac sense of a lost central European past, one evoked by Patrick Leigh Fermor's accounts of his pre-war walk down the Danube,* and, in a different register, by Hergé's account of Tintin's adventures in

---

* *A Time of Gifts*, London: John Murray, 1977.

70

Syldavia in pursuit of King Ottokar's Sceptre.* I remembered what we had been told at Oxford about the similarities between the Serbian tradition of oral poetry, with its formulaic composition, and that of the poet or poets now known as Homer. And I wondered about Hadrian's legions, marching and counter-marching up and down what had become one of the great trunk routes of an earlier empire – the Via Egnatia. From Belgrade we went on up the flat valley, passing Turkish truck after Turkish truck, to Zagreb, and over the mountains to a richer, more familiar, damper, tidier Europe. But the dust and heat of the south were now in my blood: for me, Goethe's line encapsulated every northern European's longing for the warmth of the south: 'Kennst du das Land, wo die Zitronen blühn?'

Across the Channel, up the Dover Road and on to Devon and Nottinghamshire to visit our families and show off the new baby. But I still did not know what my next job would be. Until, one afternoon, the phone rang at my mother's house: standing outside the window in the garden, I took the call from the Personnel Operations Department. We want you to start, as soon as possible, in the Foreign Office Planning Staff.

I was delighted. My only previous encounter with the planners had been when the unforgivingly cerebral head planner, Christopher Mallaby, had come to Cairo for what were optimistically known as 'planning talks'. I had been impressed by the range and depth of Mallaby's brief, looking beyond and beneath the horizon, in as many possible directions at once. I knew that the planners were clever, and were supposed to be close to the Foreign Secretary – a sort of intellectual Praetorian Guard. And I was intrigued to be working in a department headed by Pauline Neville-Jones, who already had a formidable reputation.

I was not disappointed, even though the real work started slowly. The Planning Staff had at least three roles. They produced forward-looking planning papers – what would now be called strategic think pieces – for the monthly meetings of the committee of Foreign Office deputy under secretaries (now called directors general) chaired by the

---

* Hergé, *King Ottokar's Sceptre*, London: Methuen, 1958.

Permanent Under Secretary. They drafted the Foreign Secretary's speeches, and provided drafts of those on foreign policy to the Prime Minister and occasionally other ministers. And they served as the secretariat for the private system of Cold War consultation between the four Western powers – the United States, Britain, France and Germany – known as the Quad. This system was private, not because we didn't want the Russians to know about it, or even because we didn't think the Russians didn't know about it, but to keep out the Italians, who always wanted to be at the top European table, but whose communications were, and probably still are, notoriously leaky. Of course, the Italians too knew about the Quad's existence, but, if it was secret and deniable, their pride was salvageable, when we told them that we didn't know what they were talking about.

Pauline Neville-Jones was not easy to work for, but she knew what she wanted, and liked, and was usually right. Her bark – which frightened men more than women – was far worse than her bite. Underneath the donnish exterior was an extremely kind and generous, and somewhat shy and vulnerable, person of great intelligence and sensitivity. When I left the planners, she cooked at her home in Chelsea for me and a dozen of my guests one of the best dinners I have ever had in a private house. I was the member of the Planning Staff who accompanied her for talks with other foreign ministries' central strategy units. In this capacity, I once went with her back to Cairo. As Christopher Mallaby had found, 'planning' was not a concept that came naturally to the Egyptians. But Pauline persevered, and, as a reward for our labours, decided that she and I should have a day in Upper Egypt, which she had never visited. After an exhausting morning touring the temples of Karnak, Pauline announced that she wanted me to take her to a typically Egyptian restaurant for a relaxing lunch. I found a suitable place, on the banks of the Nile. When the waiter brought the menu, Pauline waved it away. She was getting in the swing of things and was beginning to feel as though she was on holiday in the Dordogne (where she had a house). She would do as she did there, and go into the kitchen and choose direct from the food the patron was preparing. It was a *big* mistake. She entered the kitchen, to find the 'patron', clad only in a loincloth and sweating heavily, struggling to cut up a lump of blue-grey meat covered in flies. The kitchen felt like a cross between an abattoir and an inferno, awash with blood and rotting flesh and dirt and dust, and infested with cats. Pauline beat a hasty retreat and announced that she wasn't feeling hungry after all: a glass of sweet tea would keep her going until we got back to the Sheraton in Cairo that evening.

During my time in the planners, Pauline had two, quite different, deputies. David Manning was the prototypical Foreign Office mandarin: capable, unflappable and with a keen sense of the politically possible. The second, Alyson Bailes, was one of the cleverest – probably the cleverest – person ever to join the Diplomatic Service. She spoke and wrote Hungarian, and later taught herself Mandarin. But she had two flaws: she produced more good work than most lesser minds could absorb, and she hated hot climates. Alyson's early departure from the Foreign Office was a great loss to the public service.

As a planner, you were expected to think, and then write. In order to do so, you had the privilege, as a junior first secretary, of an office of your own. My work started slowly. I wrote a paper on the Philippines after the American withdrawal from the great bases at Subic Bay and Clark Field, which no one much noticed: South-east Asia was never really a Foreign Office priority, and, with America's land war in Asia over, no one then regarded military confrontation in the seas to the south and east of China as a likely possibility. A second paper, on Turkey, rather cornily entitled 'One Country, Two Continents', excited more interest, but with the usual agonising about whether Turkey could be ever truly European. Our heads told us we had to welcome it into the European fold, Islamic warts, obstinate generals and all, but our hearts were not enthusiastic. Prolonged courtship, with full consummation a distant and ever receding prospect, seemed then, as now, the preferred policy prescription.

But, then, in early 1984, I had a breakthrough. Furious at Reagan's unilateral decision to invade Grenada in October 1983, the Prime Minister, Mrs Thatcher, was fretting about what would happen if Reagan decided to do the same to Nicaragua. If she believed in one thing, Mrs Thatcher believed in the rule of law, abroad as well as at home. For her an unprovoked attack on Grenada, a sovereign state – which happened to be part of what the Americans persisted in calling the 'British Commonwealth', with the Queen as its head of state – was a gross breach of international law. As with other difficult issues during Mrs Thatcher's time as PM, the answer, her staff concluded, was to dig deeper: to hold a policy seminar at Chequers. The format was almost always the same. Outside experts, usually including Mrs Thatcher's favourite historian, the Chichele Professor of the History of War at Oxford, Michael Howard, would attend for a morning session, followed by a lunch for everyone. Then, in the afternoon, ministers and officials would go into private conclave, 'to draw conclusions for policy'. Given the Prime Minister's intellectual rigour, and her love of debate, it was a formula that worked well, and was one which later resulted in her courageous decision to reverse course and engage with the Soviet Union in general, and Mikhail Gorbachev in particular.

But in 1984 the matter in hand was armed intervention in other states. Someone had to produce a paper for the Chequers seminar, and I was given the task. I could not have asked for a more enjoyable, or more interesting, challenge. I ranged quickly across the literature on the moral, legal and humanitarian arguments for and against invading another state outside the hallowed principle of self-defence enshrined in Article 51 of the United Nations Charter. I produced a paper – a mini-dissertation really – entitled 'Is Intervention Ever Justified?' Although the Permanent Secretary's first reaction to the draft was that it was too intellectual, it was read and approved by one of those invited to the seminar, the Professor of International Law at the London School of Economics, Rosalyn Higgins. My conclusion was that, unless in self-defence, armed intervention without the authority of the Security Council could hardly ever be justified and was even more rarely wise. It was a conclusion which was to stand the test of time, and one which I had much in mind as, twenty years later, the Government for which I worked intervened in two Muslim states. In an early example of open government, the Foreign Office decided to publish, anonymously, the Chequers Seminar paper in its Foreign Policy Documents series.* I was surprised, and I confess flattered, later to find it cited in footnotes to academic articles on intervention.

---

* *Is Intervention Ever Justified?*, Foreign Policy Document no. 148, London: FCO, 1986.

The seminar came and went, without any real consequences for policy, except that the Prime Minister was reinforced in her conviction that it would be wrong (in every way) for the Americans to invade Nicaragua, and that she should tell them so – in private of course. Unlike at least one of her successors, Mrs Thatcher believed that the Special Relationship should be a load-bearing structure, capable of carrying two-way traffic. A couple of years earlier, a mole in our Washington Embassy told me, Mrs Thatcher had spent just a bit too much time and energy telling the President what she thought. Sitting beside her, the Foreign Secretary, Lord Carrington, had passed her a note which read 'Shut up, now, Margaret,' or words to that effect. The vignette says something about both the Prime Minister's and her Foreign Secretary's courage in speaking truth to their respective powers.

That spring, however, the chief speechwriter in the Planning Staff decided to leave the public service, to try his hand – rather successfully, it turned out – in the private sector. I was thrilled when Pauline asked me to succeed him.

Writing for the Foreign Secretary, Sir Geoffrey Howe, did not, however, offer much scope for great rhetorical flourishes. We relied more on the steamroller effect of remorseless legal logic. I assembled a shelf of books of jokes and quotations, with which to liven up our speeches. But the Foreign Secretary almost always substituted, after last-minute discussion in the car with his detectives, Welsh legal jokes. I realised what hard work it was going to be when I wrote the Foreign Secretary's speech for the annual dinner of the Royal Society for Asian Affairs, and proudly booked expensive tickets for the dinner, in order to hear my words of wisdom delivered by my boss. Sir Geoffrey's mellifluous Welsh-Wykehamical monotone had the effect which many of my fellow guests wanted after a large and lovely dinner, and they dozed contentedly. The balloon of my pride was properly punctured. Those of my words he had used were largely inaudible.

Speechwriting wasn't always like that. One morning I woke to the BBC news announcing that, in a speech in Bonn the previous evening, the Foreign Secretary had set a new course for Anglo-German relations. I wondered what this was, until I realised that the reference was to a speech which I had drafted for Sir Geoffrey to give to the German

Foreign Policy Association. It had been meticulously cleared, around Whitehall and with the Embassy in Bonn. In my view, it had said nothing new or exceptional. But, perhaps in order to generate some profile for the Foreign Secretary, the Foreign Office News Department had pitched the speech as being more exciting than it really was. It showed how a speech could make policy – at least on a slow news day.

My first speech for Sir Geoffrey had been one for a National Farmers' Union dinner in Exeter. With my dairy farmer uncles in Devon in mind, I put my heart and soul into a speech that disappeared without trace. No publicity, no reaction from either the Foreign Secretary or his Private Office. A speech in which he did take much more interest was one to the British Institute of International and Comparative Law, about the role of international law in foreign affairs. This speech was long and dull and worthy. It went out for consultation, to the Foreign Secretary's favourite source of outside advice, David Calcutt QC. In fact, if Sir Geoffrey was in doubt on any policy issue (and he often was), his first instinct was to consult his favourite silk. Inevitably, the speech went through interminable drafts. As it approached take-off, we moved from horizontal (or landscape) mode (which gave the Foreign Secretary plenty of scope for scribbling comments in the open acres of margin) to the vertical (or portrait) mode. Those were the early days of word processors, with printers hammering out the pages in huge sound-proof cabinets. Working for a man who was an incorrigible fiddler, I wondered how anybody ever managed without word processing.

A speech I did not have anything to do with – luckily – was one in which the Foreign Secretary, daringly and rightly, expressed doubts about the wisdom of the Reagan Administration's Star Wars initiative. Formally, the speech had been cleared by the Prime Minister, although her formidable Private Secretary, Charles Powell, wasn't clear whether he had actually shown it to her, or, as someone told us, she had fallen asleep over the draft before coming to the good bits. Either way, once the Prime Minister saw the headlines reporting that the Foreign Secretary had made a speech casting aspersions on one of the jewels in the ideological crown of the Reagan Administration, the reaction from Number 10 was fast and furious. Explanations were called for, apologies sought. The incident was one of those that gradually destroyed the trust between Mrs Thatcher and her third, and longest-serving, Foreign Secretary.

As speechwriter, I found that most officials had a tin ear when producing prose that a politician of any ambition would be prepared to use in public. Great slabs of unusable expert gobbledygook had to be turned into words that actually had a chance of penetrating the mind of a sceptical and presumed ignorant listener. Curiously, in an institution which prided itself on its drafting, only a few parts of the Foreign Office – mostly those on the policy front line – had the talent and the political sensitivity to turn out language suitable for being deployed in real political action. Gradually, experience, and plenty of trial and error, taught me what made a good – and (not necessarily the same thing) successful – speech. By successful most politicians mean plenty of publicity, whereas officials mean a speech that makes the right points persuasively to the handful of people who really matter on any particular issue. I tried to apply the principles of Greek rhetoric I had learned at school: essentially, say what you are going to say, say it, and then say what you have said. I excavated, and circulated, George Orwell's Six Rules of Good Writing.* And I drew up a Thatcher's Thesaurus – really a Prime Ministerial vocab list, full of words such as 'staunch' and 'steadfast', and 'liberty' and 'law'.

Even so, the first speech I wrote for Mrs Thatcher missed its target by an embarrassingly wide margin. It was the opening address to the Commonwealth Heads of Government Meeting in New Delhi in November 1983. I was proud of my production. After clearing it with senior officials in the Foreign Office, I submitted it to the Private Office, who duly sent it across to the other side of Downing Street. Smugly, I sat back, waiting for the expected words of praise from the Prime Minister. One weekend soon after, I was doing my turn in the Foreign Office as a resident clerk when the Duty Clerk at Number 10 rang. With thinly disguised glee, he said he wanted to give me 'a heads-up on the

---

* 1. Never use a metaphor or figure of speech which you are used to seeing in print; 2. Never use a long word where a short one will do; 3. If it is possible to cut a word out, cut it out; 4. Never use a foreign phrase, a scientific word or a jargon word if you can think of an everyday English equivalent; 5. Never use the passive where you can use the active; 6. Break any of these rules sooner than say anything outright barbarous.

THATCHER'S THESAURUS

A SPEECH WRITER'S COMPANION

Conviction - N. Belief, value, vision, confidence, purpose,
determination, firmness, steadfastness, resolution, will;
discipline, strength, challange, task; freedom, opportunity,
enterprise, liberty, innovation, opportunity, work, battle, fight;
deed; achievement, triumph; success, integrity, trust, loyalty,
justice.

Adj. - Staunch, steadfast, determined, resolved; loyal, courageous,
brilliant, marvellous, valiant, gallant, splendid, brave, noble,
tragic, poor, democratic; true.

Vb. - Work, strive, seek, find, yield (not to); resolve, fight,
compete, flourish, prosper, pledge, devote, work.

Prime Minister's thoughts on your draft'. She had, he said, reacted quite strongly, so strongly in fact that when she had written the word 'NO' across the draft her pen had gone right through the paper. The only word of my original to survive the rewriting process was 'Commonwealth'. Given the forum, there was no obvious alternative.

After that, things could only get better, and they did. Four years later, after I had arrived in Washington, I was given the task of drafting two of the main speeches the Prime Minister was to deliver during her visit to Washington to say farewell to Ronald Reagan, and to welcome his successor, George H. W. Bush. The visit, in late November 1988, just after the Presidential election which I had covered for the Embassy, was an emotional one, with the Prime Minister being given a reception just short of that for a head of state. For Mrs Thatcher, the speech that mattered most was the one at the White House dinner which the out-going President was giving in her honour. I put my all into that speech, leaving no cliché unturned, no corny truism of the love-in between Reaganite Republicans and Thatcherite Conservatives unused. I wondered whether my draft lapsed into over-heated self-parody. But Mrs Thatcher used every word, and delivered it with the controlled force that was the hallmark of her speaking style. I had been at a loss as to how to end the oration, but had eventually found, in Field Marshal Lord Wavell's anthology of poetry *Other Men's Flowers*,* the Arthur Hugh Clough poem which ends 'But Westward look, the land is bright'. The allusion to the United States, and to the West, was, I thought, clear. But, as the Prime Minister turned and, looking fondly at a Ronald Reagan who was about to leave Washington for his beloved California, delivered the words about the West, I am sure the President thought she meant that it was the land to the west of the Rockies that was bright.

Years later, to my horror, I discovered that Churchill had used the same Arthur Hugh Clough couplet in one of his wartime messages to Roosevelt from a 'former naval person'. But I suppose a cliché wouldn't be a cliché if it wasn't worth reusing.

One other event during that visit sticks in my memory. The Secretary of State, George Shultz, was to give a grand lunch in the Prime Minister's

---

* London: Jonathan Cape, 1944.

honour in the fine rooms on the seventh floor of the State Department. Just before the lunch, a team of us from the Embassy and Number 10, including the Prime Minister's detectives, walked the course. Carefully concealed in the podium from which George Shultz was due to address several hundred guests was a woman's handbag. Worried, we called security, who came rushing up. They hadn't spotted the handbag, but soon had it open. It was empty, apart from a sheaf of papers, which, on closer examination, turned out to be extracts from speeches by Margaret Thatcher dating back many years. We were puzzled, but decided to leave it there. All became clear as Shultz rose to speak after the lunch. As a token of appreciation for all Mrs Thatcher had done for the West, and for Anglo-American relations, he wanted to give her a small gift. Apparently wholly unaware of what 'handbagging' meant in colloquial English English, or of its association with a woman Prime Minister intolerant of wetness of any kind, Shultz announced that he was awarding Margaret Thatcher the Order of the Handbag. He then pulled the concealed object out from beneath the lectern and handed it to her, announcing that he had filled it with excerpts from his favourite Thatcher speeches. It was another case of two nations divided by a common language.

For interest's sake, and in order to help boost the family finances, I had become a resident clerk. It was a curious life, one night a week, one weekend in six, spent in an almost deserted Foreign Office – deserted except for a duty messenger in a cubbyhole down in the basement, and the communicators in the Comm Cen near by. At the weekend, things would brighten up, as the News and Consular Department duty officers and a duty secretary came in. If there wasn't a crisis, the Resident Clerk would cook Sunday lunch, while News Department supplied the wine. Everything that you learned in the Clerkery stayed in the Clerkery. You saw slices of other people's crises: deaths abroad, personnel problems, international incidents not yet big enough for the Emergency Rooms to be opened and manned. As foreign secretary, Sir Geoffrey Howe seemed to imagine that the clerks sat manning a console, from which they could monitor the state of the world. He would often ring in the early morning to ask what was going on. In Whitehall, we dealt mainly with the Duty Clerk in Number 10. One Saturday afternoon, Number

The plaque from the old Residence in Jeddah, which now hangs outside the house that the Ambassador uses in the British Consulate-General there, since all embassies moved to the Saudi capital, Riyadh, in the mid-eighties.

The Middle East Centre for Arab Studies, in Shemlan, Lebanon, in September 1978. The chief instructor, Douglas Galloway, is fourth from the left in the front row, with me standing behind his right shoulder, arms folded. I can count at least six future ambassadors.

River crossing, June 1980: I drive my beloved Mini ashore from the 'popular' ferry at Luxor, up on to the west bank of the Nile and towards the Valley of the Kings.

Abdul, my *suffragi*, at work in the cockroach-infested kitchen of my flat in Cairo. He carried a picture of Winston Churchill in his wallet, and adored British military Spam.

Opposite: An Egyptian newspaper report of a farewell party in my flat in March 1981 for Tony Brenton, the First Secretary (Economic), who was leaving after three years in the Cairo Chancery. Top right are the Ambassador, Michael Weir, and his wife, Hilary. Bottom left is Tony, talking to Wilfred Thesiger (who was visiting Cairo) and Mark Allen, also in the Chancery. Above, I am talking to a commentator from Al Ahram.

متحدثوا العربية بالسفارة البريطانية ينقصون واحد

المستشار الاقتصادي البريطاني يعود إلى لند

المضيف شيرارد كوبر يتحدث مع الأستاذ سيد ياسين مدير مركز الدراسات الاستراتيجية

السفير البريطاني سير ميشيل سكوت واير والسيدة هيلاري حرمه

توني برنتون يتحدث إلى ويلفريد سيجر المؤلف البريطاني المشهور والذي كتب عدة كتب منها « الرمال العربية » و « مسيرة العرب » وهو مقيم منذ فترة طويلة مع القبائل الأفريقية في كينيا وكان في طريقه من نيروبي إلى لندن حيث يقضي ثلاثة شهور كل سنة . وإلى اليسار مارك الن المستشار السياسي للسفارة البريطانية يستمع إلى حديثهما

والذي يصعب ضبطه متلبسا بالتحدث باللغة الانجليزية الا مـع الأجانب ، فمن المعروف أنه يتحدث العربية بطلاقة ، ويجدر بنا أن نذكر أن عددا آخر من الدبلوماسيين البريطانيين في القاهرة من بينهم مارك الن ، يتحدثون العربية بطلاقة .

بعد ثلاث سنوات قضاها في القاهرة وعمل خلالها أولا كمستشار صحفي للسفارة البريطانية ثم جذبته الاحداث الاقتصادية فترك مجال الصحافة واصبح مستشارا اقتصاديا تقرر نقل تـونى برنتون ، واسمه الحقيقى انتونى برنتون من القاهرة الى لندن . توني برنتون سوف يبدأ عملا جديدا في وزارة الخارجية البريطانية حيث يلتحق بإدارة السوق الاوروبية المشتركة .

بمناسبة سفر تونى اقيمت له حفلات تـوديـع عديدة حضرها الكثيرون من اصدقائه الدبلوماسيين الاجانب ورجال الاعلام المصريين .

ومن هذه الحفلات تلك التى اقامها شيرارد كوبر الملحق الصحفى البريطانى

مدير المعهد الفرنسى للتغليف يتحدث غدا فى الميريديان

فى السابعة والنصف مساء غد .. يتحدث بيير لوى الخبير الدولى ومدير المعهد الفرنسى للتغليف ورئيس مجموعة المعلومات بالاتحاد الاوربى للتغليف .. وذلك فى المؤتمر الصحفى الذى يعقده فى فندق الميريديان .. وسوف يعقب المؤتمر الصحفى حفل كوكتيل .

ويتحدث بيير لوى عن اهمية التغليف والمواد والآلات الحديثة التى تستهدف تطويره .. وسوف يجيب عن الاستفسارات الفنية التى يحددها رجال الاعمال والمتخصصون فى صناعة التعبئة والتغليف فى مصر ■

On top of the world: on my twenty-seventh birthday, 8 January 1982, I climbed the Great Pyramid of Giza with a colleague, Christopher Prentice, later Ambassador in Amman, Baghdad and Rome. We did so, quite illegally, in the before-dawn dark, to avoid detection.

Bringing back the bag: one of the pleasures of winter in Egypt was weekends spent with Abdul Gader in Wadi Natrun, in the desert half-way between Cairo and Alexandria, shooting the (very) occasional duck.

President Sadat cancelled a state visit to Austria in order to attend this dinner on board the Royal Yacht *Britannia*, when she visited Port Said at the end of the Royal honeymoon cruise in August 1981.

The Times took this photograph in October 1983 to accompany a piece about the Foreign Office Planning Staff by Peter Hennessy. The head planner, Pauline Neville-Jones, is at the centre, with me (sitting on a pile of telephone directories) to the left, and, on the table to the right, her deputy, David Manning.

Taxi for Mr Mound, Shanghai, June 1985: the PUS, Sir Antony Acland, and the Consul-General, Trevor Mound, on the steps of the Consulate-General, bracketed by Jeff and Jean Harrod (who provided the rest of the post's British staff).

The Permanent Under Secretary's Office, July 1987: this picture was taken on my last day as I handed over to my successor, Geoffrey Adams (on the right). Also pictured are the PUS, Patrick Wright, in the centre, and the two other members of the team, Jeff Harrod and Lorraine Harrison, between him and me.

Bobby Kennedy's son, Congressman Joe Kennedy, was one of HMG's most persistent critics on Northern Ireland, but somehow I established a working relationship with him.

Mrs Thatcher comes to town:
I escort the Prime Minister
through the government US
guest house, Blair House,
during her visit to Washington
in November 1988 to say
farewell to Ronald Reagan and
to congratulate the President-
elect, George H. W. Bush.

Blair House again, June 1991:
relaxing with the best of bosses,
Antony Acland, after the Queen's
state visit. I am sporting the
alligator skin boots that the
American Protocol Chief gave
me, with 'SCC' painted in gold
down each side.

Hong Kong, 1994: Chris Patten's faithful political adviser, Ed Llewellyn, makes a point in the Government House private office.

The Governor's private secretary, Martin Dinham: no one worked harder, or was more unfailingly cheerful.

The 'Mayor of Hong Kong': Chris Patten looks down on Hong Kong Harbour, with the Island behind, from a helicopter of the colony's own mini-air force – the Royal Hong Kong Auxiliary Air Force.

10 rang to say that the Prime Minister had been speaking to Mr Robert Maxwell about his plan to have the *Daily Mirror* charter a British Airways plane to fly food (and Maxwell) to the victims of the Ethiopian famine. Mrs Thatcher wanted the FCO to help: would I ring Mr Maxwell? I did, and spoke to the great proprietor at his home in Oxford, Headington Hall. I said that, if I was to obtain flight clearances for the *Mirror* mercy mission, I would need the aircraft's tail number. Maxwell said grandly that BA's Chairman, Lord King of Wartnaby, had all the details. Naively, I took him at his word. Somehow, I extracted Lord King's home number, in Leicestershire, from the BA control centre at Heathrow. Eventually, I got through. King was furious. He had just got in from hunting and knew nothing whatsoever about 'bloody Maxwell's charter', let alone the tail number of the aircraft. Such operational matters were far below the Chairman's pay grade.

I would happily have stayed on in my day job as speechwriter almost indefinitely. I loved writing, and being able to combine that with politics and policy was a dream fulfilled. But early in 1985, after I had been doing the job for less than a year, I was told that the Permanent Under Secretary, Sir Antony Acland, wanted to interview me for the job of his private secretary. I hardly knew him, having met him only once or twice, including in Egypt when he and his wife had accompanied the Carringtons on a short winter cruise up the Nile. I was amazed even to have been considered: the man in the job was eight years older than me, and a consummate courtier. And to be honest, I had heard mixed reports: Sir Antony was said to have a short fuse, to be something of a snob and to be no intellectual.

It turned out that all of those claims had, as Antony would have said, elements of truth to them. But they were only a small part of a much bigger and more positive picture. I can't now remember much of the interview, and still don't know why Antony chose me, although I suspect that, recently widowed, he may have hoped that I might help cheer him up. I worked for him, in London, and then Washington, for the best part of the next six years. I came hugely to admire him, above all for his judgement, of people and of policies, but also for his kindness, for a mischievous sense of humour too often obscured by shyness, and for courage and conscientiousness of the highest order. He was the best of public servants, and a worthy recipient of the Garter eventually bestowed on him.

The transition from the languorous life of the Policy Planner to the unforgiving intensity of acting as private secretary to the man at the head and heart of Britain's foreign policy machine was not easy. For a start, the work rate was punishing, especially for a junior diplomat with a young and growing family (two toddlers, and two more children born during my time in the PUS's office). For two and a half years, I was always in the office before 8 a.m., sometimes well before 8 a.m., and I almost never left before 8 p.m. In those days, Foreign Office staff obliged to work until after nine were entitled to a cab home. More evenings than not I would find myself collapsing into a taxi at ten o'clock, dog tired. What made the job bearable was that, apart from reading a few papers, my weekends were largely untroubled: as I was not working for a politician (that was to come later), I was not on call on Saturdays and Sundays.

My boss's full title was Permanent Under Secretary of State and Head of the Diplomatic Service. On a visit to Japan, one of his predecessors was said to have been introduced by an over-literal interpreter to a mystified Japanese Foreign Minister as the immortal junior typist of the Foreign Office. The PUS was head of a great department of state, in charge of a worldwide network of nearly 400 diplomatic posts, employing some 5,000 UK-based staff and at least the same number hired locally. He had to oversee senior appointments in the Diplomatic Service, at home and abroad. He was the Accounting Officer for the Foreign Office budget, and for those of the BBC World Service and the British Council. He was responsible for a diplomatic estate worth billions, with buildings and compounds of huge historic interest and value in the world's great cities. He was the Foreign Secretary's principal adviser on policy. He kept in touch with his opposite numbers in the world's main foreign ministries. He was the Foreign Office's chief representative in Whitehall, in dealing with other departments, ranging from Number 10 and the Cabinet Office to the Treasury. He was the docking point between the Foreign Office and the British economic and commercial establishment. Less publicly, he had a role in overseeing the work of the two overseas intelligence agencies, the Secret Intelligence

Service, then based in Lambeth, and Britain's signals intelligence agency, GCHQ, based in Cheltenham. In 1985, the government still refused officially to avow that either agency – or the domestic intelligence agency, the Security Service – actually existed. Finally, the PUS managed the overseas aspects of the British ceremonial and honours systems: wearing a dark-blue diplomatic uniform adorned with gold oak leaves, he would be present when foreign ambassadors to the Court of St James's presented their credentials to the Queen. It was he who had to handle the sometimes absurd abstractions of the honours system as applied to those who served British interests abroad. The only aspect of foreign policy the PUS didn't deal with – at least not directly – was Parliamentary politics, an activity I was to see much more of when I worked as principal private secretary to the Foreign Secretary, Robin Cook.

Done well, or even not so well, it was a huge job. To help him, the PUS had a private secretary (me), an assistant private secretary (usually a high-performing main-stream officer), a diary secretary and two personal assistants. Vital to the team, but not actually in the Private Office, were our messengers, and the drivers from the Foreign Office car pool. The messengers at that time were a couple of ladies from south London who were based in a little cabin outside our office. They provided endless cups of tea and coffee. They delivered and collected urgent papers, either by hand or through the elaborate network of pneumatic (or Lamson) tubes that at that time still linked different parts of the Foreign Office to our communications centre, and the Foreign Office to the other side of Downing Street, and to the Defence Ministry across Whitehall. We were based in the corner offices on the ground floor of the west side of the Foreign Office, looking out across Horse Guards and St James's Park. We were immediately below the Foreign Secretary's even grander suite of offices on the first floor.

As private secretary, or PS/PUS, my job was to make the PUS's job easier. I had to manage the flow of information in to him, and the flow of instructions or comments out from him, to keep his diary properly paced, to make sure that records of any significant conversations he had, in person or by telephone, were made and transmitted to all who needed to know, and to keep my eyes and ears open for bumps in the road ahead or things he might not find out himself, but would need to know. Twenty-five years his junior, I was in many respects his official alter ego. It was utterly exhausting, but exhilarating too. I learned more, more intensively, in my two and a half years in the PUS's office than at any other time in my career.

Inevitably, given the pressure of business, the PUS couldn't do everything. He had to prioritise and delegate. The Foreign Secretary, Sir Geoffrey Howe, for whom he worked, was almost obsessively interested in detail, anxious to have every relevant fact at his fingertips before making a decision. But Antony was lucky that the FCO had a political director of extraordinary ability in Julian Bullard, a fellow of All Souls College, Oxford, to whom much of the 'routine' policy work could be entrusted. Wisely, Antony concentrated on a few key issues of especial political salience or sensitivity: the negotiations over the future of Hong Kong, for example, relations with the Soviet Union and the transatlantic relationship.

Relations with Geoffrey Howe were not helped by the fact that he had a private secretary who acted as an amplifier rather than a shock absorber for some of his boss's work-creating traits. One of Antony's successors as PUS once commented to me that a good private secretary, or at least a good private secretary to Geoffrey Howe, should always have a large pending tray, into which the overnight musings of the Foreign Secretary could be put, to see if they really deserved to go any further. Sir Geoffrey was a great man for coming into the Office in the morning, having worked diligently through his overnight box of papers, with all sorts of queries and questions. A good private secretary would try to select only those that required or deserved immediate action from those better left to moulder and mature in the pending tray. But Sir Geoffrey's over-anxious acolyte seemed to insist on turning all his boss's musings into requests (which were effectively instructions) for further advice from a policy machine already under great strain. Antony struggled to get the team upstairs to filter out some of the Minister's more ephemeral enquiries, but with only partial success.

This aversion to risk, the tendency to want to examine every possible aspect of any issue, was one of her Foreign Secretary's characteristics that seemed most to annoy Mrs Thatcher. In 1985 she was well into her stride as prime minister, aided by a new private secretary for foreign affairs of exceptional ability and energy, Charles Powell. It had quickly became apparent that he and Mrs Thatcher were made for each other. Powell's ruthless efficiency, his golden pen, his intellectual rigour, his visceral scepticism towards Europe or at least towards ever greater union, and his profoundly Atlanticist views all played into his boss's view of the world. But what he really did for Mrs Thatcher was to give her instincts on foreign policy the intellectual respectability and bureaucratic coherence they needed. Charles knew exactly when to amplify, and when to absorb, the messages that the Prime Minister diligently inscribed each night on the papers put in a box which she almost always finished.

The Foreign Office as a whole was slow to recognise the potency of the Thatcher–Powell combination. Antony's successor as PUS even tried, vainly, to fight it, seeking to have Powell posted abroad, initially and incredibly, to Berne. But Antony at once saw quality and power at work, and made it his business to work with Charles Powell in the wider national interest, as well as that of the Foreign Office. Once a week, Charles would come across for a private talk with the PUS, which I would prepare and attend. As the relationship between Prime Minister and Foreign Secretary deteriorated – it was said that, as with Chancellor Kohl, Mrs Thatcher could hardly bear to have Geoffrey Howe in the room with her – these meetings became more important. The Foreign Secretary was still supposed to have a weekly bilateral of his own with the Prime Minister. But the reports of them that reached us, admittedly mainly from Charles, suggested that, rather like the treatment of Piggy in *Lord of the Flies*, Mrs Thatcher was subjecting her Foreign Secretary to weekly ritual humiliation. 'I know what you are going say, Geoffrey,' is how she was said to have begun one meeting, 'and the answer is *no*.' At other times, the Foreign Secretary would come padding back from Number 10, still clutching the brief we had prepared for him, only to confess that the Prime Minister had not had time to see him, and so he had had a session with Charles instead.

On many or perhaps most issues none of this mattered too much. There were other channels of conducting business, including the relentless efficiency of the Cabinet Office Overseas and Defence (OD) Secretariat. Antony found his own ways around the Prime Minister's deep prejudice against what she persisted in seeing as the Ministry for Foreigners. Filming outside Number 10 one day, a cameraman asked her to shift her position out of the shadow cast by the great government building opposite. 'Oh, typical Foreign Office,' she retorted. 'They always shut out all the light!' At the time, an FCO budget set in fixed quantities of pounds was suffering badly from the falling value of sterling and rising inflation around the world. An effort by the amateur traders of the Foreign Office Finance Department to buy Forex forward had met with mixed success. Something had to be done. The answer was an Overseas Price Mechanism, which compensated the FCO when the markets moved against it, but which surrendered any gains to the Treasury when conditions were more favourable. Geoffrey Howe would have had great difficulty in persuading Margaret Thatcher to agree to such an open-ended arrangement. But Antony did, arranging (via Charles Powell) to have himself invited to tea at Chequers one weekend and charming the Prime Minister, partly by taking her a brace of pheasants. Even if he didn't know it (and he probably did, but was too discreet to say so), he was exploiting Margaret Thatcher's softer side. She enjoyed the company of men who were clever or good-looking or preferably both. Often, after an official dinner at Downing Street, the PM would ask Antony to stay behind for a whisky and a gossip. When Antony's first wife had died, almost the first condolence message he had received had been a handwritten card from the Prime Minister, accompanied by flowers she had picked herself from the Chequers garden.

The other link between Number 10 and the Foreign Office was the Foreign Affairs Adviser Mrs Thatcher had appointed after what she saw as Foreign Office failures in the run-up to the Falklands War of 1982. Throughout my time in the PUS's office, the Adviser was the austerely cerebral Sir Percy Cradock, former Ambassador to China and the godfather of the Sino-British Joint Declaration on Hong Kong of 1984. He had much less of an idea than Charles Powell did of what was on Mrs Thatcher's mind on any particular day, but his weekly sessions with the PUS were like having a ringside seat at a doctoral seminar on world politics. It was a privilege just to be able to sit and listen.

Mrs Thatcher's weakness for clever men extended beyond Britons and Americans. Charles gave a wonderful account of an incident during her return visit to Moscow in March 1987 to see Gorbachev, after she had entertained him at Chequers and concluded that he was someone with whom she could do business. According to Charles, the Russian leader tried to replicate in the Kremlin the country-house fireside chat he had so much enjoyed at Chequers. Dinner was served in a small oak-panelled room with a roaring fire. An oil painting of a stormy sunset, which our Ambassador had not seen before, adorned the wall. Throughout the meal, which was just three-a-side, Mrs Thatcher and her host argued, passionately, about whether capitalism or Communism was better. As they rose to leave, Gorbachev pointed to the painting and said that the stormclouds in it resembled their disagreements over dinner. 'Ah, but Mr General Secretary,' responded Mrs Thatcher, as quick as a flash, 'the light is coming from the West.'

Reading the records of her exchanges with President Mitterrand in those years I got a rather similar impression of an almost sexual subtext to those meetings. One discussion stuck in my mind, with Mrs Thatcher telling the French President that she was 'passionate' about what was then known as the Channel Fixed Link (later the Channel Tunnel). It was Mitterrand who was said to have described the British Prime Minister as having 'les yeux de Caligula, mais la bouche de Marilyn Monroe'. Several years later, after Mrs Thatcher had left office, I was sitting next to her on a sofa after dinner with Chris Patten in Government House, Hong Kong. Fortified by a bit to drink, I said to her that, reading the records of her exchanges with Mitterrand, I had often wondered whether there had been an erotic charge to her encounters with the French President. I woke the next morning, mortified at what I had dared say. But then I recalled that the night before Mrs T had in fact been enormously flattered by my question. Drawing herself upright, nostrils flaring, she had replied, in her most archly flirtatious manner, 'Do you know, Mr Cowper-Coles, I think you may be right.'

Like her decision to engage with Gorbachev's Soviet Union, Mrs Thatcher's decision to negotiate with China over the future of Hong Kong after Britain's ninety-nine-year lease over the New Territories expired in 1997 was another case of her head ruling her heart. Taken carefully through the facts of an issue, she could be rational as well as courageous. In theory, Britain could have kept the island of Hong Kong on as a colony even after the much larger New Territories reverted to Chinese sovereignty. Some diehards argued that case, and many more felt strong emotions about handing the six million people of Hong Kong over to Communist rule. But careful work by Sir Geoffrey Howe, at his forensic best, supported by a team of officials led by Percy Cradock and including Trevor Mound, persuaded her to see where the national interest lay. The whole Hong Kong negotiation was handled superbly, using the proper processes of government, with a Hong Kong sub-committee of the Overseas and Defence Committee of the Cabinet taking all decisions on the basis of closely argued papers covering every aspect of an immensely important negotiation, of great complexity and political sensitivity.

The Sino-British Joint Declaration on the Future of Hong Kong was agreed by Mrs Thatcher and China's paramount leader Deng Xiaoping during her visit to Beijing just before Christmas 1984, on the basis of 'one country, two systems'. Not long afterwards, in early 1985, Mrs Thatcher went on a tour of South-east Asia. My boss, Antony Acland, went with her, as part of a large official entourage. One leg of the journey took her to Singapore, where she met the formidably bright Prime Minister of Singapore, Lee Kuan Yew, the self-appointed mentor of many world leaders. He told Mrs Thatcher how, on hearing the previous December that the Hong Kong agreement had been signed, he had sent a message to his Foreign Minister, asking for a copy to be brought over to the Prime Minister's office as soon as possible. While he was waiting for it to arrive, Lee made a list of all the points he judged such an agreement should cover, in order to maintain confidence in the territory, before and after the handover. Once the text arrived, he had gone through it. He told Mrs Thatcher that he had been able to tick off every one of the points on his list. He congratulated the Prime Minister most warmly on an historic achievement. Antony said that Mrs Thatcher blushed: a compliment from Harry Lee meant a lot to her.

Although the Prime Minister's office was by far the most important part of Whitehall with which the PUS and his small team dealt, it wasn't the only one. Close to Number 10, but not part of it, was the Cabinet Office, headed at that time by Sir Robert Armstrong. Sir Robert was the acme of high officialdom, the mandarins' mandarin. He was the only

Permanent Secretary for whom Antony inserted a 'My' in front of 'Dear' when writing to him officially. It wasn't just that they had both been at Eton, or that the Secretary of the Cabinet and Head of the Home Civil Service was, in a sense, Antony's domestic counterpart. It was something more subtle than that: both Antony and Robert shared a high-minded view of the sacred duties of government service and of the proper despatch of public business. Both knew that there were apparently effortless ways of getting things done, with minimum fuss. As a junior official, watching this from ground level, I was full of admiration. Mostly, I think I admired the speed and clarity with which Robert could distil the most complicated issues into papers ministers could understand and respond to. I could always tell what he had written himself, and what he had had drafted for him. And, given some of the issues with which we were wrestling, it was usually a relief when he took personal control and prepared that steadying, calming, crystal-clear analysis of the problem and of possible solutions that panicking politicians needed. His fine italic hand added to the impression of serene good sense.

The two subjects on which we dealt most with the Cabinet Office were honours and intelligence, and sometimes, and most painfully, the overlap between the two. At that time, in the corner of the PUS's office there was an ancient safe, about the size of a washing machine, in which we kept papers, dating back to before the Second World War, too sensitive to be filed in Foreign Office departments. In two and a half years, I never had time – or cause – to go through them all. But some of the dossiers I do remember extracting. A file of letters from a retiring public servant of great pomposity, who should have had more taste and discretion, arguing that a life peerage wasn't good enough for him, and that a hereditary title was what he deserved. An attempt – apparently unsuccessful – to discover if there was a Soviet mole in MI6, and, if so, who it might have been. A desperately sad record of investigation and interview, confirming that another senior SIS officer had, for decades, been a secret homosexual, at a time when such things would have led immediately to withdrawal of security clearance. Complaints from ambassadors about the behaviour of members of the royal family visiting their parish. Records of secret subventions to long-deposed colonial rulers in whose debt HMG was, or for whom we felt some guilty sympathy. The safe is no longer there: I have often wondered what happened to it and its explosive contents.

In its way that safe symbolised the thrill of the PUS's office: at the centre of almost everything, at the intersection of the worlds of intelligence, appointments and honours, as well as high policy. One of my jobs was to help prepare for meetings of the Permanent Secretary's Honours Committee, which trawled through recommendations from ambassadors, and also from the FCO's own personnel department. Another was supporting the work of the No. 1 Selection Board, which made recommendations to the Foreign Secretary on who should go to the top embassies, on which the Foreign Secretary then consulted the Prime Minister, before putting the names to the Queen – after all, they were Her Britannic Majesty's ambassadors. Inevitably, given their seniority, the deputy under secretaries who made up the membership of both the Honours Committee and the appointments board were themselves candidates for the awards and jobs they were distributing. When such conflicts arose, the DUS – or occasionally PUS – being considered for an honour, or a job, would solemnly leave the room for the time it took the others to decide his fate. As a junior official it struck me as rather farcical. So did the way in which the deputy under secretaries, meeting one week as the senior policy committee advising the Foreign Secretary, would take one decision – for one real example, to increase our diplomatic and consular presence in the United States – and then, meeting the next week as the Foreign Office's management board, would decide to cut the funds available for such expansion. The truth was that all serious decisions were taken by ministers, not by senior officials, and that in those days we had not brought together in a coherent fashion decision-making on policy and resources.

Sitting in the PUS's office I would often learn of sensitive issues affecting friends. One particularly upsetting instance was when a friend and colleague who happened to be gay was tricked into propositioning a Vice Squad officer in a club in London. The police reported him to the Foreign Office's Security Department, who ruled that his security clearance had to be withdrawn – as indeed it had, given the rules at the time. But rather than being dismissed he was allowed to find a job outside, and resign, without anybody who hadn't been involved in the case being any the wiser. You would have thought that the Metropolitan Police had better things to do than hang around gay clubs. We forget now just how paranoid the security people could be in those days: at least two colleagues were investigated because they were suspected, quite unfairly, of being Communist sleepers.

As the PUS's private secretary, I was allowed to see all the intelligence my boss saw, except one stream. For that, the FCO official responsible for liaison with SIS, Peter Wallis (who had been my first boss), would come across from SIS's then headquarters, Century House near Waterloo, bearing a locked briefcase. Peter would sit with the PUS while he read the papers, and then take them away afterwards. I did not know what this reporting was about, and didn't ask. Suddenly, however, the meetings with the man from Century House became more frequent, and I decided that we had to give them a name. Unwisely, I suggested to the Diary Secretary that we block them off in the diary as 'Boris' meetings, only to receive a quiet but sharp suggestion from SIS that the name wasn't appropriate.

I soon discovered why. The intelligence reports in question had been from Oleg Gordievsky, a KGB officer who had become an MI6 agent in 1974. In 1985 he was nominally a counsellor in the Soviet Embassy in London, but was in reality the acting KGB Resident (that is, head of the KGB Station in the UK). According to his own account,* in May 1985 Gordievsky was suddenly recalled to Moscow, because his masters suspected that he was spying for the West. That wasn't because of any failure in SIS tradecraft, but probably because he had been betrayed by, Gordievsky thought, Aldrich Ames, a CIA officer who had become a Soviet agent. Either way, back in Moscow in July Gordievsky gave the prearranged signal to the SIS Station there that his life was in danger, and that he needed to be exfiltrated. The SIS recognition signal – a man walking past the Kievsky underground station carrying a Harrods bag and eating a Mars Bar – was duly given. Two brave SIS officers left Moscow to pick him up in a forest outside Leningrad. On their way, they noticed Soviet security vehicles giving chase, and managed

---

* Oleg Gordievsky, *Next Stop Execution*, London: Macmillan, 1995.

gradually to accelerate away, before swinging into the side road where their prize agent was waiting nervously in the forest. They put Gordievsky in the boot of one of the British cars. Five separate checkpoints lay between them and Finland and freedom. The two officers and their wives managed to throw the border guards off the scent, literally, by chucking crisps out to the sniffer dogs, and making great play with babies and nappies. To the fury of the Soviet authorities, Gordievsky was successfully exfiltrated, and fully debriefed. The two SIS officers were granted a private audience of the Queen. Each was secretly awarded the OBE – which they were not allowed to reveal for another ten years. Gordievsky had to wait even longer, until 2007, for a CMG.

Years later, as an Ambassador, I was lucky enough to have one of the SIS team as my head of Station. But he was too modest and discreet to talk even then about one of the most extraordinary episodes of derring-do by the British intelligence services.

On the other hand, Gordievsky soon surfaced, and became a public thorn in the flesh of a dying Soviet Union. But before that happened, he was required to take part in an extraordinary meeting in the UK with Reagan's Director of Central Intelligence, the colourful Bill Casey, in which Casey tested out on Gordievsky the lines his President might be advised to use with the Soviet leader at the Geneva Summit in November 1985. Gordievsky claimed that his role-playing encouraged Casey to tell Reagan that he should stand firm on the Strategic Defence Initiative (known as Star Wars). It was this, said Gordievsky, that led Gorbachev to conclude that the Americans were tougher than he had first thought, and that internal reform was the only way forward.

There were a couple of other spy scandals running in the other direction with which I had to deal during my time in the PUS's office. The first was the chance discovery, in GCHQ in Cheltenham, of a Soviet spy, Geoffrey Prime. Shortly after Prime was arrested in 1982 for sexually abusing minors, his wife handed the police a bag of espionage-related material, and told them that Prime had confessed to her that he had worked for the KGB. Prime was found to have had a radio transmitter concealed in the attic of his home. I never discovered how much damage he had done, but the ever cautious Foreign Secretary, Geoffrey

Howe, was anxious to avoid more trouble. His faithful Private Secretary sent a formal minute to the FCO Deputy Under Secretary (Defence and Intelligence), in which he recorded, apparently with a straight face, that the Foreign Secretary would be 'grateful for an assurance that there are no more Soviet spies in GCHQ'. The DUS in question, David Goodall, had a mischievous sense of humour: his reply read simply, 'Only the Deity can provide the assurance the Secretary of State seeks.'

Less damaging, but more tragic, was the Bettaney case. In 1984, a disaffected counter-espionage officer in MI5, Michael Bettaney, tried to persuade the KGB to recruit him, by stuffing highly classified material through the letterbox of the KGB Resident in London, Arkadi Guk. The Russians suspected a trap and did nothing. Bettaney then decided to chance his arm with the Russians in Vienna, but, thanks to a tip-off from Gordievsky, he was already under suspicion and surveillance. Bettaney was brought in for questioning. Confronted with reams of largely circumstantial evidence, he eventually confessed. He was sentenced under the Official Secrets Act to twenty-three years' imprisonment. Ironically, the inept Guk was then declared *persona non grata* and expelled. The Prime Minister decided that something had to be done about MI5, and a new, external, director general was appointed, in the shape of Sir Antony Duff, a senior Foreign Office official with a distinguished earlier career in the Royal Navy. Duff soon freshened up a deeply conservative and inward-looking organisation, still populated by retired officers of a particular cast of mind. After Duff had started at MI5, he came to see my boss, Sir Antony Acland. As he waited in my office, I asked Duff what he thought had been the main problem with MI5. 'The gossip factor,' he replied at once. He explained that MI5 officers had been so security-conscious that they had never gossiped to or about each other, thus failing to detect the loneliness and unhappiness that had led Bettaney to go off the rails. Bettaney had even been detained for drunkenness, and had shown Nazi sympathies, singing the 'Horst Wessel' song. But his Security Service colleagues had either not known, or not cared. In Duff's view, successful organisations needed an element of internal gossip, as a means of what would now be called team-building and as a safety valve. It was a lesson about organisations I was never to forget, and always to seek to apply.

Apart from the Ministry of Defence, the most important home department for the Foreign Office was the Treasury. Relations were never easy, as the Treasury sought to bear down on Foreign Office budgets that represented a tiny fraction of overall government expenditure but still looked to many Treasury officials like unwonted extravagance. The Treasury never forgave the Foreign Office for having done an end-run round them in obtaining the Overseas Price Movement mechanism direct from Mrs Thatcher. A particular target for them was the Foreign Office overseas estate, made up in part of hugely valuable historic properties in the centre of many of the world's great cities. Gradually, the estate was rationalised, with some of the returns being recycled back into the FCO estate budget. For most of my time in the PUS's office, the Permanent Secretary at the Treasury was Sir Peter Middleton, who went on to become deputy chairman of Barclays Bank. To Middleton's embarrassment, one of his officials copied to the Foreign Office by mistake an internal Treasury note by Peter Middleton analysing senior personalities in the Foreign Office and describing us as 'worthy adversaries'. We realised we must have been doing something right in our dealings with the Treasury.

The other government department with which the Foreign Office always had to work closely was the Overseas Development Administration – theoretically part of the Foreign Office, but at that time without a separate Cabinet minister. The ODA – after the 1997 election the Department for International Development (DFID) – always had much larger budgets than its parent department, and a different, and much more liberal, worldview. This created tensions, with the Foreign Office constantly complaining that the ODA/DFID tree-huggers spent money without regard to foreign-policy priorities, and the development experts believing the Foreign Office to be cynical and unprincipled in its operations. I was to see these differences up close during my time in Afghanistan, twenty years later.

Antony Acland took me with him on some of his overseas trips as permanent under secretary. An early visit was to Israel. Antony had a strong aversion to humbug and, understandably, to terrorism, and the combination of the two pushed him beyond the limit of his patience.

At a lunch given by our Consul-General in Jerusalem, a Palestinian guest warned that failure to resolve the Palestinian question would result in bombs on the streets of London. Antony took this as a threat and, to the consternation of our Consul-General, walked straight out of the lunch: not the way Foreign Office officials usually behave. An earlier lunch, on the other side of Jerusalem, in the Knesset, had had a rather different tone. We had been invited by the veteran Israeli politician Abba Eban, who had been the first chief instructor at MECAS, and whose funeral I was to attend as ambassador to Israel. My main memory of that lunch is of Eban's pride in the BBC comedy series *Yes, Minister*, co-written (with Anthony Jay) by his nephew, Jonathan Lynn. The series was so popular in Jordan as well as Israel that there was a tacit understanding between the state broadcasters of two countries still theoretically at war to ensure that the same episodes were broadcast in sequence. The idea was that viewers in Israel who missed an episode broadcast on Israeli television could pick it up a week or so later on Jordanian television, or vice versa. Such were the practicalities of war and peace in the Middle East.

Much more gruelling was a long trip to the Far East which Antony undertook in the summer of 1985. We started in Hong Kong. Nobody ever forgets the twists and turns of the final approach to the old Kai Tak airport. What really impressed me, however, was the large black Daimler waiting for us at the foot of the aircraft steps, and which moved us quickly across the tarmac to a waiting helicopter of the Royal Hong Kong Auxiliary Air Force. Within minutes, we were relaxing with the Governor, Sir Edward Youde, at his country retreat at Fan Ling. It was another world. Almost equally unexpected was the bird-watching expedition which the Governor mounted for us, taking his antique official yacht, the *Lady Maurine*, to a hidden valley in the New Territories up near the Chinese border.

From Hong Kong, we went on to Beijing and Shanghai, to open the new British Consulate-General. The old Consulate had been a huge building, in its own small park, just off the Bund (or waterfront) in Shanghai. But it had been ordered to close during the Cultural Revolution in 1967, after the Red Guards had stormed and set alight the Embassy in Beijing. The former Consulate was now a hostel for sailors, but I spotted a poignant relic of its British past: a rusting old lawn roller, in the bushes by the gate. The new Consulate was much more modest, in a suburban villa miles from the city centre. But the colourfulness of our Consul-General more than compensated for the drab premises in which he lived and worked. Trevor Mound, whom I had known in my first year in the Office in the Republic of Ireland Department, was already known for riding around Shanghai in a converted London taxi (necessary for his back, he said) and an Inverness cape. One abiding memory is of Antony and me sitting with Trevor on his balcony, as if in a film, as a warm tropical rain poured down, eating Gentleman's Relish on toast and listening to the World Service of the BBC. To my surprise, Antony – most uncharacteristically – had the night before accepted an offer from Trevor to have his No. 1 Boiler man perform a massage on the PUS: I could hear the thumps and groans through my bedroom wall. Earlier, as commercial counsellor in Beijing, Trevor used to tell senior Chinese officials when they came to lunch in his flat that he had not had anything to do with Chinese Communists since he had hunted them down in the Malayan jungle during the Emergency there in the 1950s.

From China, we went on to Japan. The Ambassador there, Sir Sydney Giffard, invited us to spend the first weekend with him and his wife high in the mountains above Tokyo, in the Embassy's weekend cottage at Chuzenji. This was a traditional Japanese house of wood and paper on the edge of a lake. Behind and above us were forest and flowers, and bushes and walks. It was place of extraordinary calm and beauty. But, even though we were many miles from the cities on the coastal plan below, at weekends the area still filled with visitors. As we walked through the forest, behind every bush seemed to lurk an earnest Japanese walker, in his or her weekend leisure wear, earnestly photographing a flower or a plant. It was disappointing to learn, on a visit to Japan in 2009, that the Embassy had had to give up using the house at Chuzenji, on health-and-safety grounds. Paper and wood were not fire resistant enough for the risk police back in London.

On the Monday morning, Sir Sydney took Antony Acland and me back down the mountain, in his white armoured Rolls-Royce. I sat in the front, watching the outside temperature gauge rise steadily as we twisted and turned down the mountain side, to the hot and humid plains below. Japan in June could be very sticky indeed. But it wasn't just the outside temperature that was rising. It soon became apparent that it was getting rapidly hotter inside the car as well. Sir Sydney's devoted Japanese chauffeur fiddled with the air conditioning, but, to his shame and embarrassment, without success. As the car was armoured, the windows wouldn't open. We were trapped inside a mobile sauna, and got stickier and stickier, and more and more hot and bothered. We stopped for breaks, and to remove our coats.

We were on our way to a Nissan plant. Thanks to Mrs Thatcher, Nissan were investing in England's North-east, and we wanted to do all we could to encourage them. The plan was for Sir Antony to meet Nissan's top management and to visit an assembly line. Although the temperature inside the Ambassador's Rolls-Royce was almost unbearable, we decided we had to carry on. We could not lose face with the Japanese motor executives by admitting that there was a fault with a British-manufactured car, especially a Rolls-Royce. But Sir Sydney managed to scrape together enough cash from his own and his driver's pockets for us to return to Tokyo by train, once the Nissan visit was over. We would get the Rolls-Royce to take us to the nearest station, and make our own way on from there. Sir Sydney instructed his chauffeur to reveal nothing of our difficulties to our Japanese hosts.

We arrived at the factory to be greeted by a line of smiling and bowing Japanese businessmen. In response to their enquiries, we lied through our teeth: our journey down from the hills could hardly have been easier or more comfortable. We toured the factory, watching robots manufacturing a car which Nissan called the Cedric. Sydney Giffard explained that this car owed its curious name to the fact that the Nissan Chairman had been a devotee of Frances Hodgson Burnett's book *Little Lord Fauntleroy*, in which the eponymous hero's first name is Cedric. Antony seemed to spend most of the time asking about the Cedric's air-conditioning system. At last the tour, and the lunch which followed, were over, and we returned to the Ambassador's Rolls-Royce, parked in front of the factory. To our surprise, it was surrounded by a group of Japanese mechanics, in spotless blue Nissan overalls, bowing and grinning. And then we realised what had happened: the

Ambassador's driver had ignored his boss's instructions and had given the game away. He had been overwhelmed by the desire to have his beloved Roller back in working order and wanted to avoid the shame of obliging the Ambassador and his guests to take the train back to Tokyo. The Nissan team had leaped at the chance to repair not just any Rolls-Royce, but the British Ambassador's one, and had taken it into one of the workshops. They had soon fixed the problem.

We had lost face twice over, first in having a defective car and then in being caught out lying about our journey. But after hours of suffering the relief was welcome. We abandoned our train plans and set off in a pleasantly cool car down the motorway to Tokyo.

After Japan, the final leg of our Asian tour was Korea. There too we visited a car factory, as well as a shipyard. We saw production techniques that were less advanced than in Japan, but also an economy on the move, and met a people hungry for success. We went up to the Demilitarised Zone, and peered across into North Korea at Panmunjom. We made a pilgrimage to where in 1951 the Gloucestershire Regiment had fought so bravely against the waves of Chinese soldiers pouring south, at the Battle of the Imjin River. We toured some of the sites for the 1988 Olympic Games. And Antony held the inevitable talks with his opposite number in the Korean Foreign Ministry. We learned something of how Koreans had suffered at the hands of their more powerful neighbours, and admired their fortitude and sense of fun. And I even managed my first and only taste of dog soup.

But for Antony at least the highlight of our visit to Korea was climbing into the business-class cabin of the British Airways jumbo jet for the long flight back over the North Pole to London, only to find the chief custodian of the public purse, the Permanent Secretary of HM Treasury, the Foreign Office's scourge, Sir Peter Middleton, and a bevy of his officials comfortably ensconced in the First Class cabin, sipping champagne. It was an embarrassment they were not allowed quickly to forget.

Travelling with Antony was enjoyable, because it was only when he was away from the Office that he truly relaxed, and I saw the breadth and depth of his interests. I learned so much from talking to him on those journeys together.

But his sense of humour surfaced from time to time in London too. Then, as now, the PUS's morning meetings were often dominated by the overnight news, and in particular the coverage of foreign affairs on BBC Radio 4's flagship *Today* programme. Once Antony – who was rather traditional in his speech and manner – complained that he had not heard a particular item on the wireless which everyone else seemed to have heard. One of the deputy secretaries (most of whom were rather in awe of the PUS), David Goodall, cheekily commented that 'Perhaps that was because you were listening to the wireless, PUS, while the rest of us were listening to the radio.'

Antony always complained that his diary was too full. One April Fool's Day, it must have been in 1986, I decided to give him a daily programme that began where his nightmares ended. It was all carefully set out on the card with the following day's diary that went in his overnight box. I can't now recall every detail, but I know that it involved lunch with Antony's bête noire, Dame Ann Mueller of the Cabinet Office Management and Personnel Office, to discuss 'Audit Procedures Review In Limited Foreign Office Overseas Locations'. Antony didn't detect the clue, and muttered something about having to see that woman again to discuss an incredibly boring subject. But his humour completely deserted him when he saw what was in store for him that evening: 'Dinner and Dancing with the Israeli Ambassador [whose persistence in arguing the case for a country to which Antony was instinctively sympathetic irritated him], at [the *pièce de résistance*] the Kensington Hilton'. Antony exploded. 'Why do I have to spend my whole evening with that ghastly man? Why dancing? Why the Kensington Hilton, of all places – it's nearly in Shepherd's Bush?' Taking my courage in my hands, I said simply, 'April Fool, PUS.' His face turned from fury to stunned surprise. He snapped his box shut, and said we had to get on with work. Later, he told me quietly how amused he had been by the joke, and that he had kept the fake programme for his scrap book.

Another incident was the result of a rare case of Antony misjudging a personality. After a series of interviews, he appointed, with my support, a new assistant private secretary. I had known the man in question (let's call him Jones) vaguely at Oxford. He had shared a house with a friend and seemed pleasant enough. He had joined the Diplomatic Service in the main stream. I should have realised that something was wrong when I noticed that, as a bachelor, he was staying in the office longer than any of us. It wasn't just that he was exceptionally conscientious: it gradually became apparent that he was finding it hard to cope with the workload. Another clue came when Antony asked Jones to get another Permanent Secretary on the phone and instead found himself connected to a very puzzled Turkish Ambassador in Brussels. Jones had misheard the PUS. In his typically conscientious fashion, he had gone to great lengths to track down the Turk in Belgium, without once asking himself (or me) why the PUS would want to talk to him, and about what.

But the incident that finally decided Jones's fate could have been more serious. When the PUS arrived in the morning, we would gather round him in his office, as he went through the papers in the box and asked each of us – the Assistant Private Secretary, the Diary Secretary and me – to take action on various points. One morning Antony announced that he had been speaking the previous evening to Alice Renton, the wife of an old school friend of Antony's, Tim Renton, who was then a Foreign Office junior minister. Antony announced that he had agreed with Mrs Renton that the temporary 'coatwacks' (he had a bit of a lisp) at the foot of the Grand Staircase in the Foreign Office were unsightly. (They were deployed whenever a reception was held upstairs in the Locarno rooms.) He asked Jones to speak to the Home Estates Department to see if the 'coatwacks' could either be moved or have cupboards built round them as soon as possible. Jones replied, 'Of course, PUS, I will get straight on to it.'

I thought nothing more of it until later that afternoon the larger and more voluble of the two Foreign Office handymen known, for obvious reasons, as Bubble and Squeak put his head round the door of the PUS's outer office (where Jones and I sat) and enquired if the PUS had 'gone fucking mad'. 'Why do you ask?' I replied, trying to keep calm and polite. 'Come and see,' he said. Bubble took me to the foot of the Grand Staircase, where Squeak was standing, with a clipboard and a tape measure. He pointed to the twenty-foot-high statues of the former foreign secretaries Lords Lansdowne and Salisbury which stand in front of the great pillars at the bottom of the staircase. 'What does the PUS think he is doin', continued Bubble, 'asking us to move these two – they weigh ten tons each – or build cupboards round 'em? Who is 'e suddenly to say that they are "unsightly"?' – this last word was pronounced in Bubble's sarcastic take on an upper-class accent. Amazed, I turned to Jones and asked him what was going on. The PUS had been concerned about the coatracks, not these two giant statues. Jones's face fell, as the reality dawned. Slightly hard of hearing, and again without thinking or asking, he had heard the PUS say that he wanted the 'kojaks' moved or covered up. A puzzled Jones had rushed out after our morning session to see what the PUS could have meant. Thinking of the bald television detective played by Telly Savalas, Jones had spied the marble pates of the two eminent Victorians and had concluded that the PUS's reference had been to them.

When Antony heard what had happened, he decided, regretfully, that Jones would have to be moved out of the Private Office at the earliest opportunity. The story had two other consequences. About a year later, I was looking through an album of photographs of the Foreign Office during the Second World War, brought out from the archives by the FCO historians to help ensure that the restoration programme for the main building took proper account of historical realities. To my astonishment, I found photographs of both Lord Lansdowne and Lord Salisbury encased in cupboards during the war, in order to protect them against bomb damage: I sent a copy of the photograph to an amused Antony, who by then was ambassador to Washington. And, more prosaically, cupboards *were* eventually built, years later, for the 'coatwacks' which are dragged out every time there is a big party in the Locarno rooms, and which had precipitated Jones's downfall.

In the summer of 1986, Antony was posted as ambassador to Washington. His successor, Sir Patrick Wright, was a quite different character. An experienced Arabist of great diplomatic distinction, Patrick was full of Tiggerish energy and enthusiasm. From time to time, I would find him pacing outside the PUS's office at 7.30 a.m., waiting to be let in. Whereas Antony advanced deliberately (and sometimes a bit grumpily) on a narrow front, focusing on one carefully judged thing at a time, Patrick advanced on a broad front, doing many different things all at once, always full of jokes and laughter and anecdotes. I had the pleasure of drafting the Personal telegram to Patrick in Saudi Arabia, where he was ambassador, telling him of his new appointment, and of arranging briefing visits by him to many of our key overseas posts. He was (and is, as Lord Wright of Richmond) the nicest and kindest of men, as well as an unyielding supporter in the House of Lords of the Arab cause.

Patrick's father had been a schoolmaster, and there was something of the kindly pedagogue in the didactic fashion in which Patrick passed on advice to me, at an early stage in my career. He emphasised his practice of always, on return from a diplomatic dinner, updating his meticulously tended card index of contacts. Similarly schoolmasterly was his use of Latin tags and acronyms and abbreviations (one of his favourites was 'drampers' for 'dramatis personae', for the people who needed to be present at a meeting). Patrick told me that the first thing he checked on a telegram was not the content, but the distribution. He was constantly marking papers up to the Private Secretary for the Secretary of State to see, adding careful manuscript comments and witticisms of his own. He had once been private secretary to a PUS, Sir Harold Caccia, and had his own ideas on how the job should be done. Patrick liked to do more on his own and made less use of his Private Secretary. After Caccia had retired from the Foreign Office, he had become Provost of Eton.* Patrick had visited the Caccias there, and had been a bit hurt when he had asked Lady Caccia how she was finding Eton, and she had replied that it was fine – apart from the frightful schoolmasters.

Patrick's schoolmasterly side showed too in the enthusiasm with which he accepted an invitation from the Horatian Society to speak at their annual dinner on Horace (the Roman poet) and diplomacy. Horace had not said much more about diplomacy than Virgil had said about wind-surfing, but somehow Patrick, with a bit of help from me, put together something that passed muster with the serious classicists who attended the dinner.

Patrick had suffered *alopecia totalis* (total hair loss) a few years before becoming PUS. He joked about it, telling us how a gushing lady in the

---

* As did Antony Acland, on retiring from Washington in 1991.

row behind him in the Royal Box at Wimbledon had leaned forward, tapped him on the shoulder and whispered, 'I do *so* admire your swimming.' No one seeing Patrick from the front could have mistaken him for Britain's Olympic gold-medal-winning swimmer Duncan Goodhew. But Patrick was not especially amused when he summoned the Syrian Ambassador to tell him that Britain would be breaking off diplomatic relations with Syria, over support for terrorism, and the Ambassador then went out to tell the journalists waiting outside the Foreign Office that he had just seen 'the pink potato'.

Like Antony, Patrick continued the tradition of sending a monthly Secret and Personal letter to all our heads of mission, telling them what was really going on. I helped draft the letter, drawing on contributions from around the Office. But I found that Patrick worried about leaks, so that the letter became less personal and less interesting and therefore less secret.

After an exhausting year trying to keep up with Patrick, it was my turn to follow Antony to Washington, where I was to fill the internal political slot in the Chancery. I could not have wished for a better job or a better boss.

All that remained was for Patrick to find a successor. The Personnel Operations Department submitted a list, but Patrick already knew whom he wanted – and didn't want. When he saw on the list the name of the man who, twenty-five years on, actually became PUS, Patrick commented with some force that the individual concerned was far too 'wild' to be PS/PUS. I knew that the official he did choose – a junior mandarin of promise and prudence – was the right choice when, on the day of my departure, we were discussing a forthcoming tour of South America by the PUS. Patrick asked how the centre of the drugs industry in Colombia, the city of Medellín, was pronounced. 'To rhyme with *fedayeen*, PUS,' replied my successor, with a wit worthy of Bernard Woolley, the fictional private secretary in *Yes, Minister*.

Chapter 5

Potomac Fever

Four years in Washington were my reward for the tough times working at the heart of the Office in London. Like almost everyone posted to the imperial capital, I caught Potomac Fever.

My job, as first secretary (Chancery), had three parts: to report on American politics, including the Congress; to cover Irish America; and to act as the co-ordinating point in the Embassy for the US–UK relationship, including the unending flow of royal and ministerial visitors across the Atlantic. It was, in my view and that of others, the best job in the Embassy – apart from that of ambassador.

I had never been to Washington, or indeed to the States, before arriving there in August 1987. Before I left London, a colleague, John Kerr, just back from a tour as head of Chancery in Washington, gave me lunch and three pieces of advice. 'First,' he said, 'buy an American car – preferably a Chevrolet Caprice Classic Station Wagon. They may be old-fashioned gas-guzzlers, but they are part of your American experience, and perfect for long road trips across the country.' And so, when I arrived, I did indeed buy a vast Chevrolet, more like a small aircraft carrier than a motor vehicle, with great bench seats and soft suspension, all chrome and sculpted wings and American exuberance. It was just what the family's American journey needed.

John's second piece of advice was more prosaic. We would be staying temporarily in the old head of Chancery's house – once occupied by the Cambridge spy Donald Maclean – which the Kerrs had only recently vacated. Do a deal (John was always in favour of deals) to become members of the swimming club at the hotel through the woods from his old house, for the rest of summer, he advised. You'll arrive too late in the year to make it worth joining one of the swimming clubs down by the Potomac. But this will be a good way of entertaining the children in the weeks that remain of a sometimes unbearably humid Washington summer. We did so, and were grateful to John.

The third piece of advice was the best: 'Read Lou Cannon on Ronald Reagan, if you want to understand American politics.' Reagan was then approaching the last of eight years in the White House during which he had restored America's faith in itself. Cannon was the *Washington Post*'s Reagan-watcher. He wrote with easy fluency a syndicated weekly column devoted to the Great Communicator. But he had also produced *the* book on Reagan,* which I devoured with enthusiasm before I left London. The more I read (and later saw) of Reagan the more I understood how well he had done the most impossible job in the world. He had believed in only a few things – less government, lower taxes, fighting Communism – and had not bothered himself with detail. He had chosen good people – James Baker, George Shultz, Caspar Weinberger, Paul Volcker, Alan Greenspan – to implement his ideas, and had let them get on with it. He had concentrated on doing what he did best: communicating with the American people, giving them back the confidence they had lost after Vietnam and Watergate and under President Carter. So it hadn't been so absurd for him to proclaim at his re-election in 1984 that it was 'morning in America' again. Perhaps his greatest moment had been his address to the American people on the evening of 28 January 1986, the day seven American astronauts had been killed in the *Challenger* space shuttle: 'the future doesn't belong to the faint-hearted: it belongs to the brave', he said, as he referred to the astronauts having slipped 'the surly bonds of earth'.

In the 1980s, even more than now, how America was doing mattered to London. And, to paraphrase a remark once made about French politics, everyone in London thought they knew about the politics of two countries – their own and America's. Spending the next four years writing private reports about those politics for an eager audience in London would be an immense privilege. It was a job that had first been done by Isaiah Berlin, who had been sent to our Embassy in Washington in the

---

* Lou Cannon, *Reagan*, New York: Putnam's, 1982.

war to report on the politics of the only country which could win the war for us. Churchill had so admired Isaiah Berlin's reports that he had minuted his staff that he wanted to meet 'I. Berlin' when he was next in London. The staff had tracked down the songwriter Irving Berlin, who had been puzzled to find himself being quizzed about American politics over lunch with Mr Churchill.*

Washington was only the second embassy in which I had worked, and it was of course far bigger than Cairo. What made it so huge was not the core team of diplomats, which was only slightly larger and more senior than the team we had in Cairo, but a vast British Defence Staff – a sort of mini-MOD on the Potomac – headed by a major general or an air vice marshal, while a separate British Naval Staff was commanded by a rear admiral. It at once epitomised the Special Relationship, with defence at its core, and raised questions about Britain's military dependence on America, dating back to the Second World War. In those days before the Berlin Wall came down, no one questioned the absolute priority HMG gave to our defence and security relationship with the United States.

In Washington, I was succeeding Nigel Sheinwald (who was later to serve as ambassador there from 2007 to 2012). Nigel came to meet us at the airport, and prepared the best handover notes I have ever had: so good, in fact, that I kept them with me on my desk every day I did the job. It was rare for a week to go by without my consulting them. He had written a kind of pocket guide to American politics and Irish America, along with a full directory of key contacts.

By August 1987, Antony Acland had been in Washington a year, as unaccompanied widower, besieged by the divorcees of the city. But he brought back with him from leave that summer a new wife, Jenny,

---

* The former Warden of All Souls College, Oxford, John Sparrow, once told me of a similar experience he had had with Mrs Thatcher. He had been flattered to have been asked by her to lunch at Chequers one Sunday. He had driven excitedly over from Oxford, only to find that all the other guests were Conservative Party agents and activists. Eventually, he met one also called John Sparrow, and he realised what had happened. Mrs Thatcher had said to her staff, 'Invite John Sparrow,' and they, being educated people, had thought immediately and only of the Warden of All Souls. But someone at Conservative Central Office had soon spotted that the 'wrong' John Sparrow had been asked, and so invited the 'right' one – while not daring to disinvite the 'wrong' one.

whom he had known since childhood. Their happiness together, and the quiet professionalism which they brought to representing Britain in America, illuminated the whole Embassy. Late one evening, I remember leaving the hideous 1960s Chancery building on Massachusetts Avenue for the magnificent Lutyens Residence next door, in order to clear with the Ambassador a draft telegram to London. Deep inside, in a small sitting room, I found the Ambassador and Lady Acland reading different pages of the same spread of a newspaper. One could see how fond they were of each other. It made all our jobs easier, and happier.

One change Jenny soon made was to import from the heart of England a new social secretary for the Washington Embassy. Amanda Downes was pure English oak, but with a sense of humour and of proportion that would allow her to sail through the most extreme social challenges. She had poise and class and confidence: she could – and did – treat with respect and kindness everyone from the Queen and the American President down to the most humble of Embassy domestic staff. She was utterly professional, running that great British Government Residence – now it would be called a corporate entertainment facility – as such places should be run, with taste and style, and apparent effortlessness, providing a place of contact between Americans and Britons, but also a quiet space for stressed visiting ministers to relax and refuel. And it was all done without fuss: the art, as Horace would have said, lay in hiding the art.

Almost straight away, I was plunged into Irish affairs, with a visit by the Secretary of State for Northern Ireland, Tom King. Irish America is a concept as well as a place. On St Patrick's Day, all Americans seem to become Irish. The Charles River in Boston, and the Chicago River, are dyed green. So is the beer in Boston, in New York and in many other cities. Many American schoolchildren seem to be expected on 17 March to wear green. In 1987, over forty million Americans claimed Irish descent.

But drill deeper, and the picture is rather different. Most of the forty million are in fact 'Scots Irish', descended from the Protestants of Ulster or the Scottish Lowlands. Despite the St Patrick's Day shenanigans, theirs is not Catholic Nationalist Ireland. But that did not prevent them joining the traditional Catholic Irish of Boston, New York, New Jersey,

Chicago, San Francisco and Los Angeles in taking a view of Irish history and of Britain's role there that was little short of travesty. The million or so Protestants whose ancestors had settled in Ulster some 300 years earlier were ignored. Britain was occupying Ireland against the wishes of most of the Emerald Isle's people, and should leave: it was as banal as that. They did not want to be bothered with the history or the political geography, or the efforts which the British Government had made over the previous eighteen years to find a peaceful political solution to the problem. As with America's view of disputes in other parts of the world, notably that between Israel and the Palestinians, its approach was dictated as much by American politics as by the facts on the ground.

The annual visit to Washington, and usually New York, by the British Cabinet minister responsible for Northern Ireland was part of a much wider effort, for which I was the Embassy point man, to get across to Americans the realities of Ireland. This wasn't just to prevent funds – and in some cases even weapons – being sent to the IRA via collections for Irish 'widows and orphans' through organisations such as the Irish Northern Aid Committee, or Noraid. It was also to generate political and financial support for desperately needed economic development in Northern Ireland – which, along with politics and security, was the third leg of the British Government's strategy for restoring stability in the province.

Crucial to this effort was an organisation in Congress known as the Friends of Ireland. In the wake of the Nationalist hunger strikes in Northern Ireland prisons in 1981, the Friends of Ireland had been established as a moderate counterweight to the activities of the apologists for the IRA in the Irish National Caucus led by Father Sean McManus. The leaders of the group were known as the Four Horsemen: Senator Ted Kennedy of Massachusetts, Senator Daniel Patrick Moynihan of New York, Governor Hugh Carey also of New York, and the Speaker of the House of Representatives, Tip O'Neill, from Boston. By 1987, the group was led by Ted Kennedy in the Senate, and in the House by Boston Congressman Brian Donnelly. Another young Congressman active (and inflammable) on Irish issues, whom I came to know well, though we often disagreed, was Joe Kennedy, the eldest son of the late Bobby Kennedy.* Each had a staff knowledgeable about Ireland, and broadly sympathetic to what we were trying to do. But, inevitably, they were subject to competing briefing and pressures from others, including an active Irish Embassy in Washington. They could be very critical of the British Government's policies and actions in Northern Ireland, particularly anything involving the security forces.

Central to any visit to Washington by the Northern Ireland Secretary was seeing as many of the Friends of Ireland as were available, and briefing them on the latest developments. It was also important to meet other senior politicians, including members of the Senate Foreign Relations Committee and of the House Foreign Affairs Committee. My job was to line up the best programme I could. Unfortunately, British Cabinet ministers had a more inflated view of their importance than American elected politicians did – even those with Irish interests or British connections. A lot of hard work went into securing the meetings on the Hill which the British visitor deemed worthy of himself and his office. The struggle was even harder with junior ministers, or ministers in departments responsible for subjects of little current political interest to Congress. Sometimes the Senator concerned would receive the British minister but want to talk about something completely different: the British Secretary of State for Education once called on the ancient and delightfully eccentric Senator Claiborne Pell of Rhode Island only to find the meeting devoted to Pell's interest in the comparative merits of the longbow and the crossbow – a subject on which he quaintly assumed any senior British Conservative politician would have both knowledge and views.

This particular visit by the Northern Ireland Secretary, Tom King, had two unusual outcomes. The first was that King discovered at the briefing supper which Antony Acland gave for the visiting Cabinet Minister and his team that the Speaker of the US House of Representatives, Jim Wright from Fort Worth, Texas, had ancestors in County Tyrone. In a rather peremptory fashion, the Secretary of State

---

* Joe Kennedy boycotted the Queen's address to a Joint Session of Congress in May 1991 (see later in this chapter), in protest at the 'British occupation of Northern Ireland', and used to demonstrate outside the British Embassy.

instructed officials to find a way of ingratiating HMG with Speaker Wright. Someone – I hope it wasn't me – had the bright idea of commissioning a coat of arms, complete with motto, for Speaker Wright. The arms would be prepared by the heralds at the College of Arms in London, and presented when the American Speaker took up an invitation from the Speaker of the House of Commons, Bernard Weatherill, to visit London the following summer.

The Northern Ireland Office in London agreed to pay for the new coat of arms. I contacted a friend who was a herald, Patric Dickinson. In 1987, Patric rejoiced in the title of Rouge Dragon Pursuivant.* He specialised in genealogical research, and in drafting coats of arms for newly ennobled peers and others. As I had expected, Patric rose to the challenge with eccentric enthusiasm. He came up with a device which incorporated a pale golden gavel overlaying the Lone Star, a double-headed eagle resting each claw on a boxing glove (Jim Wright's father had been a prize-fighter), and the Texas state flower. It was a masterpiece of heraldic creativity.†

The only difficulty came with choosing a motto for the Speaker. Patric's first thoughts turned naturally to Latin. Ingeniously, he came up with a sentence which punned on the Latin adjective for 'right' – *rectus*. He suggested that the Wright family motto should be *Rectam Viam Sequi* ('Follow the Right Path').

No one thought any more of it. The following summer Speaker Weatherill duly welcomed his American colleague on an official visit to London, during which Jim Wright addressed the British American Parliamentary Group and undertook other official engagements. He was an important man in American politics, and Britain wanted him on side. As part of the programme, he was taken to the College of Arms in the City and welcomed by the Duke of Norfolk, who supervises the

---

* Since 2010 Patric has been Clarenceux King of Arms.

† Patric's description in proper heraldic language of the Wright coat of arms is as follows: 'ARMS: Per pale Azure and Vert a Mullet Argent surmounted by a Gavel in pale Gold; CREST: A double-headed Eagle wings displayed and inverted Argent beaked and legged Gules langued and the talons Azure the underside of each wing charged with an Escutcheon Gules gorged with a Collar Sable charged with Mullets Or and resting each claw on a Boxing Glove proper.'

College in his capacity as Earl Marshal of England. The Earl Marshal watched as, with a satisfied flourish, Rouge Dragon laid the draft coat of Wright family arms before the hard-bitten Texan pol for his kind approval.

Speaker Wright's reaction was not quite as positive as the proudly fawning Brits had expected. Wright was no classical scholar. He neither knew nor cared about the declension of Latin adjectives. But his eye lighted on the word *Rectam*. To his untutored ear that sounded suspiciously like part of his lower anatomy. He suspected the limeys were making fun of him. He exploded. He did not want any 'fucking arsehole' in his family motto. It would have to be redone.

Speaker Wright returned to Washington. But the stormclouds were gathering: already he was the subject of an ethics investigation, which was within a year to result in his resignation. As far as I know, HMG never did present the coat of arms, though the copy in the archives of the College of Arms is inscribed in pencil with Patric's proposed alternative to *Rectam: Pacis*, giving the motto *Pacis Viam Sequi* ('Follow the Path of Peace').

The other result of Tom King's visit did more good for British interests. In 1984, the Irish winner of the Nobel Peace Prize Seán MacBride had launched the MacBride Principles – nine fair-employment rules to be followed by US companies doing business in Northern Ireland. Some of the Principles, such as guaranteeing the safety of employees on their way to and from work, were impractical. The British Government was concerned that the compulsory application of the Principles, which amounted to positive discrimination in favour of Catholics, would choke off foreign investment in Northern Ireland. And that investment was critical to economic development, which was in turn critical for establishing peace in the province. Paradoxically, the rigid application of the Principles could have the opposite effect from that intended. Britain was faced with a major campaign by various Irish lobbies in the States to make all US institutional investors observe the MacBride Principles.

In response, Britain moved to strengthen its own Northern Ireland fair-employment laws. Even so, it sounded to many as though, in opposing the MacBride Principles, we were arguing against economic justice for the Catholics of Northern Ireland. It was a tricky case to make. On arriving in Washington, I found the campaign in favour of MacBride gathering strength around the country, with bills mandating the Principles being introduced in a string of state legislatures. Up until my arrival, the British Government had tried to fight the spreading bushfire with reasoned argument, relying on calls on state legislators by British diplomats, letters from the Ambassador, articles in the local press and so on. We could also point to the fact that, whereas Sinn Fein vigorously supported the Principles (MacBride had once been chief of staff of the IRA), neither the Irish Government nor the moderate nationalists in Northern Ireland did. But, understandably enough, the latter two didn't want to use up political capital supporting the British Government on such a sensitive issue. We were on our own.

I rapidly concluded that the only way to contain the problem was to fight fire with fire: to employ professional lobbyists, in Washington and in the state legislatures. Unlike many other governments with problems on the Hill, Britain had never done this. There was some resistance in Whitehall, on grounds of principle as well as cost. But Tom King's visit persuaded him that this was the only way to go. I asked for, and was quickly given, a first-class assistant, Andy Henderson, to help manage the campaign. Over the next three years, using lobbyists judiciously, we were able to halt and then reverse the MacBride campaign. It was a quiet triumph for common sense. In the course of it, Andy and I travelled all over the Union, and learned up close the truth of Tip O'Neill's maxim that 'all politics is local'. In the middle of winter, for example, I flew to Maine's state capital, Augusta, landing in a small propeller plane on a snow-packed runway. There I discovered that the MacBride campaign in Maine was not about Ireland, but about the way in which the French Catholic Acadian shoe workers had been oppressed, following their expulsion from Nova Scotia by the British in 1755. Our toughest and most important fight was in California, where the state teachers' pension fund was one of the largest in the world. But there too we somehow managed to prevail, not by defeating the legislation outright, but by having it 'tabled' which – we soon found out – is the American for 'shelved'.

Our use of lobbyists had other benefits for Ireland. In Washington, on the Hill, we used our lobbyists to secure foreign-aid money for the

International Fund for Ireland, which promoted cross-border economic development. We also deployed them on less noble tasks. The Short Brothers aircraft company in Belfast made an aircraft – the Skyvan – that was known affectionately as the 'flying shed'. In the early 1980s, the US Air Force had bought a derivative of the Skyvan – the Sherpa – to fly personnel and supplies between its bases in Europe. When that role ended, the aircraft were transferred to the US Army, which didn't really want them. But HMG had other ideas. By the late 1980s Short Brothers badly needed another order. Sitting in the Embassy, we saw that the Sherpa was the perfect Congressional aircraft: its engines were made in Fort Worth, Speaker Wright's home district, and it was serviced in West Virginia, the home state of the veteran Senate Majority Leader, Robert Byrd. Our lobbyists got to work, and before long the Defence Appropriations Bill which emerged from the Congress, and was signed by the President, instructed the US Army National Guard to acquire ten more Short Sherpas, now designated the C-23B.

The main lesson I learned from these exercises in pork-barrel politics was the importance of the House–Senate conference, at which the different versions of a bill are reconciled. It is there, behind closed doors, in smoke-filled rooms, that the real deals are done. Senators and Congressmen are seldom present. But their all-powerful staff members and the lobbyists are, in force. The sums we wanted for Ireland were relatively small, and were completely overshadowed by the eye-watering amounts being negotiated by lobbyists for Israel and the big US corporations. While we had successfully exploited the system in the interests of Britain, the episode did leave me with doubts about the constitutional wisdom of giving so much power over the public purse to elected legislators, constantly seeking re-election and the funds with which to secure that.

Irish-American politics could be rough. Americans' underlying sympathies were with the Catholics of Northern Ireland, and the Protestant voice was seldom heard. In those days, the Unionists did not bother to make the efforts they later made to get Americans to see both sides of the story. The MacBride campaign ebbed and flowed, but, thanks to the blocking action which HMG took in the state legislatures, never achieved the critical mass for which its supporters hoped. I had personal experience of the fight when, in 1990, I gave a private briefing on Northern Ireland to a conference in Rhode Island of pension fund administrators. Speaking off the record, I explained that there were a million Protestants in Northern Ireland, and half a million Catholics. The Protestants were of Scottish settler stock, and, like the Israelis or the South African whites, they could not be moved out or ignored. They had to be part of a political settlement. Also at the conference, arguing for the MacBride Principles, was an aide to that notable honorary Irishman Mayor Koch of New York. He saw that he could make mischief for the British Government by selectively leaking what I had said about the Protestants. To my horror, a few days later, following my return to Washington, I was rung by the Foreign Office News Department to say that the pro-Unionist Belfast paper, the *Newsletter*, was running a story headlined 'Envoy Slams Unionists'. My words had been twisted to imply that I had compared the Unionists to the Zionists or the Afrikaners, when my objective had been the opposite. Sensing an opportunity to attack the Foreign Office, which the Unionists had always suspected of being pro-Nationalist, the Democratic Unionist Leader Dr Ian Paisley jumped on the bandwagon, issuing critical statements, and even calling in the House of Commons for my dismissal. It was a terrible time, and my first, but not last, experience of the symbiotic relationship between papers in search of a story and politicians in search of a headline. Antony Acland and the team in Washington, and the Northern Ireland Office, could not have been more supportive, as they knew the realities of Irish and Irish American politics.

Throughout my four years in Washington I worked to secure the extradition to Northern Ireland of Joseph Patrick Doherty, a member of the Provisional IRA already sentenced to life imprisonment for his role in the killing of a British officer, Captain Richard Westmacott of the SAS and the Grenadier Guards. Westmacott (whose cousin Peter succeeded Nigel Sheinwald as ambassador to Washington in January 2012) had died on 2 May 1980 in an ambush in Belfast at the hands of what was known as the 'M60 gang', on account of their use of a massive M60 machine gun smuggled from the United States. He was awarded the Military Cross posthumously. My job, working with the US Department of Justice and the US Attorney for the Southern District of

New York, Rudolph Giuliani, was to help the US authorities persuade the US court system that Doherty's offence was criminal not political, and that he should therefore be extradited to Northern Ireland to complete his sentence. He had joined the IRA at the age of seventeen. He had been arrested after the ambush, but had managed to escape in May 1981 just before his trial concluded. Two days after his escape, Doherty was sentenced to life imprisonment *in absentia*, with a recommendation that he serve at least thirty years. Travelling via the Irish Republic, he had entered the United States illegally on a false passport in 1982, and had remained there, working as a bar man in New York. In 1983, the FBI arrested him. Doherty tried to claim political asylum in the United States, and indeed in 1985 Judge Sprizzo of New York ruled that he could not be extradited, as Doherty had indeed committed a 'political offence'. Eventually, after many twists and turns, the US Supreme Court overturned a US Appeals Court decision. He was finally deported back to Northern Ireland in February 1992, after nearly eleven years on the run, and several months after I had left Washington. But he served only six years of his sentence: in November 1998, Doherty was released from prison under the terms of the Good Friday Agreement. He became a community worker.

The Doherty case attracted more attention in America than it did in Ireland or Britain. The City of New York named after Doherty a street outside the Metropolitan Correctional Center in Southern Manhattan where he was incarcerated. His extradition was opposed by Cardinal O'Connor of New York, Mayor Dinkins and 130 members of Congress. One of them, Gary Ackerman of New York, offered to have Doherty work in his Congressional office if he could be released on bail. A decade before 9/11 American attitudes to terrorism, or at least Irish terrorism, were different. I tried not to let my emotions affect me, especially when I had to show the judge in New York the RUC photographer's album of pictures of Westmacott's bullet-riddled body in an Ulster mortuary.

One of the first British diplomats in Washington to have the task of dealing with Irish America had been Cecil Spring Rice. He wrote later of his work countering the 'Fenians' of America in the late nineteenth century. He went on to become ambassador to Washington during the

First World War, and author of the patriotic hymn 'I vow to thee, my country'. His greatest American friend was Teddy Roosevelt. It was Roosevelt who spoke most passionately against those of his country-men who remained 'hyphenated Americans', preserving ties to a home-land that were the fruit more of imagined memory than of present reality.

Another group of hyphenated Americans of whom I saw much during my time in Washington was the Greek-American community. The reason for this was that the second part of my job – covering US politics – meant that I was tasked with following the Democratic Party's candidate for President in 1988, the former Governor of Massachusetts Michael Dukakis. Since at least the 1972 Presidential election, the British Embassy in Washington had sent political officers to accompany the candidates during the campaign. The purpose of this was not so much to get to know the candidates themselves – they wouldn't have had much interest in a junior diplomat – as to observe the candidates in action and, even more important, get to know their key advisers. The first British diplomat to have done this had been Pauline Neville-Jones, in the 1972 election: coincidentally, that campaign also produced the first book – *The Boys on the Bus** – about the press pack accompanying a Presidential candidate, even though in practice more time was spent on the campaign plane than on a bus.

Dukakis had to jump through several hurdles before he could secure the Democratic Party's nomination. After the Iowa caucuses in early February (at which Dukakis had come third), the first of these was the New Hampshire primary in the middle of the month. I spent extended periods in the state, still under six inches of snow, in the early weeks of 1988. Americans made the political ground war fun. For example, the eccentric Democratic Senator from Illinois, Paul Simon, with a differ-ent bow tie every day but no realistic hope of the nomination, handed out ice-scrapers inscribed 'SIMON CUTS THE ICE'. I collected bumper stickers and buttons and badges. I attended meetings in diners and drawing rooms, in church halls and convention centres up and down New Hampshire. My main interest was in the Democratic race, as we

---

* Tim Crouse, *The Boys on the Bus*, New York: Random House, 1973.

were all but certain that Vice President George Bush would win the Republican nomination. But that didn't stop me meeting the crusty old Republican Senator Bob Dole, seeking the nomination yet again. When he learned who I was, he spoke warmly of Mrs Thatcher, the only British politician apart from Churchill of whom most American politicians had heard. I sampled up close the creepy evangelical snake oil of Pat Robertson, as I temporarily attached myself to a television crew making a documentary about him. And I met Ed Stourton, standing in L. L. Bean boots in the knee-deep snow, recording a piece for *Channel 4 News*. With him was his producer, Richard Clemmow, whom I had last seen aged twelve, when we had together edited a sweetly pretentious prep school poetry magazine we had called *Espresso*.

Trudging through the snow I also met Dukakis's foreign policy adviser, a Georgetown academic called Madeleine Albright, and her deputy, another academic, Jim Steinberg, just back from time at the International Institute for Strategic Studies in London. We guessed that both had bright futures. Albright went on to serve as Clinton's secretary of state, and Steinberg as an official in both the Clinton and Obama Administrations, ending up as deputy secretary of state to Hillary Clinton. That was exactly why we sent a junior diplomat to New Hampshire: to make contacts which would be of long-term value to the British Government. I was even able to be of some use to them, briefing Madeleine Albright on Northern Ireland.

As Governor Dukakis gradually built up his delegate count, I travelled with him across America. To Ohio, to New York, to California. We knew that once he became the clear front-runner, and even more so once he was the Democratic nominee, he would disappear into a cocoon of US Secret Service bodyguards and Democratic Party grandees. So those early weeks of the campaign were critical for access. On board the Dukakis campaign plane, an ancient Boeing 737 entirely 'coach' class, there was a clear pecking order, as the passengers spread the length of the aircraft. The candidate, and Kitty Dukakis, when she was with us, rode right at the front. Then came the senior personal advisers, mostly from the Boston Greek-American mafia. Then other campaign and policy advisers. Then, somewhere in the middle, me (there were no other diplomats). Right at the back of the aircraft sat the press pack, known variously as the 'zoo' or the 'reptiles', growing all the time as the Dukakis campaign gathered momentum. Depending on the pilots' performance, the hacks cheered or booed each landing, and rolled oranges up and down the central aisle. The Governor was not amused. In Cincinnati, Ohio, Dukakis's staff arranged an impromptu party in his hotel suite, to celebrate a year since he had announced his candidacy. The hotel chef turned out to be a proud Greek-American, and insisted on cooking a whole lamb, Greek fashion, for the son of Greece now running for president. After a long day's campaigning, we gathered awkwardly, and waited for the candidate to appear: Dukakis's campaign chairman, Paul Brountas, a lawyer from Boston; his chief assistant, Nick Mitropoulos; one or two other staffers; senior political correspondents from all the main papers travelling with us, including the *New York Times*, *Washington Post* and *Boston Globe*; and I. Dukakis appeared late. The double doors were thrown open, and a triumphant chef wheeled in a whole lamb, spreadeagled across a platter. Sparkling wine was produced. In one of the silences that followed, I tried to lighten the atmosphere and wish Dukakis well, by citing a line in Greek from Aeschylus' *Agamemnon*: 'may the good prevail'. Dukakis refused the lamb, refused the champagne and winced at my attempt at Greek joviality (which Brountas at least was good enough to acknowledge). After five stiff minutes, Dukakis announced that he and Mitropoulos needed to leave for their evening power walk. The candidate's failure to spend time cultivating the national press, in a private setting, and his refusal of a national dish prepared for him with such enthusiasm by a fellow Greek both showed the lack of emotional intelligence that was at the root of his eventual failure to win the American Presidency. With his interest in the arcana of welfare policy, Dukakis was a decent man who might have taken the top job in a Scandinavian social democracy. But he did not have what it takes to be the elected monarch of the American Republic.

That awkward evening in Cincinnati gave plenty of clues. But it wasn't decisive. Not long afterwards I was with Dukakis in New York, for the primary there. We travelled across the boroughs of the city, meeting Irish-Americans and black Americans and Polish-Americans. Then we headed north, on a pilgrimage to the capital of New York State, the Victorian Gothic city of Albany, where the enigmatic and talented Governor, Mario Cuomo, had yet to reveal whom he was backing for the nomination. At a joint press conference, Cuomo praised Dukakis, but did not endorse him. Dukakis was asked what role he saw for Cuomo in a Dukakis administration. In a rare flash of humour, Dukakis referred to Mario's mother having always wanted her son to join the Supreme Court. Cuomo blushed. It was praise, but not praise enough – a clever riposte to Cuomo's reluctance to commit himself.

Dukakis went on to win the nomination, and was crowned at the Democratic Convention in Atlanta that July. As with the Republicans in New Orleans a few weeks later, the choice of candidate was never in doubt: the real speculation was over the choice of running mate, and over exactly how the candidate would pitch his acceptance speech. This was my first American political convention. Foreign diplomats were not part of the real action, but there was plenty to see and hear, plus carrier bags full of campaign buttons and ingenious political trash. To give his campaign the gravitas it needed, particularly in the South, Dukakis picked the venerable Senator Lloyd Bentsen of Texas as his running mate. It was a smart move, which justified itself in one of the moments that defined the 1988 campaign. In a Vice Presidential debate, Bush's less than convincing choice, the gaffe-prone ingénu Senator Dan Quayle of Indiana, tried to associate himself with the young John Kennedy. Bentsen's rebuff – 'I knew Jack Kennedy, Jack Kennedy was a friend of mine. Senator, you're no Jack Kennedy' – entered American political history. I got to know Bentsen's press secretary, Mike McCurry, who went on to serve as White House press secretary under Bill Clinton – another example of how the British Government's practice of having political officers track the Presidential campaigns paid dividends later.

Dukakis's acceptance speech was timed to coincide with prime-time television, and was the Democratic candidate's first real chance to address the nation. The plan was partly derailed by a lengthy introduction from a relatively unknown Southern Governor, Bill Clinton of Arkansas, who spoke for far longer than his carefully allotted time. I wanted our report of Dukakis's speech to reach London for morning meetings the next day – beating the reports in the following day's press.

But the time difference between evening in Atlanta and morning in London was tight. So, having somehow got hold of an advance copy of Dukakis's speech, I drafted our report even before the candidate delivered it. I was impressed, and said so. The telegram's summary read: 'Dukakis delivers tour de force.' As soon as he sat down, I faxed my draft telegram to Washington, for onward transmission to London and other posts interested in American politics. The Ambassador's deputy changed only one word of my draft, so that the summary now read 'Dukakis delivers tour d'horizon'. It was difficult to know whether to laugh or cry at my editor's tin ear.

Somehow, the Democrats seemed out of place in Atlanta. But the Republicans gathering in New Orleans for their Convention struck an even more incongruous note. They were just too respectable and too white for a city (and a culture) defined by an overwhelmingly black population, by poverty, and by the seedy delights of the French quarter. Even then the Republican Party was becoming more Southern and more Christian, as the 'Reagan Democrats' changed sides and abandoned their traditional, post-Civil War allegiance to the Democratic Party. I met Charlton Heston, there in his capacity as a lobbyist for the National Rifle Association. Bush duly stunned the convention with his choice of Dan Quayle, whose patchy performance in the campaign and later as Vice President underlined the oddness of choosing the Indiana Senator. But the real highlight was Bush's acceptance speech. Crafted by Reagan's speechwriter Peggy Noonan, it spoke of a kinder, gentler conservatism, of a thousand points of light in an engaged civil society, painting George Herbert Walker Bush as the quiet but good man of American politics. It had many merits – and much in common with his son George W. Bush's compassionate Conservatism, and with the Big Society, promoted on the other side of the Atlantic twenty years later by another centre-right leader. There was soaring rhetoric, but also more measured, occasionally lyrical passages. It was a triumph. And it had the merit of being authentic – authentically George Bush, and largely true.

Conventions over, the Presidential election campaign got going. Bush's victory seemed assured, though there were one or two wobbles. During one of these, the same Embassy official who had done such damage to my Dukakisgram decreed that we send a telegram to London warning that Bush might not win. It didn't do our credibility any good: London needs forecasts, not fence-sitting.

What sealed Bush's victory was a strategy of brutal frontal assault on the Massachusetts 'liberal' that was anything but kind or gentle. Dukakis was savagely attacked, for everything from the alleged pollution in Boston Harbour (which Bush visited in a small boat) to claims that he had let a black rapist – Willie Horton – out on parole. It was rough stuff. I knew Dukakis had lost the moment I saw the image of him bobbing in the turret of a tank at Aberdeen Proving Ground in Maryland, wearing a ludicrously inappropriate helmet. As Robin Cook was to learn later and perhaps William Hague too, one of the first rules of modern politics is Never Ever Wear a Hat, at least in public.

One of the Democratic Party's most energetic supporters was Pamela Harriman. There isn't space here to trace her journey, from riches to yet more riches, from a country estate in Dorset to becoming President Clinton's ambassador to France, from marriage to Randolph Churchill, through all sorts of close friendships with influential men, to a final happy marriage to Averell Harriman.* She mattered in the 1980s and 1990s as an inveterate fund-raiser, with her own Political Action Committee, known as 'PamPac'. Thanks to her friendship with the Aclands, she was one of the Embassy's best Democratic Party contacts. One of my rather less well-heeled friends in the Party described the incongruity of attending a party workshop on poverty in her house in Georgetown, sitting beneath a painting by an Old Master depicting the same subject.

Election over, the congratulations poured in, and the spoils were divided. Britain was well placed, not least because the Aclands and the Bushes had become good friends during Bush's time as vice president and as the Embassy's neighbour – the Vice President's official residence is the old Naval Observatory just up Massachusetts Avenue from the British Embassy. It was a relationship that was to serve us well over the next four years.

---

* See Christopher Ogden, *Life of the Party: The Biography of Pamela Digby Churchill Hayward Harriman*, London: Little, Brown, 1994.

But the first task was for the Prime Minister to say a proper goodbye to President Reagan. Mrs Thatcher, accompanied by Denis, her son Mark and daughter Carol, and the inevitable Charles Powell, came out on something close to a state visit. It was my first acquaintance with the plush delights of Blair House, the US Government's official guest house across Lafayette Square from the White House. The visit went well, thanks in part to the speeches which Mrs Thatcher delivered with such force and clarity. It closed a remarkable chapter in transatlantic relations, in which the partnership between President and Prime Minister really had made a difference to the course of history.

Bush then got down to choosing his new team. Jim Baker at the State Department was an outstanding choice: a man who, following Jean Monnet's dictum dividing statesmen into those who want to be and those who want to do, preferred doing – mostly in private – to being. He achieved much over the next four years, notably managing the consequences of the collapse of the Soviet Union and the Madrid Conference on Middle East peace. I had come to know one of the transition team responsible for personnel issues, a moderate Texas Republican in the George H. W. Bush mould called Chase Untermeyer. Chase was always proper and discreet, insisting, for example, on giving me a cheque for exactly half the cost of the breakfasts I would buy him at the Hay Adams Hotel once he started in the White House. One of his colleagues on the President's staff, responsible for dealing with state and local governments, was more ideological, but also became a good friend: Frank Lavin was a US Navy Reserve officer who spoke Mandarin, but had strongly conservative economic views. He taught me a lot about how the American right thinks and works.

Some time between Christmas 1988 and the New Year, when I was on local leave, the Embassy got a call from the Bush transition team to say that President-elect Bush was planning to announce the next day that he was sending his friend, and fund-raiser, Henry Catto to London as ambassador. Antony Acland explained to the President-elect that it wasn't usual to announce the appointment of an ambassador before the host government had agreed to accept him or her – what is known in the trade as granting *agrément*. But Bush was determined: Catto's job was part of a package that Bush had to announce, to show different

Republican constituencies what was being done for them. So there was no alternative to seeking *agrément* as quickly as possible. The Queen was at Sandringham for her Christmas break. Buckingham Palace faxed the papers up from London to her private secretary in Norfolk. It was the first time the Queen had given *agrément* by fax, and, probably, overnight.

The third element of my Washington job was acting as the desk officer, or official of last resort, in the Embassy for the UK–US bilateral relationship. In that capacity, I would occasionally write think pieces, or contribute to regular papers produced by the Planning Staff in London on the state of the Special Relationship – a subject of continual anxiety in London that is of little reciprocal interest in Washington. One of the last I wrote, in the summer of 1991, was about just how difficult a US Constitution which the Ambassador used to describe as 'batty' made the effective government of a polity and an economy competing in an increasingly tough world. My experience of America trying to operate in Afghanistan fifteen years later only reinforced the judgements some of us had made back then.

But the real work of the teams handling US–UK bilateral relations in Washington and in London was visits. Hundreds of them every year, by members of the Government and the royal family. Every Cabinet minister wanted to travel to Washington for consultations on their area of responsibility, and to acquaint themselves with the latest ideas from the think-tanks that lined Massachusetts Avenue. So did dozens of junior ministers, and scores of senior officials. Admirals, generals and air marshals were in Washington all the time, but were handled by the Embassy Defence Staff. Unlike other British ambassadors, who have to struggle to persuade ministers and officials to visit (as I was to find as ambassador in Riyadh), the Ambassador in Washington (like his colleague in Paris) has to spend time actively discouraging over-eager visitors from London.

Many times over those four years did I think again of the university friend who had become a rep with Thomson Holidays. Luckily, we had an excellent team of young diplomats handling the mechanics of the visits, one responsible for ministers and senior officials, another dealing with the royals. Despite the Ambassador's attempts to discourage unnecessary or unwanted official visitors, 'visits' were a full-time job for at least two members of the Embassy staff, and sometimes many more.

Only a few such visits stick in the memory. Mrs Thatcher's, of course, in November 1988 to say goodbye to Reagan and welcome Bush, and again in August 1990, to speak at the Aspen Institute in Colorado, but also to discourage George Bush from 'going wobbly' over the invasion of Kuwait by Saddam Hussein. Three months later, I was the Embassy Duty Officer on Thanksgiving Day 1990 when the Duty Clerk at Number 10 rang to say that an urgent Secret and Personal message from the Prime Minister to the President was on its way: could I have it delivered as soon as possible? I was enjoying a Thanksgiving Dinner with my family in Northern Virginia, so I got a kind colleague to take the message off the cipher machine, put it in an envelope and run it down to the White House. It was a message from Mrs Thatcher to her good friend George Bush announcing that she was stepping down as prime minister.

One memorable visit was that by the energetic Foreign Office junior Minister David Mellor, who arrived by train at Union Station in Washington on the evening of 31 January 1988. As it was the night of the Super Bowl, in which the Washington Redskins were playing, no one more senior in the Embassy volunteered to meet the Minister. So I was sent. As I drove the length of Massachusetts Avenue towards Union Station in the stretch limousine the Embassy hired for such visits, the town was deserted. But, once I had found the Minister, and we had started back across town towards the Embassy, jubilant crowds suddenly came pouring out on to the streets. The Redskins had won. But, curiously, David Mellor didn't seem to know even that the Super Bowl was on, let alone that the local team had been playing. He asked me what was happening. What were the crowds celebrating? Without missing a beat, I replied, 'Your arrival in Washington, Minister.' For a split second, the ambitious young politician seemed almost to believe me.

At the other end of the spectrum was a visit by the Lord Chancellor, Lord Mackay of Clashfern. A member of the extreme Calvinist 'wee free' Presbyterian Church of Scotland, he was a strict Sabbatarian. He refused to travel in a motor vehicle on Sundays, or to read the Monday papers, on the grounds that they had been produced on a Sunday. All this complicated the business of getting him from Southern Virginia to Washington one Monday lunchtime to deliver a major speech on the rule of law in Britain. But we did it, and the speech was a powerful rebuttal of American critics of British justice in the wake of the Birmingham Six and Guildford Four cases, of wrongful convictions of alleged IRA terrorists. We still had a hard time in explaining to the media in a land deeply attached to the separation of powers between the executive, legislative and judicial branches of government how in England a Scottish peer could be not only the Cabinet Minister responsible for the administration of justice, but also the speaker of the upper house of Parliament and at the same time Britain's chief judge. In other words, the diffident Lord Mackay was the living antithesis of the separation of powers, a sort of secular embodiment of the doctrine of the Trinity.

There were plenty of royal visits too. For one, by the Prince of Wales, at about the time of his fortieth birthday, it was decided that we would invite to lunch at the Embassy twenty or thirty 'interesting' Americans of about the same age as His Royal Highness. After extensive research, and consultation with our consulates around the country, we managed to put together the most interesting guest list the Embassy had ever compiled. We found a female astronaut, a black mayor, a marine biologist, an architect and, as a chief guest, a man who thought in many ways like Prince Charles, Senator Al Gore of Indiana. Steve Jobs, spotted by our Consul-General in San Francisco, was on the target list, but wasn't available. On other visits, the Prince of Wales promoted his interest in architecture, at a major convention in Washington, and in sustainable development, at a conference in Charleston, South Carolina. He was a big asset for us in America, in the years immediately after his triumphant visit to Washington with the Princess of Wales in 1985 for the Treasure Houses of Britain exhibition at the National Gallery.

Diana also came to Washington, but on her own. She graced a gala dinner to raise money for the London City Ballet, and visited an AIDS refuge. The latter caused us problems, because the Mayor of the District of Columbia, Marion Barry, had been caught on camera taking drugs and had an appalling reputation. The last thing we wanted was for him to be associated with the visit: we could see the British tabloid headlines screaming 'BEAUTY AND THE BEAST'. But of course association with the Princess was just what the Mayor wanted to help rehabilitate his reputation. We didn't invite him, but he turned up all the same. Only muscular diplomacy by the Embassy Press Counsellor, Francis Cornish, kept the beast out of the same shot as the beauty. Francis was the man who nearly ten years earlier had casually ordered me to clear Kate Adie and others off the roof of the Suez Canal Authority building in Port Said, to enable the Princess to stroll on deck before dinner. Getting Francis to do the same to Mayor Barry was revenge, served cold.

Most of the last six months of my four years in Washington were spent working on the biggest visit of them all: a state visit by the Queen and the Duke of Edinburgh, planned for May 1991. The Queen had previously visited President Eisenhower (in 1957) and President Ford (in 1976, to mark the American Bicentennial), and was to go again in 2007, to see President George W. Bush, for the 400th anniversary of the Jamestown Settlement. Her parents had paid an historic state visit in June 1939, travelling to Washington and New York, and helping in their quiet way to shore up American support for Britain in the world war that broke out three months later.

But the 1991 state visit was the big one. It had four stages: a Washington leg, which was the state visit proper, followed by official visits to Florida and then Texas, and finally private time in Kentucky, staying with the Queen's friend and fellow racing enthusiast Will Farish (who was later to serve as American ambassador in London). Almost every step taken by the Queen and the Duke of Edinburgh had to be meticulously choreographed. Having had some experience of royal visits in Cairo, I thought I knew how they were done. But a two-week state visit by the Queen and Prince Philip to America was of an entirely different order. Every last detail had to be prepared, reconnoitred, scripted, thought through. I found myself drafting everything from elevator manifests (who would ride in which lift) to a whole series of speeches. We had to work closely with Buckingham Palace, who were the model of professionalism and efficiency, but also with the American authorities: the White House, the State Department Office of Protocol, and then the local authorities in Texas, Florida and Kentucky. Plus the US Secret Service, which, working with the royal detectives, would be responsible for protecting the royal visitors throughout. Sometimes it seemed as though six months would not be nearly long enough to get everything right. Americans, perhaps especially the White House, don't share Brits' preoccupation with planning everything months in advance. But we were lucky in the State Department team, led by the wholly unflappable (and extremely well-connected) Agnes Warfield, a political appointee from the moderate branch of the Republican Party which prospered under Bush senior but all but disappeared under his son. It was a measure of Agnes's discretion that the media never discovered that the American mainly responsible for the detailed organisation of the Queen's visit came from the same respectable Baltimore family – the Warfields – who had provided the Queen's uncle Edward VIII with his bride.

After all the preparations, and a lengthy reconnaissance visit led by the Queen's Deputy Private Secretary, Sir Kenneth Scott, the visit got under way on 14 May 1991. And that was when the fun started. It was a steamy Washington day. President Bush, apparently suffering from a thyroid condition, wasn't feeling 100 per cent. After delivering his speech of welcome on the White House lawn, his job was to pull out a small 'riser' or platform, for the Queen to stand on as she delivered her response. But Bush forgot, and all that the world saw, through the copse of microphones crowning the Presidential lectern, was what the American media immediately dubbed 'the talking hat'.

Over the private lunch for the Queen which followed, Barbara Bush told her husband exactly what she thought of his forgetfulness.

As it happened, however, a minor setback was turned by the Queen into a public relations triumph. She was apprehensive about her address to an expectant Joint Session of Congress. To lighten the atmosphere, she decided to start, rather unusually, with an unscripted joke. As she stood below and in front of the Speaker of the House and the Vice President (in his capacity as speaker of the Senate), and waited to begin her address, the Queen looked around, and, in a completely deadpan voice, said simply, 'I do hope you can all see me from where you are sitting today.' The chamber erupted in gales of laughter and a standing ovation. She had broken the ice. The cynical Congressmen and Senators, all surprisingly in awe of the Queen of England (as they called her), loved it.

For the Washington leg, we tried to ring the changes on a standard programme for a state visit. So we took the Queen to one of the poorer, and predominantly black, parts of the District of Columbia, to meet some of the people who lived there. As we walked in the blazing sun up an unmade-up dirt track between modest wooden cottages, a jazz band played. A police SWAT team staked out roofs near by, and a helicopter hovered overhead. One of the Queen's courtiers expressed what we were all thinking, but not saying. 'This is just like a Commonwealth visit,' he observed. The Queen took tea with a large and kindly black lady, in her tiny front room. As the Queen approached, her hostess, overcome by emotion, embraced her gently. The British tabloids turned this into 'QUEEN CRUSHED IN BEAR HUG BY BLACK MAMA'. It really wasn't like that at all.

Playing to President Bush's interests (he had captained Yale at baseball), and with the West Coast television audience in mind, we arranged for the President to take the Queen to watch a match in Baltimore between the home team, the Orioles, and the Oakland A's from California. The Presidential helicopter, Marine One, took the President and the Queen straight from the White House lawn to Memorial Stadium in Baltimore, with the rest of us following in a couple of giant US Marine Corps Sea Stallion helicopters. The President escorted the Queen down to the dugout to meet the players and out on to the pitch. And then they sat for a bit and watched. It had been my job to write the brief on baseball for the Queen. The first line read 'Baseball is not cricket. But, like cricket, it is a form of secular religion.' An Embassy expert had then helped me with the rules. I would have done much better just telling the Queen that baseball was like rounders – a game with which she must have been familiar.

I also had to prepare the more general briefs for the Queen. One that sticks in my mind was on Washington DC. In 1990 the homicide rate in England and Wales outside London had been 1.5 per 100,000, in London 2.5, in Northern Ireland 7.5, in Chicago, Los Angeles and New York 25, but in the District of Columbia it had been 75 murders per

100,000 of the population per year. A truly shocking statistic that spoke volumes about the social decay in America's inner cities.

As usual with such visits, there was an exchange of banquets. A glamorous state dinner at the White House, the menu and guest list for which were pored over by the social writers of the *Washington Post*, was followed by a return match at the British Embassy, plus a garden party, English-style. That worked pretty well, although some of the American guests almost came to blows in their efforts to get close to the Queen, and even to touch her.

From Washington, the Queen flew south, on the Concorde which had brought her from London, to Miami. Because the royal wardrobe trunks were too large for Concorde's cargo hold, a C-130 Hercules of the US Air Force followed with the royal luggage. In Florida, the Queen was able immediately to embark on the Royal Yacht *Britannia*. We managed to use the ship to the full. Once on board, the Queen hosted a dinner, followed, not preceded, in the traditional fashion, by a much larger reception. Three former American Presidents came to dinner: Ford, Reagan and Carter. So did the cream of Florida society. We had worked with our Consul in Miami to draw up the guest lists. But it was a thankless task. Everyone who was anybody in Florida wanted to be invited: up until the moment the party began, they were calling asking for invitations, and offering large sums to secure one. Nor were they ever satisfied. One of Florida's most successful businessmen rang to complain bitterly that he and his wife were going only to the reception on *Britannia*, not the dinner: what could he do for me to change that? But these were the problems of success, not failure. The evening ended with the Royal Marines Band Beating Retreat under floodlights on the quayside. Their display sent frissons of pride down my spine.

A day of official engagements in and around Miami, designed mainly to reach out to the Hispanic community, followed. From there, the Queen set sail on *Britannia* for a private weekend at sea, rounding the Florida peninsula, passing through the Keys, before regaining land, and the official programme, at Tampa, on Florida's often forgotten Gulf coast. In planning the visit, we really had been determined to reach places as well as communities that other state visitors didn't usually reach.

From Tampa, the royal party flew to Texas, to begin a gruelling four-city tour of the Lone Star state. I flew on, in advance, to Austin, the state capital, only to endure the lowest point of my time working on the visit. For the Florida and Texas legs of the tour I had invested in something more suitable than my usual grey suit. I had been to Brooks Brothers and bought, with great pride, a seersucker suit, with blue and white stripes, of the kind I had enviously observed Nigel Sheinwald wearing four years earlier on my arrival in Washington. I was so proud of that suit, and put it on the morning we went out to greet the Queen on her arrival in Texas. I stood in line at the bottom of the aircraft steps. The Queen and Prince Philip appeared, just behind them, the Foreign Secretary, Douglas Hurd, as minister in attendance, and just behind him, his Private Secretary, Richard Gozney. The disembarkation went smoothly. We climbed aboard the motorcade, for the first engagement, a welcoming ceremony in the Texas State Capitol. Gozney got in beside me. 'Sherard,' he said, 'I think you ought to know what the Queen whispered to Prince Philip as she looked down from the top of the aircraft steps.' I waited, expectantly. His *Schadenfreude* barely concealed, Richard continued: 'She said, "What *is* that man wearing?"' I was mortified, and never again wore the damn suit on that side of the Atlantic.

The Texas visit was most fun, and full of contrasts. The ceremonies in Austin were miniature replicas of what had happened in Washington a week earlier. With its sleepy southern bohemian atmosphere, and its jazz quarter beside the river, Austin felt both quaint and cool. So, in a different way, did the Spanish-American city of San Antonio, where the Queen took a boat tour along the canals running through the city. There, at the Alamo, she was received by the formidable Daughters of the Republic of Texas, proud of their state and its brief period of independence, when it had even had its own embassy in London. Dallas was different again, with a wonderful classical concert in the great symphony hall. And the official visit ended in Houston, with a tour of the Johnson Space Center, where the Queen met a British astronaut, Michael Foale. It all ended with a grand dinner given by the Queen in the Houston Museum of Fine Art, to say thank-you.

The next day, the Queen flew on for her private time in Kentucky, and the rest of us relaxed. One of the oddities of the Texas leg of the visit had been that, unusually, the Queen had stayed in hotels. One of my jobs had been to help choose them, in Austin, Dallas and Houston. I have never been looked after quite so attentively.

On the last morning of her stay, the Queen had asked to see each of the British–American team who had worked on her visit, to thank us for what we had done. I was lucky enough to be made a Lieutenant of the Royal Victorian Order, awarded for personal services to the sovereign. I felt proud to have been part of an exercise which had successfully promoted British interests in the United States, thanks mainly to the faultless performance of the star of the production, the Queen. The Americans also had had presents to give. President Bush's colourful Chief of Protocol, Ambassador Joseph Verner Reed, had ordered for the Duke of Edinburgh, for the Queen's grandsons, and for me, alligator-skin cowboy boots from the best bootmaker in Houston. Prince Philip's had 'Prince' and 'Philip' inscribed in silver letters down each side, mine a more modest 'SCC'. I was too self-conscious to wear mine much, though my exuberant eldest son makes good use of them.

After all that, the remaining weeks in Washington were something of an anti-climax. But they gave me time to recharge my batteries before the return to England, and another job in the Foreign Office. My family was now seven strong, with our youngest son, Myles, having been born in Washington a year earlier. At the Columbia Hospital for Women, the woman in the bed next to Bridget's brought in with her a small bag of soil, which she solemnly placed under her bed. She was doing it, she explained, to ensure that her child was truly a Texan. It was a Texan too who had gushed to me, over dinner in the Embassy, about how much she just loved my accent. When I had replied that I loved hers too, her puzzled response had been 'But Ah don't have an accent.' It was one of those 'only in America' moments that I would miss so much during the next six hard years in London.

Chapter 6

Back in the Office

So, in August 1991, I tried to do for my successor in Washington, Jonathan Powell, what Nigel Sheinwald had done for me four years earlier: leave him the best possible guide to doing what we all thought was the best job in the Washington Embassy. As I wrote my notes for Jonathan, with lists of contacts and comments on them, I compared them with what Nigel had left for me. My main achievement, thanks mainly to the time I had spent with the Dukakis campaign, had been to acquire a range of contacts in the Democratic Party who would acquire some importance if George H. W. Bush were, against expectations, to lose the 1992 election, just a year later. In the late summer of 1991, most people in Washington assumed that Bush would win a second term. They underestimated the skills of the man – William Jefferson Clinton from Arkansas – who would become the Democratic nominee, and they overestimated how much a tired and, some say, sick Bush wanted another four years in the job.

I knew Jonathan only a bit. The youngest of four remarkable brothers, he used to joke that, as a pretty successful fast-stream diplomat, he was the failure in the family. I could understand that: I had met another brother, Chris, who had been so successful in advertising that he had bought my sister-in-law's old school as his country house. But Jonathan's main distinction seemed to be that he insisted on pronouncing his name to rhyme with 'bowel', not the more refined 'bowl' of his eldest brother, Charles, Mrs Thatcher's Private Secretary. I was not surprised when in 1994 Jonathan left the Foreign Office to become Tony Blair's chief of staff, nor that he stuck at the job throughout Blair's ten years in power. His main book about those years – *The New*

*Machiavelli** – is an outstanding political primer, but also an insight into a man whose unusual mix of diffidence, ability and moral courage made him an ideal chief of staff, as well as a successful peace negotiator in Northern Ireland.

While Jonathan took over my job in Washington, I took over one of his roles in London. Not his day job, but the post of secretary of the Diplomatic Service Association. The DSA was an odd combination of trade union, for the fast-stream members of the Diplomatic Service, and a professional institution. As secretary, I had a platform for communicating with the members, all round the world, and for engaging with the Foreign Office Administration, in negotiations on all kinds of issues. There was a committee, a chairman, occasional half-hearted elections, and an office run by a full-time assistant secretary, Christine Berman, who was the heart, soul and conscience of the organisation.

But my real job in London was dominated by the fallout from the collapse of the Soviet Union: as assistant (the quaint Foreign Office term for deputy head) in the Security Policy Department – the team that dealt with the politics of defence, covering NATO, plans for a European defence capability, nuclear issues and conventional disarmament. Although I didn't know much about defence policy, I found that I really enjoyed politico-military affairs. I knew I had to spend a short time as a deputy head of a department before getting one of my own, and, given a free choice, I would have chosen this area anyway. I was lucky. I loved dealing with the military, and found the combination of rarefied deterrent theory and real defence practice especially alluring. Luckily, I had a rather introverted boss who loved debating, mainly with himself, deterrence and disarmament, while sketching out wiring diagrams for international military command structures, leaving me to cover NATO and European defence.

In the autumn of 1991, NATO's world was starting to unravel. The Organisation had lost an enemy and was in search of a role. I saw parallels with the way the disappearance of the Persian threat had led ancient Athens to turn its voluntary mutual defence pact, the Delian League, into a compulsory empire. And I noted how the removal of any

---

* London: The Bodley Head, 2010.

real threat to imperial Rome had led to the slow disintegration of that empire, and quoted Cavafy's poem: 'And what now shall become of us without any barbarians? Those people were a kind of solution.'* Well before the Cold War ended, there had been much speculation in NATO circles as to whether the Alliance could ever operate 'out of area', but in 1991 such talk of 'OOA' was still too daring, a step too far for an inherently conservative institution. Anyone who had suggested that ten years on the Alliance would be launching – and then effectively losing – a decade-long land war in South-west Asia would have been regarded as utterly mad. Instead, as the Iron Curtain melted away, the Soviet Union dissolved and Germany reunited, the focus was on redefining the Alliance's mission to make it more inclusive, as a mutual defence organisation for free European states in and beyond what was then becoming the European Union. NATO would reach out to the countries of the former Warsaw Pact and gradually bring them into what George Bush had called a Europe whole and free. Trouble in the Balkans was brewing, and would in time give NATO a role in its own backyard. But in 1991 that was obvious only to a few of the more perceptive observers (including a young officer in my department, who had served in Belgrade, and warned us all what would happen as Yugoslavia came apart and its constituent republics sought their independence). But ministers weren't listening, and in any case in the autumn of 1991 they had enough problems to cope with on the geopolitical front.

Those two years working on politico-military affairs in the early 1990s taught me much about what really mattered to Britain in the Atlantic Alliance. It was, for example, important to HMG that the new command structures gave Britain's armed forces roles in NATO on land, at sea and in the air which could be used to justify their size, and in particular created as many senior jobs for British generals, admirals and air marshals as could be obtained in the painful 'flags to posts' negotiations between NATO chiefs of defence staff (known colloquially as CHODs). Thus Britain became the 'framework nation' for the new

---

* 'Waiting for the Barbarians', 1904, in *The Complete Poems of Cavafy*, trans. Ray Dalvern, London: Hogarth Press, 1961.

Allied Command Europe Rapid Reaction Corps (or ARRC), based at the old British Army on the Rhine headquarters in Rheindahlen, enabling us to justify for another two decades a military presence in Germany whose real raison d'être – deterring a Soviet invasion of the West – had disappeared in 1989.

A second objective was to keep as close to the Americans as we could, and to keep them close to us, while accepting the form, but not the substance, of Europe's ambitions for a serious defence capability of its own. Then as now, our particular obsession was preventing the French and Germans doing anything serious to create a 'European Army', still less the 'European Defence Community' for which Churchill had once called. As we saw it, defence was for NATO, while security could some-times be for the Europeans. In the run-up to the Maastricht Treaty of December 1991, which turned the European Communities into the European Union, and did much else, France and Germany had launched an initiative pressing for Europe to go further and faster in defence matters. They went on to announce the creation of a Franco-German corps, which soon became the Euro-corps, into which was folded an existing Franco-German brigade. Instead of relaxing, and treating these moves as the gestures they were, Britain felt it had to react. And we reacted in a way which caused great mirth in Paris and Berlin, and no doubt elsewhere: we got into bed with the Italians, and launched an Anglo-Italian European defence initiative, to counter the Franco-German one. The improbable combination of the British Foreign Secretary, Douglas Hurd, and his Italian colleague, the fun-loving Gianni De Michelis, met at a restaurant outside Rome to finalise the initiative. With much amusement, I listened in on a call between Hurd, who still had some Italian from his time as a first secretary in our Embassy in Rome, and De Michelis, a Venetian chemistry professor who had once written a guide to the nightclubs of Italy and was later convicted of corruption, before being elected to the European Parliament. Our move carried little weight and less credibility, and I wonder now why we bothered. But twenty years on it is difficult to recall the paranoia with which European defence was then regarded in London. A wiser policy would have been to call our French and German partners' bluff: welcome their moves, and invite them to put real resources where their rhetoric was. Anything that added to the sum total of European capability should have been welcomed.

All this led, in December 1991, to the tortuous wording of Article B of the Treaty of Maastricht, which stated that the new Union would 'assert its identity on the international scene, in particular through the implementation of a common foreign and security policy including the eventual framing of a common defence policy, which might in time lead to a common defence'. The last three phrases read even better in French: 'notamment par la mise en oeuvre d'une politique étrangère et de sécurité commune, y compris la définition à terme d'une politique de défense commune, qui pourrait conduire, le moment venu, à une défense commune'. The key words in all this were 'eventual/à terme' and 'in time/le moment venu', and each was fought over long and hard. The Foreign Office Political Director handled the final negotiations in Maastricht, but was talked through every step of the way by a team of us in London led by the Under Secretary for Defence, John Goulden. Subsequent history, and several military campaigns, including one off and over Libya in 2011, have shown that, sadly, 'le moment' has still not 'venu' for Europe to develop a serious defence capability of its own.

This was my introduction to the world of multilateral diplomacy, where form often matters almost as much as substance, and where the *tour de table* (or table round of speakers) can be more important than what is actually on the table. But buried beneath all the *bella figura* were and are serious issues. As the NATO commander in Afghanistan, General David McKiernan, was to observe to me sorrowfully fifteen years later, 'There is only one thing worse than having allies, and that is not having allies.' Whatever the merits of any particular intervention, in Bosnia, Kosovo, East Timor, Iraq, Afghanistan or Libya, we were far better off with allies than without them. The issues on which we – or the Americans – could operate comfortably on our own, even with a UN mandate, were few and far between. The Falklands, Grenada, Panama and Sierra Leone are some of the exceptions over the past thirty years that prove the rule.

One of our ambitions in the Security Policy Department in 1991 was to modernise and eventually abolish a curious self-defence organisation known as the Western European Union. The WEU predated NATO, having been created by the Brussels Treaty of 1948 (NATO was brought into being by the Washington Treaty of 1949). It bound Britain, France and the Benelux countries, and later Germany and Italy, into a mutual defence pact. Despite long having been overshadowed by its much more successful younger sister organisation, it kept going, with a full-time secretary general and secretariat in Grosvenor Street, London and offshoots in Brussels and elsewhere. Giving the WEU a dignified exit from the international scene took absurd amounts of time and effort. Although it was already on life support in 1991, and later moved to Brussels, it was not until June 2011 that the WEU was finally killed off.

The Security Policy job brought me into contact with the upper echelons of the Ministry of Defence, which I enjoyed. In those days, the star policy brain was the Deputy Under Secretary for Policy (known as DUS(P)), Richard Mottram. He brought to the job many qualities, high intelligence above all, but also an infectious sense of humour, a sobering sense of proportion and an ability to suffer fools in and out of uniform gladly. He made policy-making fun. Richard worked closely with Lieutenant General Thomas Boyd-Carpenter, one of Britain's more cerebral generals. But Boyd-Carpenter's donnish manner counted against him with some of his military colleagues, who, suspicious of his intelligence, accused him behind his back of thinking like a civilian. This formidable pair, working with senior officials in the Foreign and Cabinet Offices, and in our NATO delegation in Brussels, did much to steer Britain through the shoals of developing and implementing a credible defence policy when the only serious enemy against whom we had to defend ourselves was dissolving before our eyes. But it was not long before new threats, real and imagined, emerged in the Balkans and in the Middle East to give our defence planners something real to chew on.

These years also gave me a not always edifying view of how senior Foreign Office officials conducted themselves. I remember one very senior diplomat telling me that he had signed off my draft telegram of instructions (on some arcane aspect of NATO policy), but 'didn't agree with it'. He wanted to be able to stay on the fence, or rather on both sides of it. Similarly, we spent much time sending detailed instructions to the UK Delegation to NATO on the renegotiation of every line of a document at once of existential importance to NATO and of supreme irrelevance in the real world: NATO's new 'Strategic Concept'. A colleague remarked that a particular official in our team in Brussels seemed to want instructions from London just to blow his nose.

If in those days the high officials and generals in Whitehall were worrying about 'whither NATO', just as they are today, so were the thinking soldiers on the ground. They brought to the debate a degree of common sense and practical experience often missing from the more ethereal exchanges in Whitehall. In 1992 Britain still had three full armoured brigades in Germany, as the heart of the British Army of the Rhine. Each of the brigadiers decided in turn to have a brigade study day, to get his officers to address some of the big politico-military issues then unfolding. Each competed with the others for the best cast list of outside speakers. I was invited to each day in turn, as the warm-up act from the Foreign Office for the real stars. Typically, Brigadier Arthur Denaro, who had returned two years earlier from leading (with a hunting horn) the Queen's Royal Irish Hussars in the first Gulf War, took the prize, with Martin Bell and two Canadian nuns just back from Sarajevo as his top billings. We were all invited to stay with the Denaros and have dinner the night before. I was met at the airport by the liaison officer whom Arthur had asked to look after me during my visit: a languid fop from one of the smarter cavalry regiments. On the drive in from the airport, I asked him what he did at Rhine Army Headquarters. 'Well,' he drawled, 'my main job is to organise the Rhine Army summer [horse] show, but I run a couple of hunter trials in the winter too.' I am told that his semi-official title was General Staff Officer (Jumps).

With my military geek's interest in equipment, I asked him about the tanks then deployed with the Rhine Army. I had long believed that the British Army desperately needed a fast and mobile modern armoured reconnaissance vehicle to replace the Scimitar light tanks which even then were twenty years old (and are still in service today). What he said was music to my ears: the Challenger Main Battle Tanks kept breaking down, and weren't really suitable for deployment in numbers in any likely scenario for modern war: what the Army needed, he said, was a new armoured reconnaissance vehicle.

On my return to London, I did a short note to my boss, reporting my conclusions, referring to these and other conversations in general terms, without naming names. He copied it to our Ambassador to NATO, who copied it to the British Military Representative to NATO. He in turn copied it to the Chief of the General Staff back in London, General Sir Peter Inge, who exploded. A reprimand was send to the Commander of the ARRC, who in turn sent a reprimand down to Arthur Denaro: the British Army's equipment was no business of the Foreign Office, and officers were not to tell visiting diplomats what they really thought on such issues. Although I didn't know it at the time, it was a foretaste of how thin-skinned senior officers can be, and how they can overreact to constructive military interest from civilians who are after all supposed to be setting the security and defence policies within which they work. At least that was the theory, as I used to tell the audiences in eastern Europe whom I visited on lecture tours at the time. I would explain to them how in Britain we had civilian democratic management of defence. In our ministries, civilian politicians and their official advisers told the military what to do, not the other way round. If they wanted to join NATO, they needed to do the same. It was another fifteen years before I discovered, in Afghanistan, that the reality was more complicated.

My time in the Security Policy Department came, sadly, to an end in the spring of 1993, but there was a year or so to go until the department for which I had been chosen – Hong Kong Department in the run-up to the colony's return to China in 1997 – came free. I filled the time in two quite different ways, each of continuing interest to me.

The first built on my time dealing with politico-military affairs in Whitehall. I was sent, as a research associate, to the International Institute for Strategic Studies in London to write a paper on British defence and security policy after the Cold War. The IISS Director, John Chipman, had immediately seen the point of the project, and backed it and me. The precise subject doesn't seem at all original now, but it was at the time. I researched, and then wrote, about the changing role of Britain's armed forces, as they moved from defending territory to generating security more broadly defined for the United Kingdom. I looked at earlier periods of change in defence policy, and saw how difficult it was to change an institution, or rather a series of institutions, so instinctively conservative, so deeply woven into the fabric of British society, so much part of Britain's image of itself. I saw how the system of county regiments and of territorial recruitment created bonds between particular cities, towns and villages and their own regiments. I saw the links between the Royal Navy and its home ports, and between the Royal Air Force and its own hinterland, particularly the famous air stations which bracket the A1 Great North Road almost all the way from London to Newcastle.

Before I went to the IISS, I thought I could write. But once my draft had been through the mangle of their sub-editors I knew I couldn't – at least not without help and practice. My sub-editor there didn't just tidy up my grammar and smooth out my syntax: she asked me what my words really meant. The result was a much improved article, published not long afterwards in *Survival*, the IISS quarterly.* I was pleased to find it on the syllabus for the MOD's Higher Command and Staff Course, as something for the future leaders of all three armed services to chew on, as they too adjusted to a post-Cold War world.

Being back in an academic environment taught me much. At one level, I saw and heard just how rude academics can be, not just about each other's work, but also about each other. But, more important, for the first time since the Planning Staff, I was reminded how much academic experts knew about international relations that government should really have known but didn't. In the United States, academic experts on international affairs, of whom perhaps the most prominent recent examples have been Henry Kissinger and Madeleine Albright, rotate in and out of government. But Britain's foreign policy machine has no set mechanism for tapping the expertise of our academic communities. On the one hand, think-tankers and academics specialising in international relations kept *saying* that they wanted to be 'policy-relevant' but somehow they shied away from the compromises and complications which political reality imposed. From the other side of the street, policy-makers in government *said* that they wished they knew more about the issues on which they were expected to advise ministers but often found that too much knowledge of the realities of,

* 'From Defence to Security: British Policy in Transition', *Survival*, vol. 36, no. 1, Spring 1994.

say, Bosnia or Iraq or Afghanistan only complicated the job of giving politicians the honest advice they needed. Too much knowledge could be an awkward thing.

But the difficulties of inserting more knowledge into the business of developing and implementing foreign policy didn't mean that it shouldn't be tried. And that was the theme of the other half of my mid-career gap year. I was asked to undertake an 'Efficiency Scrutiny' of the work of the Foreign Office research analysts and librarians. These 'Efficiency Scrutinies' were a Thatcherite tool of good government, introduced by Sir Derek Rayner of Marks & Spencer when he was the Prime Minister's efficiency adviser. By the time I was asked to do my study, he had been replaced by Sir Peter (later Lord) Levene, and it was to him that I reported, in three sessions in the Cabinet Office: to explain my plans, describe my emerging findings and report my conclusions – all in the space of ninety days.

What I found was that the Foreign Office research analysts knew more about almost every foreign policy issue than any regular diplomat. They formed a specialist cadre inside the Diplomatic Service, recruited for their academic expertise. They were not subject to the same mobility obligation as ordinary diplomats, and often spent many years working on the same subject, with all the advantages and disadvantages that this implies. They were grouped together in a single large department – the Foreign Office's Research and Analysis Department – in the Old Admiralty Building, separated by Horse Guards Parade from the main FCO building. The cadre's origins dated back at least to the Second World War, when Arnold Toynbee had been recruited to inject into the Foreign Office some of the expertise badly needed as the world went to war.

Separate from the research analysts were the Foreign Office's librarians, who were custodians of the great collection of books in the old Colonial Office Library on Whitehall, and a small group of historians, who regularly published collections of documents on British diplomatic history, and knew about the history of the Office. One of them, Kate Crowe, was for many years the person who brought the magnificently restored Old Public Offices to life, through countless tours and lectures.

The more I learned about these remarkable people the more I came to admire them. They were dedicated professionals, doing a good job quietly. But they were not getting the bureaucratic engagement that they deserved or that the Office needed. Ministers and their chief advisers were not drawing on their expertise as effectively as they should.

In a report entitled 'The Need to Know', I concluded that the research analysts should be moved out of their single metaphorical ivory tower and distributed in small research units around the FCO's geographical and functional commands. They needed to be kept in groups, so that they had a degree of professional mutual support and were not simply sucked into the daily business of departments, drafting briefs and answers to Parliamentary Questions. They should be positioned much closer to the front line of diplomacy. I also favoured linking them to the central Policy Planning Staff, to provide an alternative line of expertise and advice with a strong central sponsor.

Most of the recommendations in my report were accepted and implemented. The one that wasn't – of linking the research analysts with the planners – reflected the reality that, although senior officials always say they want a strong institutionalised challenge function, to question the assumptions on which policy rests, in reality they prefer a quiet life. In the short term at least, it is easier to give ministers the advice they want to hear, and not to bother them too much with inconvenient realities about the intractable foreign policy problems on which Britain often struggles to make any real difference.

Over the years I had come to rely heavily on the quiet professionalism of the intelligence services, and to trust the judgement of their officers. I was flattered to be asked each year to lecture the new entrants to SIS on 'Topics of professional gossip' – advice from an FCO insider on how they should live their Foreign Office cover. SIS officers in London usually pretended to be working in the Foreign Office, and it could be embarrassing if they were not able to offer friends and family convincing details of their cover 'job', or were even unsure where the Foreign Office was. As their careers progressed, however, they could be a bit more open, at least with trusted contacts, about what they really did. Later on, they might masquerade as a businessman or a consultant. I met one intelligence officer at this time who told me that he had eight telephones in his office, each connected to a separate land line, each handset carefully labelled with the identity he was supposed to assume when he answered it. But in the early years of a career as an intelligence officer it was vital to be able to operate under diplomatic cover abroad without fear of being rumbled.

Despite the stress they placed on secrecy, SIS, rather like the SAS, actually quite liked the limelight, and put themselves about more than their sister agencies. They thought of themselves as slicker, and more worldly-wise, than the introverts at GCHQ or in MI5. While they admired the technical capabilities of the former, they regarded the latter as little more than rather pedestrian secret policemen. Much of that has changed, but the underlying professional defaults remain. SIS put quite a lot of effort into marketing themselves in Whitehall, inviting senior 'customers' down to their training establishment in an old Napoleonic-era fort on the south coast for courses and seminars. And, occasionally, extravagantly, they would fly senior guests down by helicopter. They loved to impress visitors with what they called 'tradecraft'. One trick was to have an apparently innocuous gardener, watering the rose beds outside the lecture theatre, suddenly appear in the theatre and remove his cap, wig and overalls to reveal a senior SIS officer in disguise. For most outside visitors, the best bits about a visit to the Fort were the cloak-and-dagger arrival, meeting your hosts in a car park in a council estate on the south coast, and the military-style system of 'chits' for paying for drinks. To keep visitors entertained, there was a museum, most of which outsiders were allowed to see, and plenty of interesting Cold War case histories. I don't know if all this not quite so subtle showing off impressed the Treasury, but the James Bond atmospherics certainly worked wonders on wet and weedy diplomats, many of whom were SIS wannabes.

After a couple of mid-career breaks more interesting than most, it was time to move on and up the ladder. In the Diplomatic Service, taking charge of a department is rather like commanding your regiment in the army or your first warship in the navy: at last you have a team of your own, a degree of independence and the ability to make a real contribution. For the ambitious, you matter and are noticed. For me, leading the team at the London end responsible for handing Britain's last significant colony – and six million people – back to China met all those criteria.

Chapter 7

Chinese Take-Away

'Governor,' I said, 'you really ought to have a strategy, to take you through to June 1997.' 'Sherard,' retorted the Governor, 'you don't understand. I'm a politician. My strategy is to get through till lunch.'

Chris Patten was my kind of politician: liberal, educated, intelligent, with a sense of fun and of the absurd, just right of centre on economics, just left of centre on social policy, sensibly pro-Europe. Governor Patten was the main reason why I was so pleased when the Foreign Office's personnel department suggested that once again I follow the official whom I had succeeded in the Security Policy Department, this time as head of the Foreign Office's Hong Kong Department. The plan was for me to take over in March 1994, three years and three months before Hong Kong reverted to Chinese sovereignty, at midnight on 30 June 1997.

The historical background was that Hong Kong Island and small parts of the Kowloon Peninsula on the mainland had been ceded by China to Britain in perpetuity after the First and Second Opium Wars of 1842 and 1860 respectively. But the much larger New Territories on the mainland had only been leased by Britain, for a period of ninety-nine years which expired at midnight on 30 June 1997. Hong Kong proper was not viable without the New Territories, not least because it needed water from the mainland. Already in the 1970s, people in Hong Kong – and, equally important, investors there – were starting to ask what would happen after 1997. Mrs Thatcher had visited Beijing in September 1982 to start the process of working that out. In the talks that followed, it had soon become clear that British hopes of continuing to administer Hong Kong under nominal Chinese sovereignty would not be acceptable to China. Deng Xiaoping and the Chinese leadership believed – with some justification – that a weakened China had ceded Hong Kong to Britain under duress, and they wanted it all back. But, as the talks continued, it emerged that China might be prepared to allow Hong Kong a high degree of autonomy as a Special Administrative Region of China. This concept – of 'one country, two systems' – was enshrined in the Sino-British Joint Declaration which Mrs Thatcher signed on a second visit to Beijing, in December 1984. Nearly ten years on, in March 1994, there were many aspects of Hong Kong's future that Britain and China had still to sort out.

That substantive agenda was the other reason why I was so enthusiastic about the new job. I knew that managing the handover of Hong Kong from London would be the kind of challenge I would enjoy. The objective was clear, the timetable agreed, and the policy issues huge and highly political. Our diplomacy would thus have a shape and focus absent from many other areas of foreign policy-making. We were deciding – or at least greatly influencing – the political, legal and economic future of the six million people Britain would be handing over to Communist rule.

My biggest worry about the job was China. I knew virtually nothing about the country or the culture. At prep school, we had all written to the Chinese Embassy for our copies of Chairman Mao's *Little Red Book*. Later, thanks to an enlightened history master, I had spent a year on an optional course studying the horrors the Great Helmsman had inflicted on the country. From the Planning Staff and from the PUS's office, I had seen something of the negotiation of the Sino-British Joint Declaration and its aftermath. I was vaguely aware of the proposals for enlarging the democratic franchise in Hong Kong which Chris Patten had made shortly after his appointment in 1992. But I hadn't followed the details, and, in so far as I had a view, my sympathies were with the Governor. What worried me most about taking the job was that I wasn't a Sinologist and would be dependent on those who were. I had no feel – at least no positive feel – for China.

I was therefore a bit surprised to learn that one factor in my appointment was precisely that I wasn't a Sinologist: Chris Patten had had enough of what he called 'Sinological claptrap'. He had apparently expressed a strong preference for the head of the department support-ing him in London to be from a background other than China.

To prepare for my new job, it was agreed that I would spend a month or so in Hong Kong and Beijing in the spring of 1994. For the first leg, in Hong Kong, and as happened throughout my time as head of the department, Chris Patten invited me to stay in Government House. Of course, there was a degree of self-interest in this: getting to know and influence me was important for him and his team, although perhaps less so for them dealing with a relatively junior official than for me working with a senior former Cabinet minister. But Chris Patten didn't have to have me to stay every time I was in Hong Kong over the next three years: it was a generous gesture, much appreciated.

Even before I reached Hong Kong Island, the Governor's invitation to stay had unexpected and welcome consequences. The approach to Hong Kong's old Kai Tak airport was one of the wonders of inter-national air travel until Chek Lap Kok opened in July 1998. From my only previous visit, with Antony Acland in 1985, I remembered the sharp right banking turn as the mountain-side painted with a warning black and white chequerboard came up fast on the left; the final approach skimming over and past the lines of washing hanging from the tenement blocks of Kowloon; then down with a bump on to a runway which, as several pilots found over the years, led straight out on to the dark and dirty waters of Hong Kong harbour. A long taxi back into the terminal followed, with the 'GOOD HARVEST' air freight company's wonky signs visible from the left of the aircraft. The air-conditioning system started to suck in the warmly reassuring smells of dank tropical vegetation.

After the twelve-hour flight from London, I was looking forward to a shower and a sleep in Government House. I felt and looked scruffy. At the bottom of the aircraft steps, as the other Club Class passengers – mostly sharply dressed British expatriates returning to a Hong Kong they regarded as home – scrambled on to a bus, I was embarrassed to be pulled aside by a Royal Hong Kong Police officer and asked my name. Once I had confirmed who I was, he invited me to follow him, not as I feared to a police car but to a black Daimler limousine parked a few yards away on the tarmac. As I climbed aboard, I noticed that the car had no number plate: just a gold crown on a red plate. I sank back into the vast back seat, helpfully covered in cooling white cotton, and wondered if there had been some mistake. But the police officer, who climbed in beside the driver, was reassuring: he explained that he was the Governor's ADC. As one of 'HE's' house guests, I was entitled to VIP treatment at the airport. A Government House driver would follow with my hold luggage. And so we glided out of the airport, escorted by a RHKP car with a blue flashing light, through the Harbour Tunnel and up to Government House on the lower slopes of Hong Kong Island. The sentries saluted, the gates swung open. As the Daimler rolled to a stop beneath the portico, a bevy of Government House stewards in white tropical uniforms, with brass buttons and red tabs, rushed down the steps to greet me. Those loyal stewards – all of them Hong Kong Chinese – were one of many reasons why staying at Government House, Hong Kong, was such a privilege.

I was soon installed in a first-floor suite with a vast balcony. The bookcases were full of the latest books from London and New York (many, I suspected, presents from grateful house guests), the tables adorned with bowls of tropical fruit and dishes of the trademark Government House cheese straws. Chris and Lavender Patten made all their guests feel part of an extended family that included three daughters, the two terriers Whisky and Soda, and Chris's young political adviser, Ed Llewellyn. Chris's Private Secretary, Martin Dinham, whom Chris had brought from the Overseas Development Ministry in London, was also part of the Government House circle, even though he had a family of his own. Others put in occasional appearances: Chris's priest (he is a devout Catholic), Caroline Courtauld who was helping Jonathan Dimbleby with the film and the book* he was preparing about Chris's time as governor of Hong Kong, assorted ADCs and trusted Hong Kong Government officials, and then an endless stream of fellow house guests from London – ministers, old friends and newer ones keen to spend time in what was probably the world's best government hotel.

---

* *The Last Governor: Chris Patten and the Handover of Hong Kong*, London: Little, Brown, 1997.

Breakfast – including scrambled eggs and proper bacon, if you wanted it – was served upstairs. But lunch and dinner were downstairs, and, depending on the season and the cast list, outside on the verandah, or in one of a range of dining rooms of varying degrees of formality. The food was mainly Cantonese. Chris Patten had come to love Chinese food, and Chinese antiques. Those Government House Chinese dinners hold so many happy memories for me: of the Governor speculating on the future of China, or being deliciously indiscreet about the upper echelons of a Conservative Government back home being put through the mangle on Europe and the economy; of Lavender reporting on her latest visit to the parts and people of Hong Kong few other VIPs seemed to reach; of the girls asking to leave early, to go out partying in Lan Kwai Fong.

On coming to power in 1990, John Major had made Chris Patten chairman of the Conservative Party, with the tough task of winning the next election for the Tories. As things turned out, Chris had won the 1992 general election for Major but had lost his own seat in Bath. There were stories of Conservative right-wingers cheering news of the defeat and departure from Parliament of a 'wet' whom they both despised and feared. This was ironic, since, as Mrs Thatcher's environment secretary, Chris Patten had loyally implemented the hated Poll Tax – something that had not endeared him to the electors of Bath. But a grateful re-elected Prime Minister had offered his friend Chris Patten a choice between a safe seat at an early by-election, followed by a return to the Cabinet; moving straight to the House of Lords; and taking over as governor of Hong Kong. Patten was soon spotted in a bookshop perusing books about the colony, and it was not long before it was announced that he was to succeed Sir David Wilson as governor. As private secretary to the Permanent Under Secretary, I had played a minor part in Wilson's selection: the two governors could not have been more different.

Wilson had been chosen in a hurry, in 1986, when the then Governor, the much respected Sir Edward Youde, had died suddenly and unexpectedly of a heart attack while visiting Beijing. Youde had earlier been ambassador in Beijing and was an old China hand. But he was also regarded as someone of authority who had stood up robustly for the interests of the colony during the negotiations on the Sino-British Joint Declaration. He gave the formidable leader of the British negotiating team, Sir Percy Cradock, another former ambassador to Beijing, as good as he got. As the PUS's private secretary, morning after morning I would arrive in the office to find a long Secret and Personal telegram from the Governor of Hong Kong, fighting the colony's corner. Youde was given the Hong Kong equivalent of a state funeral: the television images of the bearer party found by the 1st Battalion Coldstream Guards slowly easing the Governor's coffin up the steps into St John's Cathedral made a lasting impression on me.

Back in London, the priority was to find candidates to succeed Teddy Youde for the Foreign Secretary and the Prime Minister to consider. On Mrs Thatcher's instructions, a list of nearly fifty names was drawn up, with the Prince of Wales followed by the Duke of Westminster at the top of it, and the FCO Assistant Under Secretary for the Far East, Dr David Wilson, near the bottom. David Wilson was a distinguished Sinologist, a diffident Scot with a strong academic record who had taken time out of the Foreign Office to edit the *China Quarterly* and to write a doctorate at SOAS. After rushed deliberations, the finger of fate lighted on him: he was immediately knighted and sent out to govern a colony which he both knew and loved.

David Wilson was a good governor, a much better governor than his detractors allowed. But he was unlucky. The crackdown in China following the events in and around Tiananmen Square in 1989 changed everything, greatly damaging confidence in an already nervous Hong Kong. In London, ministers became nervous too, and blamed Wilson for not doing more to shore up confidence in the colony. Urgent measures were announced, including plans for a new airport. This was agreed during a visit to Beijing in September 1991 by an anxious and reluctant John Major. The Prime Minister resented having been told by Sir Percy Cradock and others that he had to deal with the Chinese leaders responsible for the crackdown. In doing so, he became the first Western leader to visit Beijing since Tiananmen, and to inspect a guard of honour there. Members of the Prime Minister's party briefed the accompanying press against David Wilson, and said that he would need to be replaced by a politician, as Hong Kong's last governor. But they didn't yet have any clear idea of who that politician might be – something which Percy Cradock, who was by then the Prime Minister's Foreign Policy Adviser, found rather bizarre.

It was against that rather unpromising background that the electors of Bath unwittingly made available to the Prime Minister someone who must have seemed like the close-to-ideal political candidate to succeed David Wilson.

Most of this I knew but had not really understood before I left for my familiarisation visit to Hong Kong. After wondering what present a house guest should give Governor Patten, I lighted on a recently published anthology of poems posted on the London Underground. All the good things I had heard about Chris Patten were confirmed when, two days after I gave him the book, I overheard him reciting one of the poems in it over dinner: here was an unusual politician, of great cultural curiosity, enjoying poetry because he was interested, not because he needed to impress.

Based in Government House, I could work outwards from the centre. Even in ordinary times, the political and social life of the colony would have revolved around the Governor. But Hong Kong 1994 was not ordinary times. The new Governor had arrived in July 1992 with the world's media paying close attention. They were interested as much in his style – no uniform, three beautiful daughters, a master of retail politics – as in the substance of what he planned to do. But it was on substance that he surprised everyone, including some ministers back in London, by launching in late September proposals to expand democracy in the five remaining years of British rule further and faster than anyone, especially in Beijing, had imagined. The Chinese had rejected the proposals out of hand. They had launched a furious campaign of ludicrous public attacks on Chris Patten. Privately, he had been taken by surprise by the strength of China's reaction and was even said to have contemplated resignation. Eventually, the Chinese had agreed, reluctantly, to talk. Seventeen fruitless rounds of negotiation, lasting most of 1993, had followed. Against that unpromising background, the Governor had concluded, with the support of the Government in London, that he had no option but to put the proposals before the Hong Kong Legislative Council (or LegCo) without Chinese consent.

This he was preparing to do as I arrived in Hong Kong in the spring of 1994.

The two advisers closest to Chris Patten were Ed Llewellyn and Martin Dinham. In their different ways, each was the perfect foil to his master. Both were totally loyal and incredibly hard-working – in Martin's case so much so that he often seemed physically sick from exhaustion. Both were also master diplomats, hardly ever losing their cool, always cheerful and charming. They were 100 per cent dedicated to the Patten cause. In the three years up to the handover I spoke to one or other, often both of them, almost every working day. Even when there were tensions between London and Hong Kong, they were unfailingly courteous. They were – and are – true professionals.

The main difference between them was that Ed was a political appointee, whereas Martin was a British home civil servant on loan to the Hong Kong Government. Ed came firmly from the same One Nation tradition of Toryism as his boss. His job was to give the Governor the political support and advice he needed, in Hong Kong, but also back at Westminster and, occasionally, in Washington. But Ed's easygoing charm disguised a ruthless streak that did what needed to be done when the going got tough. Martin's job was to make the Hong Kong Government and Whitehall machines work in the ways the Governor wanted them to work. This was the pair with whom Chris Patten sat in the Private Office at Government House to chew the political cud, through some pretty difficult times.

Beyond that inner circle, there were many concentric and overlapping rings of advisers and high officials on whom the Governor depended. One was his spokesman, a combative and highly effective Australian called Kerry McGlynn. Another was his Political Adviser, a Foreign Office secondee, who acted effectively as Hong Kong's foreign minister. For Chris Patten's first year or so, this had been William Ehrman, but for all of my time a friend and Foreign Office contemporary, Bob Peirce, filled the job. Both were Sinologists. Negotiations with China on the implementation of the Joint Declaration were handled by the Sino-British Joint Liaison Group, the British side of which was led by another Foreign Office Sinologist, formerly Tony Galsworthy, but throughout my time Hugh Davies. Other senior Brits in the colony included the Senior British Trade Representative, my old friend Francis Cornish, who would take over as the first British consul-general (and thus senior British diplomat) in Hong Kong under Chinese sovereignty. The Commander British Forces was Major General Bryan Dutton: I had known him in Northern Ireland, where his sensible approach to commanding the Belfast Brigade of the British Army had led me to persuade him to come to Washington to brief the Congress – not something many British officers would be good at doing. A senior officer was in charge of the substantial British intelligence presence in the colony.

And then there was Hong Kong's colonial Government, headed by a chief secretary. By the time I arrived in Hong Kong, the former Chief Secretary, Sir David Ford, had moved to London, as the Hong Kong Government representative there. In a double first, he had been replaced by a Chinese woman, the feisty Anson Chan. She was supported by secretaries (who were really ministers) in charge of all the different departments. First among these was the Financial Secretary. But, from London's point of view, the most important were the Secretaries for Constitutional Affairs (which was really political development), Security and Justice. One way or another, however, we found ourselves dealing from London with most of the secretaries.

The British and Chinese civil servants in the Hong Kong administration worked well enough together, but came from different backgrounds and had different perspectives on the future. The Brits were mostly career members of what was still called Her Majesty's Overseas Civil Service. They had spent most of their working lives in Hong Kong or other colonies and were devoted to the place. In many cases, they had risen further, and been rewarded better, than might have been the case had they been in Whitehall. The older ones had lived through the verbal and other assaults which Communist China had launched against the colony during the Cultural Revolution. Few of them spoke good Chinese. Understandably, most of them mixed deep pride in what had been achieved in Hong Kong with profound suspicions of the Communists to the north. That suspicion extended to Foreign Office Sinologists who were not, as they saw it, robust enough in standing up to China: what Chris Patten used to call, deliciously, the Foreign Office tendency towards 'pre-emptive cringe' – the willingness to kow-tow to the Celestial Throne. Britain's first envoy to China, Lord Macartney, had allegedly refused to do so in 1793, and Chris Patten wasn't going to start two centuries later. Most of the senior British Hong Kong civil servants were planning to leave Hong Kong in or before 1997, taking advantage of generous retirement packages, which included, in some cases, passage home on a luxury ocean liner.

The senior Chinese civil servants in Hong Kong were different. All were extremely able, the cream of the cream of Hong Kong's merito-cratic education system. They were hard working, and loyal to 'His Excellency' and their colonial masters, to a fault. To the best of their ability, they did what their bosses instructed them to do, promptly and well. But, with some honourable exceptions, they were less good at thinking creatively, and at saying what they really thought. Unlike the Brits, the Chinese would be staying on after 1997, and would have to work for the territory's new masters. But they did not let that affect their attitude to their current bosses: rather the reverse in fact, with many seeming to try even harder to do what the British wanted.

And then there were the judges. Once I was installed in the Hong Kong Department, I found in my safe reports on judges' performance which my predecessors had had to complete. It was, frankly, a mixed picture. The papers gave the impression of a Bench more colourful than its London counterpart. As if in corroboration, a colleague visiting Hong Kong from London told of staying with one of the colony's senior judges, and of going down to the kitchen in the early hours of the morning to fetch a glass of water, only to be confronted by his host (who was a man) wearing a dress and tottering around on high heels. Thankfully, the Foreign Office was no longer expected to assess the Hong Kong judiciary. But we were expected to offer the Foreign Secretary advice on the Governor's recommendations for senior judi-cial appointments. As our information was less than complete, the safest course was to go along with whatever Chris Patten suggested. Gradually, he was populating the top ranks of the judiciary with judges of Hong Kong Chinese origin, of at least as much intellectual horse-power as their British counterparts. All had, of course, studied law in England. I had only occasional direct dealings with Hong Kong legal circles. Trying to mimic what I imagined were their conservative ways,

I once began a letter to a senior figure 'Dear Carter', omitting the 'Mr' (as used to be customary, as a sign of respect between equals). But the gesture backfired: 'Carter' was Australian, and thought the bloody pom FO were patronising, not flattering, him.

The rule of law was at the heart of everything we were trying to do in Hong Kong. It was what most distinguished Hong Kong from mainland China, and was what gave the territory the competitive advantage as the gateway to China and the region it still has – despite the rise of Singapore and Shanghai. The fact that commerce there was regulated by rules, and that those rules were enforced relatively cheaply and efficiently, was of incalculable value. And it wasn't just trade protected by law: it was also the basic human rights set out in the Joint Declaration and in many associated documents. Making sure that all this endured after 30 June 1997, under the rubric of 'one country, two systems', was HMG's top objective for Hong Kong. It would be our most precious legacy to the six million people of the future Special Autonomous Region of China. As part of this, keeping good judges mattered.

Formally, the colony was governed by the Governor, operating through his Executive Council (or ExCo), which met once a week, reporting to the Legislative Council (LegCo), whose members were appointed or elected through a byzantine system of limited franchises. How those franchises should be developed up to and beyond 30 June 1997 was the focus of the stand-off between Britain and China. The dispute with China was in essence about how many real people should be allowed to vote in the 1995 elections to the Legislative Council, which would then be allowed to ride the 'through train' to Hong Kong under Chinese sovereignty.

LegCo could be lively, and really did hold the Hong Kong Government to account. Chris Patten had introduced a Governor's Question Time similar to Prime Minister's Questions at Westminster – but with the crucial difference that there was no formal Opposition. In fact, in many ways LegCo was the opposition. It represented the broad trends in Hong Kong opinion, ranging from vocal and courageous democrats through rather less courageous members from the business constituencies to unashamed apologists for Communist China.

In reality, however, the key decision-making body in the colony was the Governor's Ad Hoc Group. This met, at Government House, two or three times a week, and was the forum in which the Governor and his key advisers debated and decided all the important issues. Chris Patten dominated the meetings, using steely charm and cruel humour to make what he thought and wanted very clear. It was a brave member of the Ad Hoc Group who disagreed with the Governor for long or on anything of substance.

So much for the government of Hong Kong, in its executive, legislative and judicial manifestations. Behind and beneath all the froth and flummery of liberal British administration, the fact remained that it was a colony, and that the colony was in the end run by one man, the Governor. Chris Patten used to describe himself as 'Mayor of Hong Kong', but no mayor of any city in the developed world could ever hope to dominate his city state in the way the Governor of Hong Kong did – particularly a governor with such advanced political talents as Chris Patten.

On the other hand, one of Hong Kong's main strengths was that, while its governance was good, there was not too much of it. As the expatriates used to insist, the business of Hong Kong is business. An essential part of my briefing was getting to know the Hong Kong commercial community, in Hong Kong and back in London. Two British family businesses dominated the colony's commercial life, even though, with the rise of competition from the mainland and elsewhere, their relative economic importance was probably falling. Both had forebears who had laid the foundations of their trading empires in the nineteenth century. Each had a deep tribal knowledge of China and the China trade which British ministers and officials could never hope to acquire, in their relatively short periods of responsibility for the Hong Kong dossier. The better known of the two families were the Keswicks, who controlled the great trading house of Jardine Matheson. Less well known were the Swires, who led the group of companies of the same name, including Hong Kong's airline Cathay Pacific. Each group had its own house style. Both recruited their senior managers from the more adventurous parts of the upper strata of British – and especially Scottish – society. Both enjoyed remarkably good political connections in

London, Hong Kong and Beijing. But there were differences, exemplified in a way by the London lunches to which I was treated before I took up the new job. At one, a butler offered champagne and cigars. At the other, waitresses refilled bottles of London tap water. One house had at first endorsed Patten's reforms. The other had endured in pained silence what they saw as a major strategic mistake – but would never comment publicly.

Although Jardines and Swires were the heart of the British Hong Kong commercial establishment, they were only a small part of a huge and extraordinarily diverse business community, ranging from Chinese billionaires through to British expatriates of varying degrees of colourfulness and, it has to be said, seediness. What some people called, unfairly, the Failed In London Try Hong Kong syndrome. I have vague memories of a dinner party given by an old friend from Oxford – a courageous single mother who had moved to Hong Kong to work as a solicitor to retire her mortgage and pay for her children's education – attended by an eccentric Old Etonian wearing a black silk Mao suit who lived alone on one of the smaller islands in the archipelago and claimed to have ordered Douglas Hurd around in the school Officer Training Corps. Another character who had been at university with us arrived drunk and late, allegedly a fugitive from justice, with his main base in the Philippines. My memories of a dinner put on by the Hong Kong alumni of my old school, Tonbridge, to coincide with one of my visits are even hazier, though I do recall some senior officers in the Royal Hong Kong Police expressing themselves exuberantly and at great length as to what should be done about the Foreign Office and about China. It was at events like these that I met Brits who didn't accept that the end of the lease on the New Territories on 30 June 1997 necessarily meant that Britain had to return Hong Kong Island to Chinese sovereignty – even though the Island would be quite unsustainable without its mainland hinterland.

As head of the Hong Kong Department in London, dealing mainly with the politics of the handover, I was to have little to do directly with the Hong Kong business community. But it was important to keep in touch with them, particularly with the senior representatives (or *taipans*) of the great trading houses in Hong Kong, and the top management back in London. And the banks mattered too – HSBC (formerly the Hongkong and Shanghai Banking Corporation), above all, but also Standard Chartered and the big American and European banks. One unexpected pleasure was meeting Simon Murray, the colourful and courageous banker, adventurer and retired member of the French Foreign Legion who was at the time running Deutsche Bank's Asia Pacific Division.

There was a buccaneering spirit of enterprise in the business community that you could only admire – and envy. They worked hard, but also played hard, with most enjoying a lotus-eating existence in and around one of the world's most exciting cities. Life for them was a heady cocktail, a party that had been going on for decades and which nobody wanted to end. And that was probably why so many of them, with notable and honourable exceptions, were so hostile to Chris Patten. Most spoke with real venom of the ignorant politician from London who had come out to Hong Kong and rocked the boat by upsetting the territory's new masters with proposals for more democracy that were non-negotiable. I got nowhere, trying to explain that there were two sides to the story, and that Britain had certain obligations to the ordinary people of Hong Kong. It was all summed up for me when, during my first briefing visit, Chris Patten invited me to join the Governor's party at the races. He confessed, apologetically, that racing wasn't really his thing, but he was expected to present the Governor's Cup. His priest was one of our party – I assumed because he was Irish and loved the horses. An evening meeting at the Happy Valley Race Course was a spectacle to behold: tens of thousands of ordinary Hong Kong Chinese, obsessed with gambling; the smarter stands, full of expatriates dressed as though they were attending an Asian Ascot; the no-expense-spared facilities of the Royal Hong Kong Jockey Club; everything under bright floodlights, and bathed in a sticky tropical heat. It was magic.

As our party arrived in a motorcade, and we alighted from the cars and made our way through the crowds to the Governor's box, I could see at once where Chris Patten's natural constituency lay. The poor Chinese – the *mafoos*, or stable lads, in particular – greeted the Governor like a god. But the richer, the whiter, the people, the more reserved they were. And at the top of the Hong Kong social pecking order, it was clear that there was a distinct coolness between the British politician and the local tycoons, Chinese or European. That gulf between the Governor and the Hong Kong business community was to last the rest of Chris Patten's time in Hong Kong, and never the twain did meet. I remember evenings sitting with him in Government House as he spoke with acid humour, occasionally mimicking their cut-glass English accents, of a group who had pressed London to appoint a politician as governor and then complained, bitterly, when he had done what democratic politicians do.

The final act on my first official visit to Hong Kong was for the Hong Kong Government translators to give me an official Chinese name, of three characters. The result was the vaguely similar sounding 'Ku Poi Kan', which, I was told, meant Mr 'Abundantly Diligent Ku'. They then proceeded to have printed double-sided bilingual business cards (reproduced in the end paper) of the kind I hadn't had since Cairo – but this time without the mistake.

From Hong Kong, I flew to Beijing, for the second leg of my familiarisation visit. There, the softly spoken Ambassador, Robin McLaren, explained to me how China worked, and thoughtfully provided a pair of opera glasses with which to spot the personalities on the Standing Committee of the Politburo as we sat in the gallery of the Great Hall of the People for a major Chinese Communist Party event. Beijing felt richer, but less free, than it had been when I had visited nine years earlier. Robin was an old China hand, who had served as political adviser to a previous Governor of Hong Kong. He knew what he was talking about. Not for him the black-and-white certainties of Chris Patten's supporters or critics. Whatever his private views on what had happened in the summer of 1992 (he had been on leave at the time), he knew that his job now was to do the best with the Chinese we could in the circumstances. He had led the British side through the gruelling and ultimately unsuccessful negotiations of 1993. Even when making points unwelcome in Hong Kong, his tone of quiet, measured argument earned Chris Patten's respect, and was much missed when he was replaced by an ambassador whose eagerness to please all sides resulted in him pleasing none. Robin McLaren's performance was a textbook example of how officials can preserve their professional integrity while helping ministers implement misconceived policies.

The familiarisation visits over, I flew back from Beijing to London, to start work.

The first thing I did on formally becoming head of the Hong Kong Department was to get the Foreign Office's Information Technology Department to programme our computers so that when we logged on each morning, we were told how many days were left until 30 June 1997. Of course, under the Joint Declaration, just as China had an interest in how the colony was run before the handover, so Britain would have a continuing interest in Hong Kong after the handover. In practice, however, the essence of the job would have been done by 1997. Our economic stake in Hong Kong, and the tens of thousands of Hong Kong people who would still have British passports after the handover, gave us a locus – even though in practice most of the holders of the British National (Overseas) passports would not have right of abode in the United Kingdom. It was reassuring form, without real substance. Britain's only real leverage over China's behaviour in Hong Kong after the handover was economic – and international – confidence. As both Chris Patten and the Chinese leadership knew (though the latter didn't always show it), one significant false step could destroy that confidence, and, with it, the goose that kept on laying the golden eggs.

The pattern of work in London soon emerged. Arriving in the office early in the morning, I would usually find a raft of incoming telegrams from Government House, Hong Kong, and from the other British posts in the colony and beyond – the Joint Liaison Group, the Senior British Trade Representative and, most important, the British Embassy in Beijing. The eight-hour time difference meant that cables sent from the Far East towards the end of their working day reached us at the start of business in London. We could then spend our working day preparing replies, and getting them approved at the right level, before sending them off as we left the office, so that they were in Hong Kong in good time for the opening of business there the next morning. It was an efficient system, and only occasionally did we drop catches. Once I prepared a draft telegram of 'instructions' from the Foreign Office to the Governor: in the draft, I made a number of assertions, underneath each of which I inserted, '[FCO Legal Advisers please supply supporting arguments]'. Unfortunately, the legal advisers did not always work at the pace policy-makers did. Somehow, with the help of the new communications technology then just coming in, my secretary managed to transmit the draft telegram to Hong Kong with all the square brackets left in. The Government House team had a good laugh at London's expense: the draft confirmed their view that we fitted the legal advice to the policy, rather than the policy to the legal advice.

As head of the Hong Kong Department, I reported to an assistant under secretary for the Far East, and he in turn reported to a deputy under secretary for the whole of Asia, Africa and the Americas. The latter's formal boss was the Permanent Under Secretary, who, given the high political sensitivity, tended to follow Hong Kong issues more closely than many other subjects. Much of my work went, via the AUS, direct to the Foreign Secretary – Douglas Hurd until July 1995, Malcolm Rifkind from then until the Labour Government, with Robin Cook at the FCO, took over in May 1997 – less than two months before the handover. On a day-to-day basis, the politician to whom I reported was one of the junior ministers in the Foreign Office, for most of my time the Minister of State Alastair Goodlad. In many ways, Alastair was the ideal political boss: his shrewd instinct for the mood of the Conservative Party, and of the House of Commons, led to him later being given the thankless job of Government chief whip for the last part of John Major's time as prime minister. With me in attendance, serving the wine and crisps, Alastair spent many evenings reassuring anxious members of both Houses of Parliament and all parties that the Government knew what it was doing in taking on China over democratic development in Hong Kong. One of my first jobs was to draft a magazine article for Alastair explaining what we were up to in Hong Kong, and rebutting the charge, from Sir Percy Cradock and others, that we had made a strategic error over the elections package. Both Alastair, and Chris Patten, seemed pleased with the result, which was approved without amendment. In all honesty, this was the only aspect of political supervision by Alastair Goodlad that worried me: I don't remember him questioning a single word of the written advice I submitted to him over several years.

In practice, it was Chris Patten who decided Hong Kong policy. Both the Prime Minister and the Foreign Secretary were in some degree in his debt. He had helped with Douglas Hurd's (unsuccessful) campaign to succeed Mrs Thatcher as Tory Party leader in 1990. More successfully, as Party chairman, he had played a major part in winning the 1992 election for John Major, against expectations. He was a big political beast. Both men were therefore content to give him a large measure of autonomy on matters Hong Kong. Nevertheless, the formal position was that major policy issues had to go through the Hong Kong Sub-Committee of the Cabinet's Overseas and Defence Policy Committee. So I often found myself drafting papers for the OD(K) Committee, as it was known, explaining as clearly as I could often complicated Hong Kong politico-legal issues. The Cabinet Office secretariat edited the paper, and it was circulated, usually on the Friday before the meeting, so that ministers could digest it over the weekend. Although I didn't attend the ministerial meetings, those who did reported real discussion, with the Deputy Prime Minister, Michael Heseltine, taking a much more pro-China and sceptical position than others present. Whenever possible, the Governor flew back to London to make his case to his political colleagues in person. This was Cabinet government as it should be.

Chris Patten visited London every few months or so, often combining a major speech or lecture with meetings with ministers, media interviews and some careful lobbying of selected Parliamentarians. He and his entourage based themselves at the lavish Hong Kong Government Office in Mayfair, but his advisers at least would be in and out of the Hong Kong Department in the Foreign Office. One of them – his Political Adviser – remarked that, until I had taken over and given it a role, of sorts, in offering ministers independent advice on Hong Kong, the department had been 'little more than a wash and brush-up shop for the Governor in London'.

What made everything so difficult at this time was the constant, and very personal, sniping at Chris Patten by the architect of the Sino-British Joint Declaration, Sir Percy Cradock. I had known, and admired, Sir Percy when he had been the Prime Minister's Foreign Policy Adviser at the time when I had been the Permanent Secretary's Private Secretary.

A man of rare intellect, great rigour and utter integrity, he did not suffer fools gladly. He was deeply, but quietly, patriotic. Those who had worked for him, in the Embassy in Beijing, or in London, were utterly devoted to him. But he was highly critical of the course that Chris Patten had followed since becoming governor of Hong Kong in the summer of 1992. There were suggestions that his private advice to the new appointee had been ignored. What he really resented, however, with some justification, was the sneering at him from the Patten camp as an 'appeaser'. He was infuriated by the suggestion that, in advocating the only possible course – negotiation with China over the future of Hong Kong – he had somehow been guilty of betraying his country's interests. After all, Mrs Thatcher herself had followed the remorseless logic of the need to work with China in securing Hong Kong's future. Over my three years dealing with Hong Kong, Percy continually attacked Chris Patten in public, and in increasingly personal terms – referring at one stage to the 'incredible shrinking Governor'. Although I knew Percy from before, and, following a chance meeting at a think-tank, he had asked me to lunch as I took up the job, I decided, regretfully, to have nothing to do with him. It was more than my official life was worth for me to have any contact whatsoever with a man so bitterly critical of government policy. But I fear that even so, when later I had to advise ministers that the Governor's policy was wrong, I was suspected by Government House of covertly colluding with Percy. I regret that I never saw him again before, after suffering the ravages of diabetes, he died in January 2010. Percy may have been right on substance, but he had handled the issue surprisingly clumsily, becoming too personal in his attacks on the Governor. There was plenty of fault on the other side, however, and he was treated somewhat shabbily by politicians who should have behaved better towards a genuine patriot who did more than any other Briton to secure Hong Kong's long-term stability and prosperity.

Another important aspect of my job was enlisting the support of third countries for what Britain was trying to do with the handover of Hong Kong. We needed to be able to show the world – and the people of Hong Kong – that we had their support, especially in our push for democratic reforms in the last few years of British sovereignty. We did this in a number of ways. I gave regular briefings to key Embassies in London, but also to a smaller group of like-minded countries with more direct interests in Hong Kong. The members of the group selected themselves: each had a substantial economic stake in Hong Kong, and most had taken in significant numbers of immigrants from Hong Kong – and would be liable to take in more, if things went wrong. I am not sure how effective we were as a lobby. But the meetings, and other briefings, did ensure a degree of understanding and support for what HMG was about. If nothing else, they gave us important moral support during an anxious few years. It is difficult to recall now just how much worry there was about the whole handover going wrong, with confidence in Hong Kong collapsing.

The Sino-British Joint Liaison Group held plenary sessions three times a year, usually in London, Beijing and Hong Kong. Those formal sessions had always been thoroughly prepared, in extensive meetings between Hugh Davies and his team in Hong Kong and their Chinese opposite numbers. We came to know and respect the Chinese negotiators, and their bosses back in Beijing, including the elderly, expert and unforgiving head of the Hong Kong and Macao Affairs Office of the State Council, Lu Ping. In the end, we shared the same objective, of a smooth transition, in which the stability and prosperity of the territory were preserved. But as we argued over every detail it didn't always seem like that, and tensions rose. Chris Patten always followed the negotiations anxiously and at one remove. The war of words between him and China meant that he never went back to China, after a torrid visit to Beijing in October 1992 when he had formally presented the proposals which he had already announced in his inaugural address to LegCo earlier in the month. One of the tragedies of his time in Hong Kong was that his early, and courageous, decision to take on China over democratic development in Hong Kong had had the unintended effect of removing him from almost all direct contact with China. That didn't stop him spending many hours reading, talking and speculating about a country which he did not know at first hand. He read – and understood – more about China than many so-called experts. But that knowledge sometimes seemed to be coloured by a certain hostility to China, and scepticism about the country's long-term prospects informed more perhaps by wishful thinking than by genuine acquaint-ance. In some ways, his attitude reminded me of the way Israeli 'experts' on the Arab Middle East talk about a region of which they have little or no direct experience.

In June 1994 LegCo approved the Governor's electoral package by 32 votes to 24. But the critical test had come earlier, when an amendment watering down the package had been defeated by only one vote. It was a damned close-run thing. Sitting in London, we had watched with admiration, and waited nervously, as a skilful Government House-led whipping operation pushed the deal across the finishing line. There were good reasons for believing that one of Chris Patten's most enthu-siastic supporters among the business elite, later to become one of his fiercest critics, instructed a reluctant (and conscience-stricken) employee on the Council to cast his ballot the right way in the critical vote, by waving the 'iron rice bowl' of his continuing employment in front of him. However delivered, LegCo's endorsement of the Patten package was a huge relief, but with consequences that were to over-shadow the whole of the rest of the period of British sovereignty over Hong Kong. It meant that the legislature elected under British rules in 1995 would be abolished by the Chinese at the midnight stroke on 30 June 1997 and replaced by a wholly appointed puppet Provisional Legislature. But, whatever the rights and wrongs of the decisions taken in 1992, at least the 1994 LegCo vote settled the question of the future of Hong Kong's legislature, as far as Britain was concerned.

There was plenty else for us to worry about. Doing all we could to ensure the future rights and freedoms of the people of Hong Kong after the handover was the most important. But we also needed to press ahead with building the new airport, and the associated road and rail links to central Hong Kong, in the face of Chinese foot-dragging based in part on their hostility to the Patten proposals for more democracy, in part on natural Chinese caution about government borrowing.

Long before I had arrived on the scene, it had become a tradition for the JLG negotiators to take a day out from their labours, on a touristic trip organised by the host side. I doubt that these excursions did much good, but we at least made great efforts to come up with ideas that would give the Chinese pleasure, and, we hoped in vain, make them more flexible. Once, we took them to Oxford, where they went punting on the Cherwell, and to Blenheim, and gave them tea at Cliveden. Most spectacularly, on another occasion we somehow persuaded the contractors building the Channel Tunnel to take the two teams through to France and back again, months before the Tunnel was officially opened. It was also a tradition that the host side offered the visitors a banquet. In Beijing, we could tell how we stood with our hosts by the quality of the food we were given, and where the banquet was held: if the interminable courses of any Chinese banquet included whole ducks' feet and something that tasted (and smelt) like boiled wellington boot, we knew we were out of favour. Unfortunately, sea slugs were on the menu whatever the political weather. In London, we tended in the other direction: the worse things were going, the more generous the hospitality. For a dinner for the Chinese in one of the great rooms at Lancaster House, the Government Hospitality Fund decided to go the extra mile, by offering a savoury course as well as pudding and cheese. Not content with Welsh rarebit, the GHF offered our guests 'Scotch woodcock'. Perusing the menu at the start of the banquet, the senior Chinese negotiator asked my rather stiff boss what this was. Not wanting to admit ignorance, or perhaps even unaware of his own ignorance, my boss replied that 'Scotch woodcock' was a Scottish game bird. Even the Chinese official's inscrutable features betrayed surprise when he was served with scrambled egg on toast, adorned with two anchovies. He must have thought our game birds were very small and fishy – but absolutely delicious.

Every three or four months or so I would go out to Hong Kong, to catch up with the personalities and issues. During a visit in January 1995, with two and a half years to go before the handover, I had a profound shock. Following Britain's decision to go unilateral on elections and the legislature, we had been negotiating with the Chinese on the arrangements for the judiciary, particularly a new Court of Final Appeal, after the handover. Even if we couldn't have the 'through train' originally planned for LegCo, we hoped that judges appointed under British sovereignty could stay on under Chinese sovereignty. It was a commonplace that this was important, perhaps even vital, for confidence in the rule of law in Hong Kong once China took over. We believed that the Chinese, having lost the legislative 'through train', were pretty desperate to preserve the judicial 'through train'.

Chris Patten asked to see me privately during that visit in January 1995. I remember the occasion well, as it coincided with my fortieth birthday. The Governor said that he had concluded that we would have to break off negotiations with the Chinese over the judiciary. We would go 'unilateral' by introducing a bill into LegCo in the following few weeks making future arrangements for the judiciary without Chinese consent. This was a wholly unexpected bombshell. When I expressed doubts as to whether the legislative timetable really was so tight as to mean that we had to move ahead almost immediately, I was assured that it was. I was sent to see the Chief Secretary, Anson Chan, who also argued vigorously for my support.

I flew back to London in an agonising quandary. I liked and admired Chris Patten. I had had no part in the disputes over the electoral package, and wanted none. But now I found myself under intense pressure from him to support a move which my instincts told me was neither necessary nor wise.

My first reaction was to consult two of my predecessors as head of the Hong Kong Department. One said that I had to do my duty as an official and offer ministers in London objective advice based on my best assessment of what was in Britain's and Hong Kong's interest. The other, who had followed a similar course in a different job in 1992, suggested that in my own career interests it was probably wise to go along with what the Governor wanted. I also consulted a senior Foreign Office official based in Hong Kong but back in London on leave: he was astounded when I told him the news, and blurted out his first reaction: 'The Governor must have gone mad.'

I decided I needed to know more about what had happened in 1992, and commissioned the Foreign Office Research Department to do a note. I was surprised by what I read. The background was that in 1992 the then Permanent Under Secretary at the Foreign Office had instructed officials to give the incoming Governor of Hong Kong every possible support. Most had interpreted that as meaning they were to agree with whatever the Governor suggested. The proposals for radically enlarging the franchise in Hong Kong had been worked up by a small group in Hong Kong over the 1992 summer break, in great secrecy. The plan had been for the Governor to come back to London in September for a meeting of the OD(K) Committee of the Cabinet to discuss the package, but Chris Patten had cancelled the visit. Instead, he had briefed the visiting Minister of State, who had gone along with what was proposed, without dissent. The Foreign Secretary had apparently asked what the 'plan B' was if the Chinese rejected the package, only to be told there was 'no plan B'. The only serious questioning of the wisdom of the initiative had come from the Embassy in Beijing: the Ambassador had been on summer leave, but the Chargé d'Affaires had courageously sent a telegram warning of a fiercely hostile Chinese reaction. His reward had been a personal telegram back from London, saying that advice of that kind, questioning the Governor's proposals, was not welcome and should not have been sent.

Such bureaucratic pusillanimity was bad enough. But what was really disturbing in the Research Department note was that officials in London and Hong Kong had failed to tell the incoming Governor of a private exchange of letters between the Foreign Secretary and the Chinese Foreign Minister, in January–February 1990, on the pace of democratic development in Hong Kong. The Patten package had been developed in breach and in ignorance of those understandings. Worse still, the proposals had been given to the Chinese only on 25 September 1992, with no chance for discussion before the Governor announced them in his inaugural address to LegCo a couple of weeks later. The first opportunity for substantive discussion with China had been only when Chris Patten paid that first (and only) visit to Beijing as governor, in late October that year, once everything was in the open. The Research Department note concluded that, in these extraordinary circumstances, it had not been surprising that the Chinese had reacted with such hostility to the Patten proposals, or that the seventeen rounds of negotiation which lasted most of 1993 had failed to reach agreement.

I was taken aback. It was not only the substance of the package which had been so offensive to the Chinese: the way it had been presented to them also looked somewhat inept. I could understand why the small circle of Hong Kong Government officials working for a new governor determined to make a break with the supposed bad old Foreign Office tradition of kow-towing to China had gone along so enthusiastically with the package and its handling. I could see why one or two senior intelligence officers, who should have known better, had egged Chris Patten on, thinking they would impress the new Governor and distinguish themselves from the appeasers in the FO. But I could not understand – and still don't understand – why Foreign Office officials had not done their job of formally warning the Governor, and ministers back in London, of the likely Chinese reaction to the substance of his package, and to his decision to announce it before discussing it with them. Failing to tell Chris Patten of the foreign ministers' exchange of letters had been a serious mistake: failing formally to warn him and ministers of the likely consequences of the policy and its presentation struck me as an even more significant professional lapse.

It was a mark of Chris Patten's fundamental decency that he had not dumped on officials for not giving him the advice to which he had been entitled, before allowing him to go over the top to do battle with Beijing. He was told of the exchange of letters only after he had launched his proposals.

And now, two and half years later, here was Chris Patten apparently wanting to do the same, but over the judiciary rather than the legislature. I was more worried than I had ever been in my job. But my conscience told me only one thing: I had to give ministers honest, objective advice, even if it meant upsetting Chris Patten and those around him. I made sure that the Permanent Under Secretary was aware of the dilemma: he consulted the Foreign Secretary, who said, reluctantly, that he accepted that officials working for him in the Foreign Office in London should offer independent advice, as objectively as they could. As far as I was concerned, the main criterion had to be: what would be in the longer-term interests of Britain and Hong Kong? I always had in mind the six million people of the Territory. Through our own mishandling of the situation, we were giving China (apparently to its dismay – it had wanted the predictability of a 'through train') carte blanche to dissolve the legislature elected and appointed under British rule. I didn't want to offer our opponents the same open goal on the judiciary.

Chris Patten was not happy. Understandably enough, he objected to the idea of officials in London questioning proposals made by him, and even more to officials recommending to ministers that they overrule the Governor. That was not the basis on which John Major and Douglas Hurd had sent him to Hong Kong. He applied great pressure to me, arguing that all my advice to the Foreign Secretary should be cleared with the Governor in draft and advance. Very unhappily, I resisted, but agreed that he would see in parallel whatever advice I was putting up to ministers, giving him an opportunity to comment and, if necessary, make counter-arguments.

The result of all this was a rise in tension between the Foreign Office and Government House in Hong Kong. What followed were the worst few months of my diplomatic career. I lay awake at night, worrying where my duty lay. But always I came back to the inescapable conclusion: while we had reason to believe that the Chinese would do a deal over the judiciary, it would be the height of folly to break off negotiations, still less to introduce 'unilateral' legislation into LegCo. I had to set out the arguments for ministers, who would have to decide.

Not surprisingly, perhaps, officials who had said in London that they were not persuaded of the wisdom of the Governor's course changed their view once they returned to Hong Kong. Not surprisingly, none of those attending the Governor's Ad Hoc Group meetings expressed any doubts – at least not to Chris Patten's face – about the wisdom of going unilateral before there was evidence that it was really necessary. It was the Governor himself who decided to allow the negotiators more time, while those drafting the bill worked up their proposals.

Then, almost out of the blue, one of the biggest beasts in the British Government weighed in to argue for doing a deal with China. The Deputy Prime Minister, Michael Heseltine, had his own reasons for disagreeing with Chris Patten: he was planning to take a jumbo jet full of British businessmen to China, seeking contracts. He did not want any turbulence before then. Nor was he persuaded by the arguments in favour of immediate unilateral action.

Patten stalled. Heseltine went to China, and came back, satisfied with the business done by his delegation. And then suddenly it was all over. Without any instructions, let alone pressure, from London, we discovered one morning that, with the Governor's agreement, the negotiators in Hong Kong had done a deal on the Court of Final Appeal that seemed to offer the Chinese more concessions than officials in London would ever have dared recommend. China too had made concessions. But the Governor had agreed that the new Court of Final Appeal would now not be set up until after the handover. After months of having the Foreign Secretary twisting uneasily between advice from his officials in London and pressure from his political friend in Hong Kong, there was no disagreement. After the handover, Hong Kong would have a Court of Final Appeal – and it was Chris Patten who had conceded that, while it would be set up according to British rules, it would not be formally established until midnight on 30 June 1997. The relief on both sides was palpable. To have lost continuity in the legislature was one thing: to have lost continuity in the judiciary would have been serious. My role had been to question the wisdom of breaking off negotiations in the early months of the year, thus buying time for an agreement. Contrary to what Government House sources apparently told Jonathan Dimbleby, the question of British trade with China had never entered my calculations.

Despite the efforts of Chris Patten's two faithful advisers, Martin Dinham and Edward Llewellyn, to keep channels open, his relationship with Foreign Office officials never really recovered. The course of confrontation with China on which the new Governor had embarked in the autumn of 1992 had created a deeply damaging perception that in dealing with China and Hong Kong policy there was no middle way: you either favoured negotiating pragmatic arrangements with China, and were therefore opposed to the Governor's more robust approach, or you supported Chris Patten's stance on democracy and human rights in Hong Kong after 1997, and were therefore against doing imperfect deals with China. In the eyes of Government House, you couldn't be both pro-China and pro-Hong Kong. There was much emotional talk of 'appeasement' and 'betrayal'. Until the row over the Court of Final Appeal, I had managed somehow to steer a sensitive course between the two approaches. But now the team in London were placed by Government House firmly in the camp of those who favoured appeasing China. In some ways, it was all rather childish, and, ironically for

Chris Patten, reminiscent of Mrs Thatcher's Manichean division of the world into those who were 'one of us' and the 'wets'. Within Hong Kong, as the handover approached, more and more individuals who would remain there after 30 June 1997 found themselves making their own accommodations, however distasteful, with the incoming sovereign power. The Governor became in many ways the informal leader of the opposition to China in general and, once he was nominated, to C. H. Tung, China's choice as the first chief executive of the Hong Kong Special Administrative Region. Chris Patten's approach won him few friends among Chinese or international business elites who, understandably enough, were known better for their commercial pragmatism than for their political courage.

The same agonising choice – between doing unilaterally what was in absolute terms right, in the sure knowledge that it would be torn down by China at midnight on 30 June 1997, and securing through tough negotiation the best deal you could, in the hope that it would endure after the handover, in the interests of the people of Hong Kong – occurred in other areas, notably on legislation protecting human rights in Hong Kong. But, after the parting of the ways over the elections – which neither the British nor the Chinese had really wanted – and the near-miss over the Court of Final Appeal, both the British and Chinese sides seemed more willing to negotiate constructively. Nevertheless, the default position in Government House sometimes seemed to be that, given a choice, heroic but futile gestures that played well at Westminster or in Washington were preferable to shabby compromise with China. The trick was to avoid the choice, and keep negotiations going – which was probably what most of the people who would live and work in Hong Kong after the handover really wanted. If we had flounced out of negotiations again, we might have preserved our honour, but we would have lost any genuine influence over what happened in Hong Kong after 1997.

Back in London, the Deputy Prime Minister was the unashamed cheerleader for the 'pro-China' camp. I drafted a speech for him to give at a big Hong Kong dinner, in which I wanted the Government to try to get away from the black or white distinction between being pro-Hong Kong, and therefore anti-China, or vice versa. I knew that Michael Heseltine had read philosophy (and politics and economics) at Oxford.

So I had the speech say that he remembered from his studies what logicians called the Law of the Excluded Middle – the rule that makes something either true or not true, with nothing in between – and then go on to assert that this should not apply to dealing with China and Hong Kong. You could be pro-China and pro-Hong Kong at the same time. With a great flourish, 'Tarzan' solemnly read out these words, and then announced that, come to think of it, he didn't remember the Law of the Excluded Middle at all. It was some clever dick in the Foreign Office who did, and had put it in the speech for him. He brought the house down.

In July 1995 the incoming Foreign Secretary Malcolm Rifkind seemed surprised to discover how bad relations were between the Governor and those who would assume sovereignty over Hong Kong in less than two years' time. At one point he commented that, if the Governor wasn't on speaking terms with the Chinese, then we needed to change the Governor. But there was no appetite in London for the turbulence associated with changing the Governor at such a late stage. And, whatever the difficulties Chris Patten had with certain self-interested constituencies in Hong Kong, he was still immensely popular with ordinary people there, and a powerful asset at Westminster and in Washington. His crusade for more democracy in Hong Kong enabled us to rebut charges that we were selling the six million people of Hong Kong down the river. In London, many Parliamentarians confessed privately that they had doubts about the wisdom of a policy which had the net effect of giving China an excuse to abolish an elected legislature and replace it with an appointed one, but they saw no political mileage in saying so publicly.

The end of British rule in Hong Kong seemed to approach at an ever increasing pace. Our departure would mark the close of the last significant chapter in Britain's colonial history. As I suggested to Chris Patten more than once, he was 'running for history'. With that in mind, we started quite early on to focus on the formal and ceremonial aspects of the handover. The Prince of Wales had been booked many years out. Which ministers would attend would depend on the result of the British general election, due by May 1997.

After interminable discussions within Whitehall, and with Hong Kong, it was decided that there would in fact be two ceremonies in Hong Kong on 30 June: a British-only Farewell Ceremony, followed, on both sides of midnight, by a joint British–Chinese Handover Ceremony. The former would be outdoors, in a small stadium, with plenty of British military pomp and circumstance. The latter would be inside the new Hong Kong Convention Centre. The ceremony would be focused on two huge 'flag poles', which were built to emit a breeze to keep the flags of the outgoing and incoming sovereign powers flying indoors. Somehow, I managed to extract £2 million from the Treasury to pay for the farewell event, and for a firework display in Hong Kong harbour. Assessing bids from event-management companies made a pleasant change from the daily grind of writing policy submissions and drafting briefs on politico-legal issues.

We knew, however, that, before this could happen, there would almost certainly be a change of government in London, and that final decisions would probably be taken by a set of ministers from a different political party than Chris Patten's. As predicted, Tony Blair's Labour Party won a landslide victory in the general election on 1 May 1997. I was stuck at a meeting in Canada, but flew back in time to brief new ministers that weekend. On Saturday 3 May, I was one of a stream of officials called into the Foreign Office to take the new Foreign Secretary, Robin Cook, through the key issues in the run-up to a handover less than two months away.

We recommended that the new Foreign Secretary lead a large party of British VIP guests at the event, flying out in a British Airways Boeing 747 chartered by the Foreign Office for the purpose. We set out the plans for the farewell ceremony, a grand banquet and then the handover ceremony itself. We briefed him on the fact that a naval task force would be over the horizon in the South China Sea, but that the Royal Yacht, HMY *Britannia*, would be tied up alongside the Naval Base of HMS *Tamar*, on Hong Kong Island, ready to sail off with the Prince of Wales and the Governor in the early hours of 1 July. We told the Foreign Secretary that other international guests would include the American Secretary of State, Madeleine Albright, and that there would be opportunities for bilaterals with her and others 'in the margins' of the main event – something to which he would become very used over the next four years.

The new Prime Minister, Tony Blair, overruled the Governor's advice that he should not attend, and did so, bringing not only his own wife, but his brother, Bill Blair QC, and his wife, who happened to be Hong Kong Chinese. A row with Chris Patten over whether the architect of the Joint Declaration, Sir Percy Cradock, should have been invited to the handover and, if so, in what capacity was defused when Cradock declined the invitation.

But there was also an important policy issue on which we needed a view from the new British Government. For some weeks, the Chinese negotiators in the Joint Liaison Group had been pressing for the People's Liberation Army to have a presence in Hong Kong before midnight on 30 June so that they could be there in the first moments of Chinese sovereignty. For all sorts of reasons, not least what they done in Tiananmen Square eight years earlier, the PLA's intentions in respect of Hong Kong were a subject of immense sensitivity in the territory, and in London. We believed that they planned a small, low-key, largely symbolic presence, and that they were not intending to indulge in highly visible deployments outside their barracks. We also believed, as a story by Jonathan Dimbleby in the *Sunday Times** shortly after the handover suggested, that the pressure for the PLA to be in Hong Kong at the moment of the handover came from the very top of the Chinese leadership. For them, it was an all-important question of 'face': they had to be able to show the world that China was exercising sovereignty over Hong Kong from the first moments of 1 July. A PLA presence was the symbolic way of doing that.

This had produced a reaction from Government House that bordered on the hysterical. The Governor sent a message to the effect that he would not have 'the goose-stepping goons of the PLA on the streets of Hong Kong on his watch'. There was serious talk from those

---

* Jonathan Dimbleby, 'Caught in the crossfire as China turns the screw', *Sunday Times*, 6 July 1997: 'Intelligence sources in Beijing indicated that President Jiang Zemin was himself the instigator of the proposed demarche by the PLA in what seemed like a bid to shore up his credibility with his generals.'

around him of cancelling some of the ceremonies on 30 June if any concession was made to the Chinese over this. Allowing the PLA into Hong Kong before the handover would deal a fatal blow to confidence.

The 'appeasers' in the Foreign Office took a different view. We recommended that we negotiate a deal with the Chinese whereby a token PLA contingent be allowed into Hong Kong under cover of darkness in the last hours of 30 June, in order to be able to take up their posts at the midnight stroke. Just as some of the armed forces of the outgoing sovereign power would have to remain after midnight, so some of those of the incoming power could be pre-positioned there before midnight. We advised that keeping the PLA out until midnight would generate great hostility at the highest levels in China, and might well result in the PLA massing at the border before midnight, and then streaming across it in convoys of trucks once China had resumed sovereignty. We judged that that would be much more damaging to confidence than a discreet negotiated compromise of the kind we were recommending.

New ministers in London were clear on what needed to be done. Overruling the Governor, they instructed the British team in the Joint Liaison Group to negotiate a sensible compromise whereby token units of the PLA would enter Hong Kong late on 30 June, in order to be there from midnight. That is what happened. Despite the fulminations from Government House, the world hardly noticed. Pragmatism had won.

Government House picked another fight with London, this time over a forecast prepared by the Joint Intelligence Committee on Hong Kong's prospects after the handover. Like all intelligence assessments, this one was based at least as much on open-source material as on secret intelligence. It concluded, rather unadventurously, that in general China was likely to behave responsibly towards Hong Kong after the handover, in order not to damage confidence or its own economic interests. The overall tone was of cautious and conditional optimism. This infuriated the Government House team, who sent a series of messages questioning the Joint Intelligence Committee's judgement and asking for the formal assessment to be reopened or qualified. In the Government House view, the prospects for China's behaviour towards

Hong Kong after the handover were not good. After a tussle, this too was rejected. In the event, the JIC Assessment turned out to have been nowhere near optimistic enough.

This episode showed how out of touch Government House had become in the final weeks of British rule over Hong Kong. A mutual friend bumped into the Governor's Political Adviser in the street in the last few weeks of British sovereignty. To the friend's astonishment, the Political Adviser warned, apparently in all seriousness, that 30 June would be like the last days of the US presence in Saigon, with helicopters lifting off from the roof of Government House. Perhaps such a mood of imminent loss, of anticipated grieving, was inevitable. But we had made things worse for ourselves by practising the politics of the impossible.

The handover itself went smoothly enough. As planned, the team from London left Heathrow's Royal Terminal with a jumbo jet full of VIP guests, with the Prince of Wales up front. An enthusiastic young Prime Minister put on his British Airways pyjamas and worked the aircraft. Robin Cook brought his wife Margaret. Soon after arrival, I accompanied him to his bilateral with the American Secretary of State, Madeleine Albright, on board *Britannia*.

On the day itself, Chris Patten delivered the speech of his life at the farewell parade. A violent tropical downpour only made everything even more dramatic. With his soaked uniform sticking to his skin, the Prince of Wales had difficulty in standing up to speak. He in turn played his part with dignity and aplomb. So did the bandsmen, emptying their tubas as quickly as they filled with rain, along with the 'jocks' of the Black Watch in their kilts and tam-o'-shanters bearing the Red Hackle of the Royal Highland Regiment. It was imperial recessional at its elegiac best.

The same could not be said of the handover ceremony itself, conducted in the air-conditioned clinical vastness of the Hong Kong Convention Centre. It was Party Congress meets Las Vegas sales convention. But it was soon over. Our fireworks sprayed and boomed and spluttered over Hong Kong harbour, to be followed by an even more impressive Chinese display. *Britannia* slipped her moorings and steamed slowly out into the South China Sea, with a tearful Governor and his party embarked, along with the Prince of Wales. As if in omen, the boss of one of Hong Kong's biggest British trading houses slipped and fell in the rain, breaking his arm. Some of us went out and danced the rest of the tropical night away, in the rain-soaked lanes of Lan Kwai Fong.

We reloaded the jumbo, minus the Prince of Wales, and returned to London. I flew out of Kai Tak, and have never been back, not even to see the new airport on which I spent so many hours in negotiation. I cleared my desk in the Hong Kong Department. My reward was to be four years as political counsellor in Paris.

After I had gone, however, two rows broke out involving Jonathan Dimbleby, who had played Boswell to Chris Patten's Dr Johnson during Chris's five years in Hong Kong. First came the *Sunday Times* piece that seemed to reveal knowledge of sensitive secret intelligence, on Britain's negotiations with China over the PLA's arrival in Hong Kong. There were stories of an alleged breach of the Official Secrets Act. It was then suggested that the stories had been inspired by the new Labour Government's spin-masters, to divert attention from the row which had followed Robin Cook's sudden announcement, from the VIP lounge at Heathrow on Saturday 2 August 1997, that he would be leaving his wife for another woman, as a result of a *News of the World* story expected the following day. In November 1997 the Attorney General made a Commons statement, in which he said that 'intelligence and foreign relations considerations outweighed other public-interest considerations which might otherwise have required a prosecution'.* And there the matter rested.

Then, later in August 1997, came Jonathan Dimbleby's television documentary, and the accompanying book, *The Last Governor*.† In three years dealing with Hong Kong, I had never met Dimbleby. But officials had asked about arrangements for checking the book before publication. It turned out that there were none: no politician or senior official felt able to interfere in whatever arrangement had been made between Chris Patten and his friend from Bath. Neither the book nor

---

* *Hansard*, 20 November 1997.
† Op. cit.

the films pretended to be other than a Governor's-eye view of Chris Patten's time in Hong Kong: selective, partial and, in order to achieve broadcast and publication soon after the handover, rushed. The villain of the book was Sir Percy Cradock, who responded robustly. But several other actors in the drama, including me, were criticised, often on thin or partial evidence. The Foreign Office squirmed but, probably wisely, did nothing.

Luckily for me, I had moved on, physically as well as emotionally. I was back on language training, this time in Lille, renewing my acquaintance with French irregular verbs. I followed the rows over Dimbleby only remotely. Supporting the handover of Britain's last big colony had been an exhilarating and exhausting experience. But, after nearly three and a half years, it was time for something less stressful.

Chapter 8

Death on the Seine

The priest at the church of La Madeleine spoke perfect English, albeit with a South African accent. But, being a bit of a language snob, he insisted on giving me – the newly arrived Political Counsellor at the British Embassy in Paris – my instructions in French: 'On va placer Monsieur le Ministre côté Fauchon de l'église, Monsieur l'Ambassadeur côté Hédiard.' This ecclesiastical French sounded confusing, but I could see that the man of God wanted the Minister to sit on the right-hand side of the church, our Ambassador on the left.

It was September 1997. We were arranging the seating for the official memorial service in Paris for the Princess of Wales, at the high-society church of La Madeleine, just off the Place de la Concorde near the British Embassy. I was the Embassy official responsible for liaising with the church authorities. The guest of honour was to be the colourful French Health Minister, Bernard Kouchner, the founder of Médécins sans Frontières, who had worked with Diana in the campaign against land mines. But what were this 'Hédiard' for left and 'Fauchon' for right? I could only assume that they were the French church's equivalent of port and starboard. When I got back to the Embassy, I casually mentioned this to our translators, not wanting to betray my poor vocabulary. They burst out laughing, as they gently explained that 'Fauchon' and 'Hédiard' were the names of the two famous grocery stores in their respective corners at the north end of the Place de la Madeleine, which surrounded the church. It was rather as if the priests at St James's, Piccadilly, were to christen one end of their church Fortnum's and the other Criterion. I learned something new every day.

After packing up in the Hong Kong Department three months earlier, I had gone straight to Lille, for immersion training in French – 'perfectionnement' as the Diplomatic Service Language Centre optimistically called it. I loved Lille, a Flemish city of great beauty, full of surprising treasures, ranging from the architectural jewels of the old quarter to some fine museums, of art and of natural history. The last was filled with hundreds of stuffed birds of every size and shape collected by a distinguished French ornithologist of the nineteenth century. Lille had been the only French city to have been occupied by the Germans during the First World War and had suffered terribly. The monument to the *colombophiles* (or pigeon-fanciers) of the city told its own sad story, of the brave men who had used their carrier pigeons to convey messages to the Allies and been shot for their bravery. A similar fate had befallen those who had helped a British pilot escape, only for him foolishly to fly back over the city to drop a farewell message to the German commandant, leading to the network being rounded up and shot. When I wasn't studying, I spent time at weekends making my first proper pilgrimages to the battlefields of the Great War. There I had the shock of finding my own name on a gravestone: my great-uncle, Captain Sherard Cowper-Coles of the six-month-old Royal Air Force, shot down near Ypres one month before the end of the war. I discovered that, on two earlier occasions, his aircraft had been hit by enemy fire, but his navigator had climbed out on the wing while the aircraft was in the air to repair the damage.

I worked hard at my French: there was a lot of ground to make up, even though French had been my favourite subject at school and I had once received, after spending a gap-year month in Montpellier, a 'Diploma in French Civilisation' from the Université Paul Valéry there. (One could never imagine a British university, or any other educational institution, granting diplomas in British 'civilisation' – it was not something Brits believed in.) Thanks to the efforts of a team of dedicated teachers, and the inability of the family with whom I was staying to speak anything other than rapid-fire French, I made some progress. But not enough to speak anything approaching French French, still less to cope with the priests at La Madeleine.

It had been agreed that my first day at work in the Embassy in Paris would be Monday 1 September 1997. On the morning of Sunday 31 August, I was on my way back with my children from a holiday near Perpignan, staying in a Formule 1 motel near Clermont-Ferrand. Half asleep, I flicked the television bolted to the wall over from cartoons to the news, with the sound down. Suddenly, I noticed the images of a wrecked car in a tunnel and the headline 'Mort de Diana'. At first I thought I was watching the preview of a French television drama in poor taste. But, as I dialled the volume up, the literally unbelievable horror of what had happened started to dawn on me. I immediately phoned my wife, who had gone on ahead to Paris with one of our sons. Bridget was already installed in the Gatehouse of the Embassy on the Rue du Faubourg St Honoré, which was to be our home. She had not seen the news, but said she had heard the great gates of the Residence being opened and closed all night and had seen the Ambassador's Jaguar coming and going, and had wondered what was happening. She now knew. I rushed back to Paris and reported for duty.

I found the Ambassador, Michael Jay, and his wife, Sylvia, handling a major crisis superbly. They needed little help from me, as they fielded constant calls from Buckingham Palace and Downing Street, from the Elysée (which had apparently had difficulty in tracking down the French President in the early hours of Sunday morning) and from the French police and air force. In the space of only a few hours, the Embassy was coping with a major consular incident, a massive news event and then a royal visit: the Prince of Wales would be arriving in Paris that afternoon with two of his sisters-in-law to escort his former wife's body back to England.

But, for the Embassy in Paris, the departure of the Princess's remains was only the start of a story that was to dominate much of the Embassy's work for years to come. The first question was why we had not known that the Princess was in Paris. It turned out that we *had* known, but only by chance, and only late on 30 August. After a dinner out, the Embassy Defence Attaché, Brigadier Charles Ritchie, had been making his way back to his flat on the Rue de Rivoli and had noticed a crowd outside the Ritz Hotel in the Place Vendôme. On making his way over and asking what was going on, he was told that 'Diana and Dodi' were in town and were expected shortly to leave the hotel. He continued home to bed: the Princess was now a private individual and no responsibility of the Embassy.

Within hours of the news of the terrible accident breaking, the Embassy was besieged by journalists, desperate for any scrap of information with which to fill out their reporting. They were joined by mourners, wanting the Embassy to pass their condolences on to London. They gathered under the windows of our house overlooking the Rue du Faubourg St Honoré. The French riot police – the CRS – strengthened their presence on the street. Many of the mourners had already placed flowers on the Pont de l'Alma, above the tunnel where the fatal accident had happened. In the months and years that followed, many tourists visiting Paris came to believe that the golden 'Flame of Liberty' sculpture above the tunnel was in fact a memorial to Diana. We opened a big black leather-bound book of condolence in the Residence, of the kind embassies everywhere keep in stock, for the French public and others to sign. We soon learned that the French didn't believe in just signing the book with their names: each visitor wrote 'quelques mots' in often moving personal tributes to a personality who had captured the world's imagination, and whose sudden, violent death had been a traumatic shock. For days the queues backed up and snaked down the Rue du Faubourg St Honoré. More condolence books were sent urgently from London. While the Ambassador and his wife attended the Princess's funeral at Westminster Abbey, my wife and I went to the memorial services organised by the two Anglican churches in Paris, each representative of one of the main varieties of Anglican liturgical experience: one more Roman than the Catholics, with a Requiem Mass sung amid clouds of incense, the other in the equally emotional but wholly different charismatic tradition, with lots of 'Hallelujahs' and swaying to spiritualist hymns.

Those memorial events, and that at La Madeleine, were soon over. It was then that the Embassy's real work arising from the Princess's death began: supporting the French judicial investigation, and then an inquiry by the Metropolitan Police from London which lasted, unbelievably, until 2006, and did not lead to an inquest verdict until 2008 – eleven years after the crash. The simple explanation – a driver too fond of drink, excessive speed by the car carrying the Princess and those chasing her, passengers not wearing seat belts, head-on collision with a concrete pillar in the tunnel rather than with another car – was too easy for the conspiracy theorists who now crawled out of the swamp. The obvious objection to a plot was wilfully ignored: anyone planning to have the Princess killed would have been unlikely to have left the outcome dependent on whether or not Her Royal Highness and her boyfriend put on seat belts for what was apparently an unplanned car journey by an inebriated driver. It was not long before Dodi's distraught father, Mohammed al Fayed, was asserting that MI6 had to have been involved, acting on the instructions of the royal family. Then, as part of an effort to 'out' members of MI6 operating under diplomatic cover worldwide, the disillusioned former SIS officer Richard Tomlinson unhelpfully (and wrongly) identified the 'Political Counsellor' on the Paris Embassy list – that is, me – as the head of SIS's Paris Station, a solecism that added hugely to my prestige with my children's friends. I still don't know whether to feel flattered or insulted by Tomlinson's mistake, which persists on the internet to this day. As weeks turned into months, and months into years, the whole painful process of establishing the truth about what had happened that August night dragged on and on. The answer when it came, from the conclusions by the French magistrates and of the London inquest conducted by Lord Justice Scott Baker, told most people what they had known from the start, but did little to satisfy those with a preference for conspiracy over cock-up – almost always the wrong explanation for such events.

Paradoxically perhaps, the part which the Embassy in general, and the Ambassador in particular, had played in dealing with the aftermath of Diana's death gave us a bit of a boost: here was a diplomatic mission coping calmly and professionally with a series of wholly unforeseen challenges, at the centre of world attention. We had shown what we could do. Here was another example of a truth about diplomacy that was to occur to me throughout my career: just as soldiers love a good fight (but can't say so), so diplomats love a good crisis (but won't admit it). In each case, it is what the profession is about.

A much more important boost for the Embassy in Paris, and for the whole British diplomatic effort in Europe, had come from the New

Labour landslide on 1 May 1997, and the arrival in power in London of Tony Blair's Government. In part, this was because Blair, and his Foreign Secretary Robin Cook, were unapologetically pro-European. After the agonies over Europe endured by John Major's Government, here was a fresh team of ministers, headed by a charismatic Prime Minister, ready to engage with our European partners in all sorts of positive ways. With the British Presidency of the European Union coming up in the first half of 1998, we felt that the tide of European history was at last flowing in our direction. Even though the French Government was suffering from 'cohabitation', with a Gaullist President, Jacques Chirac, just up the Rue du Faubourg St Honoré in the Elysée, and a Socialist Prime Minister, Lionel Jospin, across the river in the Hotel Matignon, we found the New Labour messages on Europe an easy sell. Britain was no longer the odd one out in Europe, the reluctant and resented curmudgeon of European integration.

But it wasn't just that Britain was no longer unpopular, it was also that we were positively 'cool'. It had been in 1996 that a friend of mine working for *Newsweek*, William Underhill, had helped produce a prescient cover story for the magazine describing London as 'the coolest city on the planet'. William was a gratifyingly uncool Wykehamist, with an air of donnish detachment that had led him to identify, in the graphics accompanying the piece, as 'cool' hotspots several nightclubs long ago closed. A Chinese diplomat whom I knew from Hong Kong, with poor English, read the story. Puzzled, he pointed out that the conclusion was wrong: several other cities, including Beijing, Moscow and Stockholm, were much cooler than London.

All this 'Cool Britannia' talk was music to French ears, at a time when the Eurostar effect was starting to get going, with London filling up with young French waiters and only slightly older French bankers. The Embassy in Paris embraced 'Cool Britannia' with enthusiasm. The Ambassador had good personal relations with many of the senior figures in New Labour. He was invited to join the Foreign Office committee working on the rebranding of Britain. Out went the old artworks in the Paris Residence, to be replaced by the best modern British art the Government Art Collection could afford – which wasn't always quite the best. But installations blinked and winked at our guests, plastic replaced paint, chicken wire instead of watercolours, oil cans in place of oil paints. It was all achingly trendy. So New Labour, so *troisième voie*. It was only a pity that, privately, our French guests had a more rigorous approach to artistic excellence than did we eager apostles of Blairism. But, after the bitter divisions with 'old Europe' over Iraq which came later, it is sometimes hard to recapture just how the early months of the Blair Government felt – at least for those charged with promoting Britain abroad. It would be only slightly exaggerating to suggest that it was indeed bliss at that time to have been one of Blair's European diplomats, and that to be young as well was very heaven.

Perhaps the most potent symbol of all this was the Prime Minister's decision to address the French National Assembly in French in 1998. We sent two of the Embassy's doughty French translators over to Downing Street, to put the PM through his paces. As you would have expected with the consummate thespian that Tony Blair was, he rose magnificently to the occasion. The substance of the speech was carefully crafted to touch buttons across most of the French political spectrum, provoking repeated applause, albeit for different reasons depending where in the hemi-cycle you were sitting.* And the delivery, while slick and assured, was artfully bashful enough to steal a few French hearts. It really was a tour de force, Blair's finest hour on the European stage.

Even then, though, you could not help noticing that, while the French welcomed Blair's Euro-enthusiasm, they were less convinced by his political philosophy. I attended an excruciatingly embarrassing lecture on the 'third way', delivered by its chief prophet, Professor Tony Giddens of the LSE, at a private club of French philosophers in Paris. With calm Cartesian precision, the French audience rose one by one quietly to dissect the contradictions and concealed hypocrisies of political calculation dressed up as philosophy. It was cruel sport. 'Triangulation' and 'progressive social democracy' were not really the French way.

---

* 'The right had decided to use his speech to make a point. Every time Tony said something New Labour they applauded loudly while the socialists sat on their hands looking glum, and every time he said something faintly left-wing the socialists clapped wildly while the right sat in silence. The right got the better part of it.' Powell, op. cit., pp. 241–2.

As in Washington in 1987, so in Paris in 1997. Once again I was working in the Political Section – the Chancery – of one of our largest and most important embassies. But this time it was one rank up, as a counsellor, with the job of leading the Embassy's political and press work. My team was larger than the total UK-based staff of most British embassies today. One group focused on French foreign policy, keeping close to the Quai d'Orsay, the French Defence Ministry and the foreign and defence policy parts of the Matignon and the Elysée. France, like Britain a permanent member of the UN Security Council, had a serious foreign policy, which reached parts of the world – mainly but not only in Africa – which we never reached. Even then, France had more diplomatic missions in more countries than we did. On a good day, their diplomats were more than a match for ours – worthy adversaries and valuable colleagues. On a few issues – relations with Iraq, defence sales, for example – we competed. But on most we co-operated, and could learn much from each other. The Embassy diligently marked all the key players in the French foreign policy establishment. The Ambassador would cover the advisers to the President and the Prime Minister, and the top officials in the Quai and elsewhere. I would mark the next level down, and the rest of the team parcelled out the remainder. We sent a constant flow of reports and analysis back to London, probably more and of higher quality than the Foreign Office needed.

Covering French politics was much the same. The Ambassador dealt with the party leaders, the *grosses légumes* of French democracy, with the rest of us working the lower levels as best we could. Unlike in foreign policy, however, we had little information to offer, nothing much to trade, so creating a load-bearing link was harder. But, once you succeeded, the rewards were immense. I was particularly proud to have become good friends with Jospin's *plume* – his speech writer.* I was even prouder that, after months of effort, I managed to persuade Chirac's notoriously reclusive communications adviser, his daughter Claude, to come out to lunch, albeit accompanied by a political chaperone. As part of our efforts to promote the British way of doing everything, we tried to interest some of the French political-campaign

---

* Aquilino Morelle, appointed in 2012 to do the same job for President Hollande.

professionals in the advertising that had helped New Labour cruise to power. They were polite about the show we put on, but you sensed that they didn't feel they had much to learn from British diplomats, or indeed from British politics.

The Embassy also had a small but skilled press team, headed by Tim Livesey, a quietly devout Catholic who went on to work in Tony Blair's Press Office, and then for the Archbishops both of Westminster and of Canterbury before becoming, in 2011, Ed Miliband's chief of staff. We covered most parts of the French metropolitan media. I am not sure our efforts made much difference to how they reported Britain – which depended mainly and rightly on their correspondents in London – but we learned more from them about the state of France than we ever did from French politicians. We also took the first faltering steps towards exploiting the new media, establishing our own Embassy website years before the Foreign Office got round to acting on our suggestion of a common template for all embassy and FCO websites. I am not sure how many hits the site received in those early days, but those who did consult it would have been well rewarded, with all the basic texts on the Anglo-French relationship, and plenty of Cool Britannia colour.

There was one issue which brought me into contact with Buckingham Palace and the Central Chancery of Orders of Knighthood back in London through most of my time in Paris. On the occasion of his State Visit to Britain in 1992, the Queen had awarded President Mitterrand the Royal Victorian Chain, which was returnable on the recipient's death. Curiously, I had dealt with the same subject in Cairo. Soon after Sadat had been killed, a letter had arrived from London instructing the Embassy to seek the return of Sadat's Royal Victorian Chain. It seemed rather hard on the descendants of the great man. But the Egyptians soon produced Sadat's Chain, and we sent it back to London. Securing Mitterrand's wasn't so easy, however. He had died in January 1996. For months, and then years, the Elysée equivocated. We couldn't understand what was going on. Increasingly strident letters arrived from London, pointing out that each Chain, made mainly of gold, was worth £75,000, and that it was made clear to each recipient, in writing, that it had to be given back when the recipient died. Eventually, we found out what had happened: Mitterrand had passed his Royal Victorian Chain on to his mistress, who, understandably enough, surrendered it only reluctantly and belatedly.

Good food, decent wine and patience played an important part in the Embassy's efforts to win French friends and influence them. Unlike the contacts I had made in Washington, who would be satisfied with a quick snack and a Pepsi before rushing back to their desks, French contacts expected a real lunch. My favourite restaurant, which I used all the time, is now, sadly, closed: it was called *Ecaille et Plume* ('fish scale and feather'), and served seafood in summer, game in winter. The patron was almost spherical. He presided over the tiny dining room, dispensing glasses of wine carefully calibrated to each course (no customer was expected to buy a whole bottle). His wife cooked, emerging only occasionally from the kitchen, blinkingly to greet a favourite client. Each day, she and her husband set a single menu: there was no choice of dishes, only of quantities. This was the perfect place not just for a proper lunch, but for a proper conversation as only the French know how, not about the weather, but about ideas. I was amazed how long my guests would linger, and how much wine even busy *députés*, about to return to the National Assembly, would imbibe, without ever obviously becoming drunk. When I left Paris, in the spring of 1999, one of my team entered two search terms in the Chancery database: 'Sherard' and 'Lunch'. He came up with scores of hits, and a rich seam of insights into France's sense of itself.

But we didn't entertain only in restaurants. For the most senior guests, the Residence was the place. Sylvia and Michael Jay ran it with an apparently effortless ease that concealed extraordinary professionalism. My favourite moment was when the Editor of *Libération* was made literally to eat his own words. He was served miniature fish and chips wrapped in edible paper on which was printed that day's edition of his paper. But the Jays also had fun with Beef Wellington, British cheeses of all varieties, good whisky which the French adored, and, perhaps best of all, sending round to the Elysée the occasional case of English beer for a President who preferred ale to wine. Just occasionally, they even served English wine, usually white and sparkling.

My family and I were lucky enough to live above the shop as well, in the famous Gatehouse of the Embassy. This ten-bedroomed establishment looked out over the French equivalent of Bond Street on one side and over the Residence courtyard on the other. All it lacked was a garden – though we were free to use the Embassy one next door whenever we wanted. It was the perfect place to live, to entertain, and from which to work. The Gatehouse had played its own small part in the history of relations between Britain and France, and had witnessed many of the comings and goings at the Embassy that had marked the ebb and flow of engagement between the two ancient enemy-allies. Until the Second World War, the Gatehouse had been used as the Embassy's Chancery – its offices. Thereafter, it had been the home of the head of Chancery. What was now the drawing room had once been the Third Room of the Chancery. In 1814, Arthur Wellesley, the Duke of Wellington, had secured the Hôtel de Charost from Napoleon's sister, Pauline Borghese. Wellington had been having too good a time with the ladies of Paris to want his wife to join him, to help choose and furnish a house. So, to avoid (or postpone) her arrival, he had taken the house with all its furniture and fittings, including the Princess's famous bed – all now the property of the British Government. At that time, as the horse inscribed above the door indicated, the Gatehouse had been the stables: it must have witnessed the scene when the Princess's former servants had been lined up to receive the house's new owner. In a final gesture of defiance, they had turned their backs on the victorious British general. His acid response was said to have been 'Gentlemen, I have seen plenty of French backs before.' By the time Wellington fought the Battle of Waterloo, following Napoleon's escape from Elba in 1815, the Hôtel de Charost was his home. Most famously, the Gatehouse has a big part in Nancy Mitford's novel about the Paris Embassy after the Second World War, *Don't Tell Alfred*, in which a former ambassadress sneaks back into the Gatehouse, establishes a rival salon and refuses to budge. Personally, I felt lucky to be there: a distant relation, Richard Lyons, had served as ambassador to Paris for twenty years in the late nineteenth century, before, during and after the Commune of 1870. He had been criticised for deserting his post during the uprising. Lyons was apparently a shy bachelor – so shy, it was said, that for two decades he had not dared tell his butler that he had preferred his breakfast egg soft boiled not hard (or vice versa). An even more distant family connection, Lieutenant Colonel Maurice Hankey, must have been there with Lloyd George during the Paris Peace Conference in 1919: it was he who, before departure for Paris, was said to have asked Lloyd George (who was at least as fond of the ladies as Wellington had been): 'Prime Minister, will Mrs Lloyd George be accompanying us to Paris?', only to receive the shameless put-down: 'My dear Hankey, I never take my own sandwiches to a banquet.'

During what turned out to be a brief stay in Paris, we used the Gatehouse as best we could to entertain as many French guests as possible. Along with the Ambassador, we were allowed to buy Pol Roger champagne at a preferential rate. This tradition dated back to just after the war, when old Madame Pol Roger (who had known and liked Churchill) had decreed this special expression of gratitude to the British Embassy in Paris. For food, we used, deliberately, a Scottish chef, Anna Murray, who catered to the racing set in Chantilly. She produced the most wonderfully original British dishes, which the French loved. The only challenge was the logistics of getting her and the food in from Chantilly: she never actually let us down, but she did once fail my successor, Simon Fraser, who, in an incident recorded with glee by Boris Johnson's journalist sister Rachel, was forced to send out for pizzas.

There are a number of vital ingredients to successful diplomatic (or indeed any other) entertainment. The first is giving the guests the sense that their hosts are enjoying it. The second is giving the guests the sense that they are among people they want to be with, or at least ought to want to be with. And the third is mixing people up, as intelligently and imaginatively as possible. Couples should never be allowed to sit together, or even on the same table. Lots of round tables work better than a single long one. And of course good food and good wine are essential. I have often encountered something close to spontaneous social ignition: guests know almost instinctively that a party is going to be fun, and the infectious sense of mutual enjoyment then spreads rapidly.

Soon after we arrived in Paris, we experienced a social disaster straight out of Nancy Mitford. We had met a charming couple, the Comte and Comtesse de Pourtalès, who had known some of our predecessors in the Gatehouse. We put their names on the list to be invited to one of the first big dinners we gave, heard that they had accepted and thought no more of it. As I was waiting for the guests to arrive, I was a little surprised to be phoned by the gate guard to be told that Madame la Comtesse de Pourtalès had arrived alone. I went to the top of the great staircase to greet her. Up swept La Comtesse, much older and more imperious, much grander and greyer, than I remembered. She greeted me warmly but formally. She was so happy to have been invited to the Gatehouse, as she had never been there before. She reeled off the names of British ambassadors to Paris she had known, and of her forebears who had lived in the Hôtel de Charost. Half an hour later, the 'right' Comte and Comtesse de Pourtalès arrived. I had realised at once that there had been a mistake. But we had to carry on as though nothing had happened. Clearly, the first Comtesse was the senior of the two. So, swiftly and secretly, we shifted the place cards around, and I found myself hosting a dinner, with the 'wrong' Comtesse de Pourtalès on one side, and the 'right' Comtesse on the other: the latter soon guessed that something had gone wrong and gave me a knowing wink. But generously she kept up the pretence throughout what turned out to be a happy evening. Later, we found out that a temporary secretary in the Embassy had mistakenly telephoned the 'wrong' Comtesse de Pourtalès to ask if she had received our invitation and was coming: she had accepted with alacrity, even though she hadn't received a card. Meanwhile, the 'right' Comte and Comtesse had replied in writing. Not unreasonably, my secretary on returning had assumed that only the couple to whom she had sent a card were coming. We had learned, amusingly, that in France many aristocrats have exactly the same title.

It wasn't just the French whom Bridget and I entertained at the Gatehouse. By the end of our time in Paris, our Peugeot people carrier could almost find its own way to the Gare du Nord, to greet hordes of newly enthusiastic friends from England being disgorged by the evening Eurostar from Waterloo. People we had not seen or heard from for years were in touch, the prospect of a few days on the Faubourg setting aside the diffidence of decades. But most visitors were genuinely welcome, and, with ten bedrooms in the beautiful heart of Paris, it seemed churlish not to fill them when we could. And the good thing was that the Gatehouse wasn't close just to the Champs Elysées and the

Louvre: there was also plenty for our teenage children and their friends, and for younger people – or people who wanted to be younger – to enjoy. One of these was the Buddha Bar, in a side street off the Place de la Concorde, the home of occidental–oriental fusion music, and cuisine. I was first introduced to it by an SIS officer, who held his farewell dinner there. Many were the evenings when we and our guests repaired there, after a dinner at the Gatehouse, and much was the fun we had. Perhaps the most improbably exuberant scene I can recall was that of two distinguished (and normally rather austere) beaks from Eton College tripping the light fantastic at the Buddha Bar, to the deep thumping rhythms of the Buddha Bar's blend of transcendental disco music. Such was the effect Paris had on people.

We didn't just entertain, however: we were entertained too, not only by the usual suspects who buzz round any embassy in any capital, but by real French people well outside the smart arrondissements of Paris. We met them in different ways, and at different times: in a French book club or a conversation class, and in Arabic refresher lessons, at a gym, through our youngest son's school, by keeping in touch with my French teachers in Lille, or via my Dutch and Argentinian cousins who lived in and around Paris. We were invited to dinner by Gaullist *députés* and socialist intellectuals, by the smart set and by those with fewer pretensions. What united them all was the quality of conversation, the strength of intellectual curiosity, the passion for ideas for their own sake. Not for our French hosts the narcissistic focus on schools and house prices encountered over lunches and dinners in south London. But the flip side of this was that one was expected to keep up, to take part, in French. In the early months at least, there were many meals at which my French neighbours would talk, politely but passionately, right across me. And it took time to pick up the nuances. One small example of how difficult this could be came during a tour of the Somme battlefields which I organised with some friends from England. We ended up with dinner in the old town of Lille, to which I invited, among others, one of my French teachers and her boyfriend Emmanuel from Guadeloupe. A man of great nobility and few words, he worked as a driver for the French Finance Ministry, at its headquarters in the Paris suburb of Bercy. One of those at the dinner was David, an English peer and City tycoon. The morning after, David said how much he had enjoyed the dinner, except that 'those French Treasury types are damned tight-lipped. I couldn't get a word out of Emmanuel on economic and monetary union.' It emerged that Emmanuel, asked what he did, had said simply and proudly, 'Je suis fonctionnaire à Bercy,' and had spent the rest of dinner stonewalling David's questions. David had not realised that *fonctionnaire* means any employee of the French state, not the high official he had assumed Emmanuel to be.

Such social insights helped with the serious work of the Embassy, as Prime Minister Blair strived to put Britain back at the heart of Europe. Rightly, he had concluded that defence was the area where Britain and France could work most easily and most profitably together. Both were serious military powers, with global pretensions and reach. For all the linguistic differences, our military officers got on well. In many ways, they came from similar backgrounds. French officers seemed more worldly than, for example, over-serious teetotaller Americans from the Southern Baptist boondocks. And, if Britain and France couldn't work together on defence, what could we work together on?

So it was that, in early December 1998, for the annual Franco-British summit, I found myself in a windswept waterfront hotel in St Malo in Brittany. There the two governments signed an historic declaration promising a new era in Franco-British military co-operation, covering intelligence, operations and even media-handling. Both Chirac and Jospin were there. The details were argued over incessantly, and seemed so important at the time: my over-enthusiastic opposite number in Washington, the Political Counsellor there, even rang to object that the proposed wording would upset the Americans. But he needn't have worried. The approach was right, the intent sincere, but, as with so much in efforts to secure real British engagement in Europe, the delivery fell short of the promise. Today, Britain and France are still talking about stepping up defence co-operation. They missed the boat (literally) over co-operating on aircraft carriers, they persisted (thanks largely to France) with building, damagingly, two competing European fast combat jets, but are now considering – seriously and rightly – working together on unmanned aircraft. Through all this, the truth that led to St Malo remains: if Britain and France don't hang together on

defence, they will surely hang separately, especially as America turns
from the Atlantic to the Pacific.

The other area where Britain and France had once been rivals but
could now co-operate was Africa: on instructions from the Foreign
Secretary in London, Robin Cook, who was developing a good relationship with his French colleague, Hubert Védrine, we worked to put
together a Franco-British joint Heads of Mission Conference in Africa,
on Africa. Our key ambassadors (or high commissioners, in the case of
Commonwealth countries) were invited, from South Africa, Kenya,
Nigeria and one or two smaller posts. On the French side were the
ambassadors from Dakar, Abidjan and Gabon, who, despite the difference in titles, often fulfilled a more proconsular function than their
British colleagues. The two post-colonial powers had much to talk, and
worry, about as they surveyed the political, security and economic
outlook across Africa.

At the top of the tree, Tony Blair worked hard to build good relations
with both Chirac and Jospin. Each was invited to his constituency, each
invited to experience British pub food at the Dun Cow in Sedgefield.
Before the dinner with Chirac, the Number 10 spokesman, Alastair
Campbell, bet the British team that Chirac would afterwards tell the
Prime Minister that the rather indifferent dinner had been the best
meal of his life. Sure enough, after dinner, Chirac got up and advanced
across the saloon bar to Blair: 'Mon cher Tony,' he said, 'zat was ze best
deener of my life.'

More serious though was the slip which the Prime Minister made
when entertaining Jospin in Sedgefield. After a liquid lunch in the Dun
Cow, the Prime Minister decided to draw on his gap year working in a
bar at Roissy to address the assembled French press, in French. With
Jospin, the austere northern Protestant, beside him, the Prime Minister
plunged straight in. He wanted the French media to know that he had
always been envious of Jospin, in whatever job he had done. Looking
meaningfully at Jospin, he announced, 'J'ai toujours envie de toi, Lionel,
même en toute position' (roughly translated, 'I have always lusted after
you, Lionel, in every position'). The French journalists burst out laughing. Jospin went bright red and hastened to explain what the Prime
Minister had really meant. It was reminiscent of an interview which

Chris Patten had given to *L'Express* magazine before leaving Hong Kong, about his hopes of enjoying his farm in France: that irreproachable sentiment had come out as something like 'I am looking forward to pleasuring my (female) farmer in France' ('Je voudrais jouir ma fermière en France').

When I got back to Paris from the St Malo Summit in December 1998, a friend in the Foreign Office in London rang to tip me off: Robin Cook had been asking what I was like. I didn't even want to think what that might mean, and so dismissed the thought. I had been promised four years in Paris and really didn't want to leave early.

Chapter 9

The Gnome Secretary

Gaynor Cook was furious. 'Why on earth did you put that stupid hat on, Robin, when nobody else did?' she demanded. We were in the Azores, for an informal weekend meeting of EU foreign ministers in May 2000. At the photo-call to mark the occasion, the proud local authorities had handed each of their ministerial guests a sample of the headgear worn by the Azoreans – a woollen bobble hat. Only the British Foreign Secretary had been foolish enough to put his on, with the inevitable result. Bored photographers had swung into action, cameras clicking and whirring. As Mrs Cook continued to scold him, the Foreign Secretary passed me the offending object. I tucked it away in the red-leather despatch box I was carrying.

Right on cue, the *Mail on Sunday* the next day carried the picture they had wanted, with the headline every sub-editor dreamed of: the bearded Robin Cook in a bobble hat, beneath the banner 'The Gnome Secretary'. A few days later I tentatively asked the Secretary of State if he wanted his hat back. 'Sherard,' said the Foreign Secretary, 'I never want to see the damn thing again.' I gave it to my eldest son, who for several years jauntily sported the Robin Cook Memorial Bobble Hat while skiing.

In so many ways, that incident summed up Robin Cook's relationship with the media: the touchingly naive vanity that led him to put on the hat, without any sense of the gesture's possible consequences; and a British press that gave him nothing like the respect he deserved and, at least in its lower reaches, never missed an opportunity to mock him, for his looks as well as his politics. In those early years of the Blair Government, when the Prime Minister was a hard target to hit, his beleaguered Foreign Secretary was easy meat for the right-wing tabloids.

It had been exactly the same on a visit to Moscow a few months earlier. Robin had had a deep affection for Russia ever since he had first been there on a schools cruise from Scotland. One of the symptoms of that affection was an ancient fur hat that he put on in cold climates whenever he could, but which made him look a bit like Vladimir Ilyich Lenin. As we landed in Moscow on a freezing February day, on went the hat and out went any camera-conscious discretion. Within hours of our arrival, he had been spotted. The *Daily Mail* was in touch with the Foreign Office press office. There had been criticism of public figures, including the Countess of Wessex, for wearing fur. The *Mail* wanted to know if the Foreign Secretary's hat was the real thing or merely synthetic. I asked Robin Cook, who neither knew nor cared. After frantically examining the hat, we concluded that it was fake and triumphantly transmitted the news back to London. Much relieved, the Foreign Office press office rang the paper, to say that they could spike the story: the hat was synthetic. But that didn't deter the *Daily Mail*. We heard that the next day's edition had apparently carried a short piece headlined 'Cook Insults Russians', explaining how the Foreign Secretary had offended his fur-loving hosts by wearing fake fur in the land where everyone preferred the real thing.

A year earlier, in January 1999, I had only an inkling that I was being considered as a candidate for the job of Robin Cook's principal private secretary. On leave in Devon, I had spotted on a petrol-station forecourt a *Sun* front page made up of a grimacing photograph of Cook beside the headline 'Would YOU sleep with this man?' Telephone numbers were helpfully provided for a public poll. The following day, the front page screamed that '966 WOULD sleep with Robin Cook'. Inside, a 'Robin Cook Pulling Kit' was assembled for readers' use: with a cut-out-'n'-keep mask of the Foreign Secretary (described as a 'Robin Hood'), plus pictures of Ferrero Rocher chocolates, the keys to Chevening (the Foreign Secretary's official country residence) and a diplomatic passport, as well as a list of chat-up lines in foreign languages. The occasion for this mass mockery of one of the most senior politicians in the land was the publication of his ex-wife Margaret's bitter memoir, in which she had claimed that the married Mr Cook had had several earlier lovers. The *Sun* coverage would have been funny if it hadn't ultimately been so sad.

Not surprisingly, when eventually I did become Robin Cook's private secretary in April 1999, the first thing I decided was that we should do all we could to stop him reading the press cuttings, let alone the papers themselves. Instead, we got the FCO press office to prepare a daily summary, as upbeat as possible, of what the Foreign Secretary needed to know about the day's media. I had much in mind that Mrs Thatcher's Press Secretary, Bernard Ingham, had done the same when they were at Number 10. And I was aware of how both Harold Wilson and John Major had undermined their own confidence – and their premierships – by insisting on seeing the first editions of the next day's papers before retiring to bed.

I hardly knew Robin Cook when I started in the Private Office. In fact, I had met him only three times before: once when I had briefed him on Hong Kong on his first day as foreign secretary, once when I had attended his meeting on HMY *Britannia* with the American Secretary of State Madeleine Albright in June 1997, and finally when he interviewed me for the job. Soon after Christmas 1998, thankfully before I had seen the *Sun* story later in January, I had been asked whether I would be prepared to be considered for what many thought was the poisoned chalice of principal private secretary to a man with a reputation as one of the most difficult foreign secretaries in recent memory. I had said yes straight away: I was up for a challenge, and was starting to feel that Paris, while fun, was not wholly serious work. I then heard nothing for weeks.

When I did hear, everything happened at once, and with the chaotic management of the Foreign Secretary's diary I came to know so well over the following couple of years. I was told that the Secretary of State wanted to interview me as soon as possible, but that the only slot available would be during a visit by him to Ghana! Could I get myself there, from Paris, at short notice? As it happened, I could, as I would be attending the first joint Franco-British Heads of Mission Conference in Abidjan* (at which the British and French foreign ministers were dropping in) only shortly afterwards.

---

* See p. 195.

Bizarrely, the interview took place in a luxury resort on the coast just outside Accra. I was taken to see Robin Cook in what was little more than an upmarket beach hut by the Assistant Private Secretary, Andrew Patrick, who hardly concealed his amused pleasure at the discomfort of the candidates. They included one of the tougher specimens of Foreign Office woman. I was sure the personnel department had put her forward just to ensure that there was one female candidate, as she was quite unlikely to have hit it off with Cook. She had appeared in Accra in a thick tweed suit and brogues.

The interview didn't last long. I took immediately to Robin Cook. He came across as highly intelligent, but wounded and vulnerable. He had a wry sense of humour and a twinkle in his eye. He was refreshingly free of cant and pomposity, and disarmingly human. I told him that, in my view, he needed a private secretary who would give him affection and honest advice, as well as loyal support. With hindsight, I think it was the mention of the word 'affection' that made up his mind. Robin Cook had a thinner skin than his critics imagined, and he felt pretty unloved.

The interview over, I returned to my post in Paris. Again, weeks passed. Then I heard that the Foreign Secretary had had a long conversation, from a car in Germany, with my boss, the Ambassador at Paris, Michael Jay. Robin Cook had wanted to know what I was really like. And the next thing after that was that I was told I had got the job and was needed in London at once. As our house in Balham was still let, I had to stay in temporary digs in London, pending my family's return. Typically, when I did start back in King Charles Street after less than two years away, my new boss seemed to have forgotten that I was coming. On my first day in the job, he appeared round the great oak door which separates the Foreign Secretary's magnificent office from the private secretaries' room. He seemed somewhat startled to see me installed behind the principal private secretary's desk in the opposite corner of the room. His only comment was something on the lines of 'Oh you're here,' and he then didn't speak to me properly for days. I wondered if I had made a big mistake.

But I hadn't. The two or so years I spent as Robin Cook's private secretary were probably the most difficult of my career. And yet they were in many ways the most rewarding and enjoyable. It was a privilege to have been chosen to be the chief assistant to someone of such enormous talent and ambition, but at the same time with such failings and faults, of which he was, touchingly, only too well aware. He knew that he needed someone like me. As the weeks turned into months, and the months into years, we found that the Scottish socialist politician and the public-school-educated English diplomat got on surprisingly well together. It is all too easy to fill the day *being* foreign secretary, receiving visitors, giving interviews, issuing statements, attending the House of Commons, holding Office meetings, travelling the world, attending conferences. It is much more difficult to use the job actually to *do* things. What I admired most about Robin Cook was his determination to do things, things that he hoped would make the world a bit better – as well as reflecting credit on him and the Government to which he belonged. If I could be of some help to him in doing that, then the job was worth while, more worth while than most in the Diplomatic Service. And with him humour, often of the gallows variety, was never far away, usually the result of accident (of which there was plenty) rather than intention.

What I also liked about him was his humility – surprising in someone so widely regarded as arrogant. Once he confided to me that he was really in politics because he needed 'approbation' (as he called it) of the kind he hadn't had from his strict schoolmaster father. He was vain about his brain, but not about his looks. At a question-and-answer session with British Council staff at their headquarters in London, one employee, eager to curry favour with the Council's political boss, asked Robin Cook which actor he would choose to play himself in a film of his life. The Foreign Secretary's flattening response was simply 'They don't make actors as ugly as me' – and he meant it. Fatuous suggestions in the media that he was vain led to another absurd saga that lasted until my final few months in the Private Office. Cook had decided that the fine portrait of a nineteenth-century ruler of Nepal which had belonged to the East India Company and had long graced the Foreign Secretary's office was out of keeping with the spirit of New Labour and should therefore be removed to the British Library, where it now hangs. In its place, over the grand fireplace, a great gilt mirror was hung.

Within weeks, the press, out to get Cook, were criticising him for his vanity, for having installed in his office a mirror in which to gaze at himself. Cook responded by having the mirror removed, leaving two great scars where the mirror had been fixed to the otherwise beautifully decorated wall. It took me the best part of two years to persuade him to allow me to do something about it. With Andrew Patrick, I chose from the Government Art Collection a suitably socialist painting by John Bratby RA of a street in north London viewed over a packet of cornflakes, and an eighteenth-century oil painting of Robin Cook's beloved Newmarket. I am not sure he ever really noticed either the gap on the wall or how we filled it.

Both personally and professionally, Robin Cook had had a rough first two years as foreign secretary. First had come the very public breakdown of his marriage, and the associated row over his plan (never carried out) to appoint his then mistress and future wife, Gaynor Regan, as his diary secretary. On policy, his announcement that the New Labour Government would pursue a 'foreign policy with an ethical dimension' was widely, and deliberately, misinterpreted as committing him to the obvious impracticality of a wholly ethical foreign policy. In the event, his record of achievement as foreign secretary did have a remarkable ethical dimension – but he would have been wiser to trumpet the achievement, not the promise. Soon after the marriage story broke, he was in hot water again, for casting a double shadow over the Queen's state visits to India and Pakistan, to mark the fiftieth anniversary of independence, in August 1997: he was attacked by the Indians for supposedly offering to mediate over Kashmir, and by the British press for returning to the UK for the weekend between the two state visits, allegedly to see Gaynor. There followed the row over whether Foreign Office officials had been aware of supposed breaches of the arms embargo against Sierra Leone by a company called Sandline. And there were other, more minor alleged gaffes, including, in March 1998, a row over a visit to an Israeli settlement site on the West Bank, which caused the Israeli Prime Minister, Netanyahu, to cancel a meeting with the Foreign Secretary. By the spring of 1999, Robin Cook had acquired the reputation of being the most accident-prone member of the Blair Government.

I had arrived to find the Private Office in a pretty battered state, but with the team gamely keeping the wheels turning. My predecessor had had a tough time coping with a Foreign Secretary beset by personal and political troubles. The whole Diplomatic Service already knew that at the best of times the Secretary of State was bad at cutting through the paperwork – at 'doing his boxes'. And these hadn't been the best of times. Moreover, the problem had been compounded by the installation in the Private Office of a large metal cupboard to hold all the papers waiting to be seen by the Foreign Secretary. Inevitably, the cupboard had rapidly filled up, with policy 'submissions' requiring decisions by the Foreign Secretary and, perhaps even more important, warrants for intelligence operations which a secretary of state needed to sign if the operation in question was to remain legal. Somehow, I plucked up courage to have the cupboard removed and later replaced with a wardrobe for my cycling clothes. I separated out the papers which the Secretary of State really had to see and sign, and sent the rest back to the Foreign Office departments whence they came.

I then began a campaign, which continued until Robin Cook's last day as foreign secretary, somehow to make sure that he processed as it came in the paper he needed to process. It was rather like getting my children to do their homework. I took every opportunity to ambush him with a folder or two of papers for signature. For the two-minute car journey from the Foreign Office across to the Foreign Secretary's official residence at 1 Carlton Gardens, or back again, I would grab a couple of folders, and ask him to sign them as we sat together in the back of the car. I would lie in wait for him in the morning outside the front door of 1CG, before he came across, and then leap into the car. 'Oh, Sherard, it's you again,' he would moan weakly, as his tormentor reappeared. I would dash into his office between meetings, with more papers for him to sign. I would carefully sort what we needed him to get through on every plane and train journey. I would make sure that he was never given too much, or too little, work. I took personal charge of packing the box in the evenings, and tried to make its contents as digestible as possible, with the papers sorted into colour-coded folders, denoting importance and urgency. Sometimes I used carrots: occasionally, for example, I would slip his beloved National Hunt form book into the box, halfway down, as a reward for good work. I would try to bury the interesting but non-urgent papers right at the bottom of the box, so that he didn't get distracted. Sometimes I used threats: once in the back of the car I told him that, if he didn't sign a particular, operationally essential warrant, I would take it to the Home Secretary. There was a huge explosion, from which the driver and the detective in the front took metaphorical cover, but he signed. On another occasion, he sat with his head in his hands at the kitchen table in the Foreign Secretary's flat, in despair at the paperwork I had told him he had to get through. 'Sherard, how can you do this to me?' he complained. For a while, Gaynor Cook banned her husband from bringing official papers home after work, in his interests as well as hers. The result was that we used to park up the official car out of sight, in front of the Athenaeum in Waterloo Place, round the corner from Carlton Gardens, while the Foreign Secretary went through the paperwork for me to take back to the Foreign Office. More than once, to the detective's fury, curious (and, I suspect, inebriated) passers-by started tapping on the car window and yelling with great ribaldry, ''Ere, look, it's that Robin Cook.' The detective leaped out, to chase them away. It wasn't that the Foreign Secretary was lazy – far from it. But he was profoundly disorganised, and he believed in concentrating on issues which interested him and/or on which he could make a difference. Rightly, he judged that most of what passes through the Foreign Secretary's box is routine government business which requires little real input from the Secretary of State.

In those days, the Private Office had – or was supposed to have – a suite of six red-leather despatch boxes, each numbered and with the Royal Arms and the legend 'Secretary of State for Foreign and Commonwealth Affairs' stamped in gold on the front. Managing the flow of boxes to and from the secretary of state was at the heart of the principal private secretary's work. After I had been in the job a week or two, Andrew Patrick confessed to me, rather shiftily, that one of the six boxes was missing: no one in the Private Office knew where it was. When questioned, the Foreign Secretary had denied vehemently that he had it. Neither Andrew nor his colleague was convinced, given the chaotic fashion in which Robin Cook ran his life: they suggested that we mount a covert search of his official flat while he and Mrs Cook were away. I reluctantly agreed, the search went ahead, and we were even more alarmed when we found nothing. We didn't dare tell the Foreign Office Security Department, let alone a Permanent Under Secretary who often seemed to think that none of the private secretaries was up to the job of managing Robin Cook. But we needn't have worried: weeks later, when one of the desks in the Private Office had to be moved, the missing box emerged from one of the darker recesses of the outer office. We, not Robin Cook, had lost it.

Achieving a faster throughput of business was a joint effort by the whole Private Office team. The inner core consisted of me, as principal private secretary, two able young diplomats as assistant private secretaries, an irrepressible Geordie lady who took no prisoners as diary secretary, and, in the outer office, a team of high-powered secretaries and clerks. Beyond the Private Office proper, there were several other elements in the team providing the day-to-day support the Foreign Secretary needed. First came three politically appointed special advisers, Labour loyalists there to maintain links with supporters in the Party and beyond, and to ensure that policy advice and presentation took proper account of political sensitivities. Two of the special advisers sat in an office beyond the outer office. Following the policy disasters of Robin Cook's first two years, one had been squashed into the Private Office itself, as a sort of political commissar to keep an eye on what we civil servants were up to. Luckily, he was almost never there. Even more important than the special advisers were the officials handling Robin Cook's generally fractious relations with the usually hostile (or so he thought) British media. The man mainly in charge of this was John Williams, who had succeeded Alastair Campbell as political editor of the *Daily Mirror* and had been hired by Cook as the politically appointed 'deputy' head of News Department when the going had got especially rough. John was conscientious to a fault, and immensely hard working and loyal. But, like his boss, he had been badly bruised by the punishment the media had meted out to Robin Cook. Sometimes he seemed to worry more than the situation warranted. The infinitely patient real Head of News Department, Kim Darroch, found himself managing John as well as Cook, but did so with amused distinction.

Closely linked to the News Department team was a speechwriter, initially an exceptionally able young official, Matthew Gould, who moved on soon after I arrived. His replacement never really hit it off with Robin Cook, mainly because the Foreign Secretary, who was obsessively punctilious about personal hygiene, didn't like working with someone who smoked heavily, and smelt as though he did. Robin once asked me to speak to the official concerned, but I funked it. In the end, we did without a single official speechwriter, but at great cost in terms of diary management. Robin Cook always over-prepared his speeches, and now cleared great swathes of the diary in order to dictate and revise his speeches himself. I always thought that his speeches, particularly those in the Commons, were too good, too polished.

As a member of Parliament and as a minister, Robin Cook also had a more explicitly political support team with whom we had to deal. His Parliamentary Private Secretary was Ken Purchase, a no-nonsense traditional Labour MP from Wolverhampton, and a fount of political common sense. Cook didn't employ a full-time secretary in the Commons, and most of his constituency work seemed to be handled, rather erratically, either from home or from his constituency, the new town of Livingston outside Edinburgh. We didn't have much to do with his Constituency Agent, Jim Devine, who was later to succeed him as the member for Livingston before being embroiled in the expenses scandal in the run-up to the 2010 election. The Foreign Secretary would spend at least one long weekend a month in Scotland, and we would speak to him between engagements in his constituency.

But the Foreign Secretary's support team consisted of much more than policy and political people. Central to the whole operation were the Foreign Secretary's 'detectives', a group of seasoned personal protection officers provided by Scotland Yard, who took it in turns to accompany the Foreign Secretary at almost all times. One of them was supposed always to be with him, or within almost instant reach. They became our friends and allies in the difficult task of managing Robin Cook. They would tell us where he was, even though on more than one occasion, walking in Kent, he deliberately gave them the slip. They were there when he ran out of money and had to go to the cash machine in Pall Mall. They were there to deal with the drunken louts who accosted the Foreign Secretary when he ran out of milk at eleven o'clock at night and had to go to the Europa Food Store on Trafalgar Square. One of them would be there, at a corner table for one, when the Foreign Secretary and his new wife went out to dinner in a restaurant. Most important, one or more of the team always 'advanced' wherever we were heading, so that we knew what to expect. They were also our link to the 'bikes' of the Metropolitan Police Special Escort Group, whom they would whistle up if, as happened only too often, the Foreign Secretary was running late and needed speeding through the London traffic.* What the detectives had, which we didn't, was 'comms' – personal radios with earpieces that kept the team connected, wherever we were in the world. The detectives carried guns, and were required to requalify on the Metropolitan Police ranges at least once a year. But they never produced them, and most of them were manifestly not the crack shots they told the Private Office girls they were. Moreover, years of good living meant that one or two of the Foreign Secretary's detectives presented a larger target to terrorists than they should have done – but, as I reassured them, that also increased the size of the human shield they provided for the Foreign Secretary.

The detectives were especially kind to me when, after a black-tie dinner in the City, I left my briefcase in a taxi as I arrived home. I wasn't used to having a briefcase with me when wearing a dinner jacket. I soon realised what I had done and spent a sleepless night worrying what would happen, as my briefcase contained the Foreign Secretary's forward programme for weeks ahead, classified 'RESTRICTED'. There was nothing in it particularly damaging, but, in the wrong hands, it could have caused political embarrassment; and we would have had to swap certain engagements around, for security reasons. On arriving in the office, I went straight to the detectives. They took it calmly and got on to their colleagues in the Met. Within a day, they had found CCTV footage of me hailing a cab outside the Mansion House and of the same cab driving across Southwark Bridge and on south to my home in Balham. Infuriatingly, however, the footage wasn't clear enough to read the cab's registration number. But the episode gave me an insight into

---

* See my book *Cables from Kabul*, pp. 106–7, for a tribute to the Special Escort Group.

how much, even in 2000, Big Brother was watching us. And it ended happily when the taxi driver brought the briefcase back, of his own accord. Relief understated how I felt. To his credit, Robin Cook had merely grunted when I had confessed what I had done.

The detectives worked most closely with the Foreign Secretary's driver, Archie, an irrepressible Cockney from the Government Car Service, who did more than any other single member of the team to keep the show, literally, on the road. I don't know how many hours the driver and the detectives spent waiting outside the Foreign Secretary's official residence in Carlton Gardens for an almost invariably late Foreign Secretary to emerge, often in a foul mood. Or how many times they cheerfully accommodated last-minute changes of plan. For overseas visits, we were helped by the Foreign Office's Ministerial Visits Section – they went on ahead and made everything work with an apparently effortless efficiency that concealed much panicky paddling beneath the surface.

For the Foreign Secretary's home engagements, we could call on many different parts of the government machine for support. The group I most enjoyed dealing with was the Government Hospitality Fund. They always seemed able to provide, at short notice, delicious breakfasts, lunches and dinners, impeccably presented and served, with special printed menus referring to 'Her Majesty's Government *in* the United Kingdom'. Such official occasions were presided over by a Jeeves-like figure who rejoiced in the title of the Government Butler. Perhaps, reverting to medieval terminology, he should have been called the Great Steward of England.

Key to everything any minister does is one of the not-so-secret secrets of British government – 'Switch', otherwise known as the Downing Street switchboard. In a basement room beneath the Cabinet Office sit half a dozen or so of the most unobtrusively professional government operatives anywhere in the world – the ladies, now joined by one or two men, of the Downing Street switchboard. They keep a vast database of numbers, and pride themselves on being able to reach almost anybody the Prime Minister wants to speak to anywhere in the world at any time. They connect conference calls, patch together ministers and the officials listening in on the calls, and generally oil the business of government with a cheerful informality that disguises an extraordinarily efficient operation. Switch means that ministers need only one number – that of the Downing Street switchboard – to connect them to whom they want when they want. In my experience, the ladies of Switch never complain and hardly ever fail to find the person being sought. At the end of my time as principal private secretary, I went to visit them, to say thank-you for all they had done to make my job so much easier and more pleasant than it might otherwise have been. They were exactly as I had imagined them from their voices – although I hadn't quite expected that their room should also have been an informal shrine to the late Princess of Wales. Years later, working as special representative for Afghanistan, I would be patched through Switch to the then Foreign Secretary: they would recognise my voice without being told my name, ask politely how I was and then get on with connecting the call. No machine can ever replace what the ladies of Switch do for the good government of our United Kingdom.

Switch weren't responsible for one of the more amusing foul-ups in my time in Private Office, and would have seen it coming a mile off. One day, the Foreign Office switchboard put through to the Private Office a call from the President of Liberia, Charles Taylor, wanting to speak urgently to the Foreign Secretary on 'a matter of great sensitivity'. We fielded several calls from the gentleman, and tried unsuccessfully to have his *bona fides* checked. Eventually, we decided we had to ask Robin Cook how he wanted to play it. We were in the middle of excitements over Sierra Leone and 'blood diamonds', and Robin would have none of our reservations. 'I'll deal with him,' he said. 'Put President Taylor on.' We did, and listened in. A very African voice said the matter was so sensitive that he needed to speak to the Foreign Secretary on his personal mobile number: our hearts sank as Robin blithely gave the caller his number, known only to a few. 'President Taylor' then revealed that he would need the Foreign Secretary to transfer $25,000 to pay for a sensitive political operation: he would be back in touch later with the details of the bank account in Lagos to which the funds should be wired, as soon as possible. The small size of the sum 'President Taylor' was asking for gave the game away: the real President would have pitched his demand much higher. We had to get Robin Cook a new mobile phone number.

Very early in my time as principal private secretary, I decided that I should keep myself as free as possible from the daily grind of handling regular policy submissions to the Foreign Secretary, to focus on helping him get through the day, to allow myself time and space to cope with crises and, if possible, to think ahead. I did not therefore take direct responsibility for any of the Foreign Office's geographical or functional dossiers, but divided them between my two assistants. The only areas I explicitly reserved to myself were intelligence, plus, inevitably and often, crisis management. This left me free to concentrate on doing all I could to help the Foreign Secretary be in the right place at the right time, and then do and say the right thing once there. It also kept me free for the domestic chores that Robin Cook constantly foisted upon me. I would have to go with him to Fortnum's to help him choose a birthday card, or to Austin Reed to help decide on a new mac. Occasionally, I would have to walk his dogs when neither he nor Gaynor was available. Worst of all, he would ring me up from his official flat to complain that 'the effing builders' who were working on the neighbouring new office block in Carlton Gardens were disturbing him and Gaynor: could I please get them to quieten down? Sadly, such was public respect for Robin that, once I had found the foreman and passed on the Foreign Secretary's request, his men seemed to start hammering even harder, and drilling even more determinedly. In one of life's little ironies, they were building the office in which I now work.

I also decided that I had to keep myself fit, and cheerful, if the job wasn't to do to me what it had done to my predecessor. So I cycled from Balham to Westminster, and back again. I kept the specially supplied wardrobe in Private Office topped up with suits, shoes, shirts and a few ties. I aimed to arrive early enough to use the Foreign Secretary's private bathroom to change, comfortably before he got in. In its Victorian splendour, that bathroom is one of the less expected perks of being foreign secretary, with its views from the throne across the spires and towers of Whitehall. My cycling routine worked well, except on the few occasions when I failed to make sure that I had the right clothes in the right place. Once, to my horror, I arrived in the Foreign Office to find that all my black shoes were at home and I had nothing to put on my feet but the trainers in which I cycled. No one at the PUS's morning meeting believed me when I said that I was wearing my trainers (with a suit) on doctor's orders. Robin Cook didn't even notice, and wouldn't have cared.

One of my main tasks as the principal private secretary was to liaise with the other parts of government that interacted with the Foreign Secretary. Within the Foreign Office, this consisted mainly of the Permanent Under Secretary, and other senior officials, plus the team of junior ministers in the FCO. In both cases, my difficulty was that Robin was not much interested. Senior officials in the FCO tend subconsciously to believe that the Foreign Secretary's main job is to have meetings – known formally as Office Meetings – with them: they troop solemnly into his vast room, compete with each other in pronouncing on the subject of the meeting while keeping a close eye on which way the wind is blowing, and then troop out again. But Robin would have as little as possible of that. He didn't believe much in Office Meetings, preferring to ring (or summon) the startled young desk officer for, say, Iraq or Chile and ask him or her what they thought. Similarly with junior ministers: throughout my time working for him I tried to get Robin Cook to have reasonably regular meetings with his team of ministers in the Foreign Office. He would agree, reluctantly, and then cancel at the last minute. Once, memorably, he began a meeting with his whole ministerial team by announcing that he had been told to have a meeting with them, but had nothing himself to discuss with them: was there anything they wanted to raise?

One of the most difficult relationships that Cook had within the Foreign Office was with his Permanent Under Secretary. I didn't know (and didn't want to know) quite what had gone wrong, though somebody once told me that Robin had picked up indications that the Permanent Secretary had a low opinion of the Foreign Secretary's work rate. The Sandline affair had also had something to do with it. Partly, it was a matter of personality, and of like poles repelling: both the Foreign Secretary and the Permanent Secretary were highly intelligent, driven Scots, with a low tolerance for fools. I also suspect that Robin didn't like having an unusually courageous and exceptionally able senior official remind him of his shortcomings as foreign secretary. He may also have guessed – correctly – that his senior official adviser didn't really approve of him. Whatever the reason, I got caught in the middle. I would go downstairs to the PUS's daily meeting, in the office immediately below the Foreign Secretary's, to tell the assembled senior officials what (selectively) I sensed was on the Foreign Secretary's mind. For much of the time that was all the insight the Foreign Secretary's most senior advisers got. It was a wholly unsatisfactory situation. The Permanent Secretary accused me of blocking his access to the Secretary of State. In reality, I repeatedly told the Foreign Secretary that he had to see the Permanent Secretary regularly. All too often Robin Cook slithered out of attending the meeting, usually, infuriatingly and probably deliberately, at the very last minute. Once, I managed to lever the Permanent Secretary into the diary on a Monday morning, as the first engagement in the Office after the Foreign Secretary had been to the dentist. My reward was to have Robin storm in, shouting at me, 'Sherard, I cannot think of a worse way to start the week – the dentist followed by the PUS.' Every so often the PUS would invite the Foreign Secretary to lunch at the Garrick. Robin Cook would be away for hours, and return mid-afternoon in exuberant form, pledging undying friendship and co-operation with the PUS. But the next day hostilities would resume, and I would again find myself dodging the cross-fire.

The contrast with how the super-smooth Chief of the Secret Intelligence Service handled the Foreign Secretary could not have been sharper. At their meetings, Sir Richard Dearlove fed a grateful Foreign Secretary a carefully prepared diet of selected intelligence reports. He handled a potentially recalcitrant Secretary of State rather as an experienced SIS case officer might seduce a prickly agent, using all the charm and flattery at his command. Highly sensitive reports, some from Iraqi agents later discredited, were produced from secure pouches with a theatrical flourish, like pots of caviar. Occasionally, 'C' would invite the Foreign Secretary to breakfast at his official flat. I was lucky enough to go along and to witness the liturgy of the meal working its magic on a senior politician not known for his gullibility. One of the Sloane Rangers whom SIS still employed at that time would run up a delicious country-house breakfast, and pass it through the hatch to me:

my main job was not to take the note, but to serve the Chief and his ministerial guest with bacon and eggs, and toast and coffee.

Number 10 was the brightest star in our constellation of contacts beyond King Charles Street. I would speak to the Foreign Affairs Private Secretary there several times a day. Just occasionally I would talk to the Prime Minister's Chief of Staff, Jonathan Powell or, even more rarely, to the Prime Minister's Official Spokesman, Alastair Campbell. But mostly they were too grand to deal with me, and spoke to ministers direct. Certainly, the tone Alastair adopted even towards a Labour politician as senior as Robin Cook was one of impatient disdain. Jonathan Powell was a bit more polite. The Foreign Secretary's face-to-face meetings with the Prime Minister were surprisingly sporadic. They would see each other at the weekly Cabinet meeting, assuming the Foreign Secretary was in London, and hold bilateral meetings when diaries allowed. There were remarkably few formal Cabinet Committee meetings for them both to attend, though they did meet quite often with like-minded senior politicians of all parties to discuss the campaign to get Britain into the euro. I was never present when the Prime Minister and the Foreign Secretary met in London, but I did listen in to their phone conversations, and see them together abroad, notably at European Council meetings. What struck me most was the fawning tone that Robin Cook adopted, in talking not just to the Prime Minister but also to Jonathan Powell and Alastair Campbell. Patched in to the call, I could sense that the Prime Minister's mind was elsewhere as the Foreign Secretary told a bored Tony Blair heading out of London to Chequers for the weekend just how well his Foreign Secretary had done on one issue or another. The faint praise received in return wasn't damning, just insincere and slightly mocking. It was a bit the same at the briefing meetings convened in the Prime Minister's hotel suite on the first morning of European Council meetings. Robin Cook, wearing a suit and tie, accompanied by a bevy of senior officials and me, all similarly dressed, would trot along to the suite at the appointed early hour, to find the Prime Minister, clad only in boxer shorts, preening himself in front of his own small coterie. I didn't know where to look. Poor Robin would drone on about the issues, while Tony Blair, looking every inch a film star, paid little attention, wrapped up in his own thoughts. Ever the diligent pupil, Cook would have mastered all the detailed issues in the briefing pack. He could be relied on to ensure the British ministers at the table made the points they needed to make, when they had to. At one European Council, President Chirac spotted that Cook was getting up to go to the gents, leaving the Prime Minister on his own staring dreamily into space, blissfully unbothered by the folder of briefs in front of him. The wily old Chirac pounced, tabling language restricting the free trade in services that Britain wanted, knowing that he could get it through while Robin was out of the room. The Foreign Secretary had quite a shock when he returned.

Robin Cook's relations with other Cabinet ministers were mixed. He and the Chancellor were hardly on speaking terms. Twice, I worked with Gordon Brown's Private Secretary to try to effect a reconciliation. We arranged for the Chancellor to invite the Foreign Secretary across to Number 11 for a drink. Cook arrived, on time, to find that Gordon Brown was 'running late'. He was left on his own to drink whisky. After about half an hour, the Chancellor appeared and ordered a glass of water. A quarter of an hour later, an official put his head round the door and told the Chancellor that he was wanted elsewhere. The insult could hardly have been clearer. On another occasion, Robin decided to ask to dinner at 1 Carlton Gardens Gordon Brown and Sarah Macaulay (I can't remember whether it was before or after they married, in August 2000). Instead of having an informal kitchen supper in the flat upstairs, Robin decided, against my advice, to have the dinner in the state rooms downstairs, with silver and candles and hovering flunkeys. He judged that the wine first suggested by the Government Hospitality Fund to entertain the frugal Chancellor wasn't good enough and asked for something more expensive. Entirely predictably, Cook's extravagant effort to impress the Chancellor and his partner fell rather flat: the Government Butler told me later that the dinner had been an awkward affair, punctuated by long silences.

This difficult non-relationship with Gordon Brown also poisoned the Foreign Secretary's dealings with the Cabinet Minister who should have been closest to the Foreign Office – the Secretary of State in the newly independent Department for International Development. Clare Short was one of Gordon Brown's political allies. From where I sat, she seemed to wage unrelenting war on the Foreign Office and all its works. I don't remember the Foreign and International Development Secretaries having a single formal bilateral meeting in two years, though Robin Cook often reported that they had traded barbs at or in the margins of Cabinet. But Robin did get on, well, with his fellow Scot George Robertson, the canny Defence Secretary. They went through the Kosovo war together in early 1999, and kept in touch when Robertson moved to NATO as secretary general later that year. Robertson was succeeded at the MOD by Geoff Hoon, who had served as a junior minister in the Foreign Office under Cook: they had a straightforward relationship, though without the Scottish intensity of the Cook–Robertson link.

Robin Cook's relations with the wider Parliamentary Labour Party were more patchy – unnecessarily so, in my opinion. The main reason was that he couldn't be bothered to work the Commons tea room or bars in the ways that he should have done, no doubt because he didn't enjoy it. Nor would he use the Foreign Secretary's considerable resources to dispense hospitality and patronage: more than once I asked him why he didn't invite Labour MPs over to Carlton Gardens or down to the Foreign Secretary's country residence, Chevening, for drinks, or lunch, or dinner. But somehow he never had the time: I suspect that he didn't like what he saw as vapid socialising with lower forms of political life, and that in any case he didn't see how it could help him.

The House of Commons occasion for which Robin Cook made most effort was what we called Foreign Office 'TOPS' – the day, once a month, when the Foreign Office was top for Parliamentary Questions. We would get the questions a day or two in advance. Cook would go through them carefully, deciding which he wanted to answer himself – usually those that would reflect most political credit on him – and which he would farm out to his unfortunate junior ministers. There would follow hours and hours of intensive preparation, including a marathon session with special advisers and the press team present. Robin would dictate, and redictate, the draft answers to his questions, plus responses to possible supplementaries. On the day itself, the whole morning would be cleared, as he rehearsed in his room, with sandwiches being sent in. At about 2 p.m., he and I would drive across to the House: the rule for this three-minute journey was absolute silence. Even if I dared mention something which I thought he really needed to know before getting up in the House, he would snap at me: he was wound up like a coiled spring. Once in the Commons, he would hunker down in the foreign secretary's room, again in absolute silence, before slipping into the Chamber just before 2.30 p.m. I would clamber into the officials' box, up behind the Government front bench. And then the combat would begin. It was an unequal contest. The Shadow Foreign Secretary, Francis Maude, struggled to land a blow on a Robin Cook determined to concede nothing. In my view, Cook came across as too well prepared, too unforgiving, too self-satisfied, in short too cocky. It was all rather unedifying political theatre, all about Cook's standing, and left nobody very satisfied. The House of Commons may respect, but doesn't like, somebody who is too good, too cruel, too polished.

Despite the drubbing he got from the press, Robin Cook did make great efforts to cultivate certain key journalists, seldom with real success. Once he asked the proprietor of the *Telegraph* down to Chevening for lunch. Conrad Black arrived, in a Bentley I think, and sat at lunch flanked by his two faithful editors, Charles Moore for the daily paper, Dominic Lawson for the Sunday. Opposite him sat the Foreign Secretary, flanked by John Williams from the Foreign Office News Department and me. I came away thinking that Black had some eccentric neo-Churchillian ideas about the forces of good and evil in world history: much of the lunch was taken up with a strange but amicable debate on strategic missile defence. In the weeks that followed, we detected no real improvement in the *Telegraph* group's coverage of the Foreign Secretary. More humiliating were repeated efforts the Foreign Secretary made to recruit the *Sun*: listening in to an ingratiating call to the self-confessedly yobbish Editor, Dave Yelland, was an embarrassing experience.

One other constituency, instinctively more sympathetic to a foreign secretary committed to 'a foreign policy with an ethical dimension', was the world of think-tanks and NGOs. New Labour even went to the trouble of establishing its own centre-left Foreign Policy Centre, headed by the irrepressible Mark Leonard. He kept bobbing up with ideas for 'progressive' projects that, to my amusement, caused the Centre's patron, Robin Cook, to groan inwardly and to try to restrain him. It was bad enough, when, in the run-up to the 1999 Commonwealth Heads of Government Meeting, Leonard suggested a study on remodelling the Commonwealth that would have upset all the other CHOGM participants. But what really had to be stopped was a proposal that the FPC should work on 'modernising Islam'. Having a New Labour think-tank try to update the immutable word of God would not have played well with Labour's Muslim supporters in Britain, or with governments and populations across the Islamic world. The project was quickly shut down.

The Foreign Secretary's most enthusiastic fan club was overseas. With his fellow foreign ministers, Robin Cook was charm itself. All the prickliness that polluted his relations with his fellow Britons, in the press or in Parliament, disappeared when he dealt with foreigners. But it wasn't just a matter of charm. Whether it was the EU, NATO or the G7, or the Commonwealth, APEC or ASEAN, Cook dominated the forum he was operating in. He was better briefed, more agile, more focused on results, than any of his colleagues. They not only liked him – they respected him. In their meetings, foreign ministers often seemed reluctant to take a view until they knew 'what Robin thinks'. My first experience of what would today be called Cook's role as a 'thought leader' came when I was listening in to the conference calls on Kosovo between the five key Western foreign ministers several times each week in the early months of 1999. The senior participant was of course the US Secretary of State, Madeleine Albright. She would often start the conversation by reading through what sounded like a checklist of points to make. She would then become more hesitant, and more often than not it was Robin Cook who saved the day, suggesting positive and practical outcomes. On one occasion the conference call was punctuated by a piercing scream. Albright asked if everyone was all right. The German Foreign Minister, Joschka Fischer, piped up, apologetically: the scream had come from him, as Manchester United had scored a goal against Bayern Munich. Though neither Robin Cook nor I had realised it, the UEFA Champions League Final was taking place that night – 26 May 1999 – in Barcelona. Manchester United had won an historic victory by scoring two injury-time goals. Fischer had been focused more on the football final than on the next round of the Balkan wars.

Robin Cook and Madeleine Albright got on exceptionally well one on one. She took considerable risks with and for Cook, notably over Kosovo and over the Lockerbie bombing. Madeleine was known for her outsize brooches, often of great originality. Each Christmas, Robin gave her one to add to the collection. One year, with my wife's help, I found one, of a large lion, in a costume jewellery shop in the King's Road. Robin duly sent it to Madeleine, and we heard no more. Later Albright went to see President Hafez al-Assad of Syria, wearing the brooch. The sceptical old man was intrigued and flattered: how clever it was of the American Secretary of State to wear a lion brooch when meeting a man whose name meant 'lion'. As a grateful Albright told Robin Cook, such was the law of unintended consequences.

Cook also had a curiously warm relationship with the French Foreign Minister, the quiet but shrewd Hubert Védrine. The fact that neither spoke the other's language didn't seem to matter. Perhaps it even helped. There was a real rapport, personally as well as in terms of policy. I used to call them 'le couple improbable'. At times it seemed almost like a platonic love affair, especially when, in a fit of enthusiasm, Robin told me that he was going to learn French in order to speak to 'Hubert' in his own language. At my request, one of the Diplomatic Service Language Centre's magnificently French language instructors duly appeared in the Private Office. But the prospective pupil had no idea that one hour of desultory French conversation every three or four weeks would never equip him to converse with Védrine in any serious way. As with so many of Robin's good intentions, this one too faded away in the face of the almost impossible pressures on the Foreign Secretary's time.

The American and French foreign ministers were Robin Cook's special favourites among his colleagues. But he had good relations with all the others. I wondered whether he had a secret crush on the Swedish Foreign Minister, the beautiful and able Anna Lindh, who was tragically assassinated in September 2003. Certainly, whenever he was dealing with her, he seemed to go all goofy, rather like Basil Fawlty in the episode when the beautiful blonde Australian woman comes to stay at the hotel. But it was the Danish not the Swedish Foreign Minister to whom Cook was speaking one weekend from his new flat in Edinburgh, where he was struggling to assemble furniture from IKEA. In some annoyance, Cook told the Dane that he was having difficulty with his 'flat-pack furniture'. It was soon obvious that 'vlat pag vurniture' wasn't in the Dane's vocabulary or experience: he sounded completely mystified as a breathless Robin Cook told him he had been wrestling with an Allen key. I couldn't help recalling Alan Clark's snobbish reference in his diary to Michael Heseltine's need to buy his own furniture. By 1999 things had come to such a pass that the Foreign Secretary had not only to buy his own furniture, but also to assemble it.

The much married veteran German Foreign Minister, Joschka Fischer, was a natural ally, though Robin Cook found some of his views perhaps a shade too Green. Robin was greatly amused to discover, when we met Fischer in Bonn, that the museum of German history near by had on show the pair of trainers Fischer had worn when he had first entered the Bundestag as a young Green MP.

After the disastrous visit to India with the Queen in August 1997, Cook made great efforts to restore his position in that country. The supremely tactful Assistant Private Secretary, Andrew Patrick, spent months patiently planning a return visit. We carefully cultivated the Indian Foreign Minister, Jaswant Singh, to whom we sent the occasional case of the fine claret that he loved. During the visit, Singh was to act as a kind of political human shield for Cook, in case of upsets. Singh was kind enough to invite the Foreign Secretary, accompanied by me, to spend a day or so with him in Rajasthan, visiting Jodhpur. There we met the Maharajah and his elegant son, duly clad in the ineffably elegant eponymous trousers. We were lucky that the unfortunate outfit, including a bizarre sun hat, that the Foreign Secretary chose for our day out with the impeccably attired Indian nabobs did not catch the attention of the British press. The whole visit was full of tension, as Cook worried about avoiding the disasters of the previous visit. In his anxiety, he took against the new British High Commissioner for arranging a meeting with a senior Indian official immediately after our arrival in Delhi (the only time the Indian, who was about to travel abroad, could manage). On one motorcade through the imperial capital, I happened to be sitting next to the Foreign Secretary, deep in his brief. He glanced up and commented gracelessly: 'Oh, it's you, Sherard. If I had known, I would have spoken earlier. But I thought it was the High Commissioner.'

Israel was another sensitive spot for Cook. Here too he was anxious to repair the relationship, and to pay another, more successful visit to Israel once the time was right. In this he was again helped by a sympathetic Foreign Minister, the notably moderate Professor Shlomo Ben-Ami. One weekend, while giving my son a driving lesson, I was listening in on my mobile phone to a conversation between Cook and Ben-Ami. At a junction, my son jerked forward, my finger slipped and released the Mute button and I yelled, 'Change down, you fool!' The Foreign Secretary's response was simply 'Get off the bloody line, Sherard!'

Just as in working up his approach to India, Robin Cook had relied heavily on the advice of Lord (Swraj) Paul, so, in dealing with Israel, he worked closely with Lord (Michael) Levy, Tony Blair's chief fund-raiser and special envoy to the Middle East. Michael worked tirelessly to ensure that the second visit, in October 1999, went without a serious hitch. Michael was very much part of the life of the Private Office. But I got to know him properly only when I became ambassador to Israel. I had first become aware of him when my boss in Paris, Michael Jay, had reported on a visit by Lord Levy to the Embassy there, soon after Labour had taken power. Before turning to supporting politicians, Michael had been one of the most successful charity fund-raisers ever, having collected millions of pounds for Jewish Care and other worthy causes. What made him unusual was the way he combined huge energy and ego with a deep religiosity drawn from his roots in north-east London. On Israel and Palestine, he took a courageously moderate view, which did not endear him either to right-wing Israelis or to some of the more conservative elements in the Jewish community in Britain. What struck us in Private Office was his tireless networking with senior government figures, from the Prime Minister down, and across the establishment. In those early years of the Blair Government, Michael seemed to know everyone who mattered. And, as far as we were concerned, he put that knowledge to good use, offering constant support and kindness to Robin Cook and his new wife. Whatever one thought of Michael Levy, one could only be impressed by his generosity of spirit. His basic humanity came through on his first visit – with Robin – to a refugee camp in Gaza: Michael was almost physically sick at what he saw, of people whose families had been cooped up there since 1948.

That visit to Israel in October 1999 broke a taboo for Robin Cook, which enabled him to return to the Middle East again, much more confident of his position with both sides. We went back to Israel a year later, in the run-up to the Biarritz European Council in October 2000, and shuttled round the region in an RAF VC10 in order to generate support for the peace deal that President Clinton had been trying, at Camp David in July 2000, to broker with the Israeli Prime Minister, Ehud Barak, and with the veteran Palestinian leader, Yasser Arafat. Despite the sense of hope at the political level, in the West Bank, Gaza and the Arab areas of Israel tensions between Jews and Arabs were rising. On 28 September 2000, the leader of the Israeli opposition, Ariel Sharon, had visited the Temple Mount in Jerusalem, escorted by hundreds of Israeli police. As the site of the Dome of the Rock and of the Al-Aqsa mosque, the Temple Mount is one of the holiest places in Islam. Sharon's deliberately provocative act set off the second *intifada*. On 12 October, two Israeli Army reservists were lynched in the main West Bank city of Ramallah. We flew straight from the Middle East to Biarritz, to report on what still looked like hopeful prospects. Thanks in large part to Robin Cook's efforts, the European Union stood ready to underwrite an Arab–Israel peace to the tune of billions of dollars: it was a real tragedy that the effort fell at the last fence, at Taba in January 2001, just as Clinton left office.

It was on one of those trips to the Middle East, this time for a European–African summit in Cairo, that Robin Cook had his only encounter with Qadhafi. The Libyan leader's speech and manner, not to mention his dress and his mad staring eyes, made it difficult to believe that he was on the same planet as we were: I assumed that he must have been on some substance or another, but perhaps it was just personality. Sensing trouble, the Foreign Secretary wisely decided to have as little contact as possible with the man whom Sadat had called the 'mad boy'. But the sight of a wary Robin Cook, small in stature, alongside the larger than life comic figure of Qadhafi in turban and flowing robes is one of the treasured memories of my time in the Private Office. In Cairo, as elsewhere, I used to help the detectives and other members of the Private Office team with informal language lessons. This led to one of our favourite close protection officers, the veteran Detective Constable Richard Restorick, telling an Egyptian police major, in Arabic (coached by me, but without Dick knowing what he was saying), that he loved the major. To Dick's surprise and embarrassment, the Egyptian police major swung back round towards Dick and, looking him meaningfully in the eye, told him, in romantically husky English, 'Dick, I love you very much too.' Dick quickly withdrew: it wasn't what he had meant at all. To my regret (but not surprise), Dick never took another language lesson from me again.

The detectives were not short in humour when the opportunity arose. One weekend in late July 1999, the Resident Clerk at the Foreign Office rang to say that King Hassan of Morocco had died. His funeral would be held within a day or at most two, in accordance with Muslim tradition. We needed to send a senior British delegation, including a minister and, most important, a member of the royal family. After several hours of difficult negotiations, the Prince of Wales and Foreign Secretary were persuaded to go, and I went along with Robin Cook. We flew in a BAE 146 of 32 (the Royal) Squadron – the unit formerly known as the Queen's Flight. With its four engines, and low noise profile, the 146 is a wonderful aircraft for short-haul operations. But it could not get to Morocco and back without refuelling. The outward journey went fine, but we had a premonition of trouble ahead when we arrived over Rabat and found that there was a queue of VVIP aircraft circling ahead of us waiting to land, as every Muslim leader and many others converged on the city. The RAF crew told us that the German President's aircraft had already been circling for four hours. We couldn't stay up that long without refuelling, so we diverted to Casablanca. On landing there, I peered out of the window to discover that the city's Governor had turned out, with a brass band, to greet the Prince of Wales and the Foreign Secretary, and to offer them tea while the aircraft was refuelled. Prince Charles was reluctant to disembark, so it was left to a grumpy Robin Cook to descend, inspect the guard of honour and sit with the Governor, with me in attendance. I dissolved into uncontrollable giggles at the sight of Robin, in a crumpled shirt and chinos, his face like thunder, being forced to strut up and down in front of the saluting soldiers, beside a Governor clad in a fez, hooded burnous and curly-toed slippers. A small band in Ruritanian uniforms thumped and squeaked their way through some tuneless paramilitary melodies.

But worse was to come. When we reached Rabat, we discovered that the funeral itself was completely disorganised. In the burning sun, we found ourselves plunging into a heaving crowd, several thousand strong. I spotted President Clinton, surrounded by his Secret Service detail, sweating heavily. Chirac emerged later. I was lugging with me a couple of the Foreign Secretary's red-leather despatch boxes, in which I had secreted, at Robin Cook's request, his unfortunate sun hat. At one point, I had to stand on a box, to see over the crowd and find our way. As we pushed through the mass of heaving VIPs, the Prince of Wales remarked, rather languidly and to no one in particular, 'This is the most frightful chaos. Who organised it?' Without missing a beat, the rather superior royal detective drawled in reply, 'Robin Cook, Sir, Robin Cook.' I turned to see a furious Foreign Secretary jumping up and down on the spot. The whole unhappy expedition was capped when on the way back we stopped in Portugal to refuel, and the local authorities refused the RAF's credit card. A further delay followed as we scrambled to assemble the necessary cash.

Nearly a year later, in June 2000, the Foreign Secretary and I found ourselves once again travelling to the Middle East in a Royal Squadron 146 for the obsequies of another Arab leader, those of President Hafez al-Assad of Syria, the father of Bashar. This time we had to stop twice on the way out, and twice on the way back, to refuel, underlining the British Government's lamentable failure to equip itself with proper VVIP aircraft. We missed the funeral itself, but paid a condolence call on a young and rather nervous new President. After opening courtesies, Bashar asked all his advisers to leave the room. Alone, he then gave the Foreign Secretary a persuasive account of the difficulties he faced in convincing some of the hard men of the regime to change. He pledged that he would do what he could to work for peace and reform. But he needed us to be patient. Assad sounded sincere. He may well have meant what he said at the time.

In those days, we relied on the RAF for most of our overseas travel. For short hops in Europe, or around the UK, we would travel in an HS125 executive jet, which seated only three or four in comfort, with the rest of the team squashed along a bench seat in the back. The 146 was much more spacious, with two large cabins, tables and, best of all, a galley, from which the RAF stewards would produce the kind of deliciously unhealthy military cuisine which both Robin Cook and I loved: huge ham sandwiches, bacon and eggs, meat and two veg. The best moment was halfway through the flight: the steward would appear with a little printed piece of paper on which the weather conditions at our destination were inscribed. It must have been what was done for their most senior royal passenger. For longer trips, we were still able to draw on the ancient VC10s of 101 Squadron of the Royal Air Force. These were really meant to be tankers and troop carriers, but, at government request (and expense), could be put into a special VIP fit. That really was the way to travel. As we landed, the pilot would push a small Union flag out of a little hatch in the top of the cockpit. I imagined us back in the days of Sir Alec Douglas-Home as foreign secretary, circling the globe in a VC10, with Lady Home always a pace behind him as he descended the steps whispering 'Moscow, Alec, Moscow,' just in case the Secretary of State forgot where he was, as apparently he sometimes did.

But while we liked the RAF I am not sure the RAF liked us. They found Robin Cook a difficult passenger. He was almost always late for departure, usually from Northolt, which set the pilots off on the wrong foot. But what they really disliked, to the extent of making an official complaint, was the Foreign Secretary's habit of remaining on the aircraft after we had landed, in order to finish his box. The reason for this was that, when he wanted to sleep on any air journey, Robin Cook would pick up the folder of papers I had put in front of him. With a wink at me, he would say that he was going to read the briefs. Within seconds, he would be asleep, and would wake up only as we came into land. Being a conscientious minister, who always made sure he was properly prepared, he insisted on going through the rest of the paperwork before leaving the aircraft. The RAF crew hated being kept waiting, especially when we had arrived back at Northolt and they wanted to get home.

The midnight stroke: 30 June 1997. The handover ceremony, in the Hong Kong Convention Centre, with Hong Kong's last Governor sandwiched between the Chief of the Defence Staff, General Sir Charles Guthrie, and the Foreign Secretary, Robin Cook. On the podium behind Tony Blair is Mrs Thatcher, and I am two rows behind her husband Denis.

The Gatehouse of the British Embassy in Paris, with our faithful Peugeot people carrier in front, and the Rue du Faubourg St Honoré outside the great green gates, beneath the Union flag.

With Alastair Campbell hot on his heels, Tony Blair lands in Paris as part of a tour of European capitals during the British Presidency of the European Union, in the first half of 1998.

Gnome Secretary: at the informal meeting of EU foreign ministers in the Azores in May 2000, Robin Cook sports the local headdress, blissfully unaware of the headline that awaits him. To the left are the German and Austrian Foreign Ministers, Joschka Fischer and Benita Ferrero-Waldner.

Travelling with the Foreign Secretary: en route to a meeting in India, with my special hardback private secretary's notebook in hand. We kept the notebooks when full, just in case we ever needed to check a record. The Foreign Secretary's chief detective follows behind, with a British diplomat beside us.

On almost every outing I took one or more red despatch boxes, full of papers for the Foreign Secretary to process. But on this occasion – the funeral of King Hassan of Morocco in July 1999 – one of the boxes concealed the Foreign Secretary's sun hat.

The standard issue official photograph that Robin Cook gave me when I left his Private Office (and he left the Foreign Office) in June 2001. Mainly because of his hectic lifestyle, he wasn't good at giving presents, but he did show his appreciation in other ways, for example by filling my annual appraisal form with compliments, some of which ('Sherard is a natural sub-editor') were unintentionally two-edged.

To Sherard, With Many Thanks! Robin Cook

to Amb. Cowper-Coles. With best Wishes,

President's House, Jerusalem, 6 September 2001: just after making a few remarks in uneven (and therefore apparently amusing) Hebrew, I hand President Moshe Katsav my letter of credence from the Queen.

With an affectionate rabbi, visiting a religious boys' home in northern Israel. Israel's more traditional communities seemed to react exceptionally positively to unexpected overtures from an ambassador who spoke some Hebrew.

In Jerusalem, July 2003: in my last week in Israel, I donated an ambulance to the Magen David Adom (Red Shield of David) on behalf of the British Jews who had funded it. Sadly, like so much else, Israel's ambulance service is divided, with the Magen David Adom for Jews and the Red Crescent for Muslims.

Preparing for war, February 2003: as the US/UK attack on Iraq neared, British Embassies in the Middle East were reduced to skeleton staffing, with dependants sent back to Britain. In the Residence garden, the Embassy core team practised donning our charcoal-lined chemical biological warfare suits. I am in the front row, with my Defence Attaché, Colonel Tom Fitzalan Howard, to my right, and the Air Attaché, Wing Commander Steve Cummings, to my left.

Dinner in the desert, spring 2004: Crown Prince Abdullah of Saudi Arabia escorts the Prince of Wales to dinner in a tent at his desert encampment. Abdullah showed an avuncular affection for Prince Charles, who reciprocated with understanding rather than prejudice.

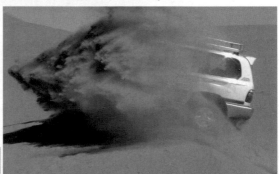

Dune-bashing: driven by an overenthusiastic visitor, my Land Cruiser crests a dune, in the desert near Riyadh. The bedu say that the Toyota is best for desert travel. Crossing soft sand means letting the tyres down.

In the Empty Quarter, Easter 2005: one of the aspects of Saudi Arabia that the whole family enjoyed most were the expeditions that we mounted across the deserts of Arabia with friends. On this occasion, we circled through the great sand sea in the south-eastern corner of the peninsula. My bodyguards' pick-up trucks can just be seen at the end of the convoy.

Camels: tens of thousands of camels still roam the deserts of Saudi Arabia. One of the largest and most expert breeders is Prince Misha'al bin Abdul Aziz, who invited me to his farm near Riyadh to see his herd.

100 degrees in the shade: for much of the year, Riyadh has a near-perfect climate – hot, but not humid like Jeddah or the Eastern Province. Only in the middle of summer does it become almost unbearably hot.

Tony Blair visited Saudi Arabia in early July 2005, four days before 7/7, on his way to lobby at the Singapore Olympic meeting for the 2012 Games to come to London. I seem to be whispering to Jonathan Powell about the princes on Crown Prince Abdullah's supporters' bench, opposite us, and out of shot.

Gordon Brown's visit, November 2005: holding one of our falcons was almost obligatory for visitors from London. The Chancellor's adviser, Jon Cunliffe, looks on anxiously as his boss (more nervous than he appears) performs for the camera.

In June 2009, as Special Representative for Afghanistan and Pakistan, I was invited by the Royal Air Force to speak about Afghanistan to the officers of No 1 Group, at RAF Coningsby. The unexpected reward was a superlative flight in a Typhoon over Lincolnshire, Yorkshire and the North Sea, which was almost as good as seeing a Spitfire of the Battle of Britain Memorial Flight come into land.

For some special overseas visits, involving the Queen or the Prime Minister, the Government would charter an aircraft from British Airways. In November 1999, the Commonwealth Heads of Government Meeting was held in Durban. Such meetings are traditionally opened by the Queen, and, on this occasion, it was decided that Her Majesty would pay a Commonwealth visit to Ghana and a state visit to South Africa itself, en route to Durban. The Foreign Secretary was to be Minister in attendance. The Queen and her party occupied the First Class cabin at the front of the aircraft, the Foreign Secretary and his party the Club World cabin in the middle, and the support staff and others the back of the plane.

Both visits passed off smoothly enough, although there were some minor hiccups in Ghana. As we flew south across Africa, the Queen's Page appeared in the Club World cabin with a silver salver, on which was a copy of the *Racing Post*. The Page said simply to the Secretary of State, 'Her Majesty thought that the Foreign Secretary might be interested in seeing this' – which indeed he was. The state visit to South Africa was short and sweet, with formal elements in Pretoria, during which the Queen met President Mbeki as well as Nelson Mandela, followed by a visit to some of the tougher townships around Johannesburg, before moving down to the sub-tropical humidity of Durban for the Commonwealth Meeting.

The Queen's gesture in passing on to her Foreign Secretary her copy of the racing paper pointed to a side of Robin Cook of which I had known virtually nothing before I started to work for him. I must have been vaguely aware that he had once written a racing column for the *Glasgow Herald*. But I had not begun to realise that his love of horses, and of the country, went far beyond doing business with his turf accountant. Even so, he liked nothing better than to go down to the paddock before a race – preferably National Hunt (that is, over jumps) – to pick a winner. He once told me proudly what a good eye he had for horses. Robin's best friend was the eccentric tipster John McCririck, with his huge sideburns and Old Harrovian bow tie, whom he used to invite to stay at Chevening. The only way I could get a reluctant Robin Cook to visit GCHQ at Cheltenham was to combine a visit there with the National Hunt Festival. Once the Queen Mother invited the Foreign

Secretary racing on a day when he had been due to visit his constituency. The Livingston Labour Party were told that urgent government
business had detained the Foreign Secretary in the south. They weren't
pleased when they saw television pictures of their Member of Parliament
standing with the Queen Mother at Sandown.

Both Robin and Gaynor Cook really enjoyed their country weekends
at Chevening – the beautiful house and estate near Sevenoaks left to the
nation by Lord Stanhope. There they would go for long walks along the
North Downs, or across the Weald, or he would visit a local livery stable
and go for a hack on a hired horse. Robin loved nature, but he wasn't
sentimental about it. Once he spotted a fox in the long grass at Northolt
RAF Station, and he told the driver to stop the car while we sat and
watched the fox work its way boldly across the airfield. On another
occasion, he was on the phone from the Foreign Secretary's official residence in Carlton Gardens, to me in the Foreign Office, when he spotted
a fox in the garden below. 'Shoot it, Secretary of State,' I joked. He
affected to be shocked, as a foxhunting man who would never ever
shoot a fox. He was unhappy about Labour Party efforts to ban hunting, and courageously refused to vote in favour.

One day, Robin came into the office and told me proudly that he had
decided to buy a dog. Thinking of the way Peter Mandelson had used a
Golden Retriever to soften his image, I hoped that perhaps the Cooks
would buy a Yellow Labrador or something similarly warm and cuddly,
with one eye on the media reaction. I had always dreamed of Robin
giving an interview to *Country Life* or *Horse and Hound*, as part of an
effort to reach parts of the British people who would, I hoped, have
been favourably surprised when they learned that the socialist Foreign
Secretary was more of a countryman than most of them. But it never
happened. To my disappointment, he bought not one but two dogs that
were small, Scottish, bearded and aggressive: rather like their owner, as
one of my colleagues was quick to point out. This pair of Scottish
Terriers became the bane of our lives. They attacked an American tourist in St James's Park: luckily, our apology did the trick, before the incident hit the media. To the horror of the staff at Carlton Gardens, Robin
put some artificial turf on the balcony for the terriers to use as an
outdoor lavatory. The smell was appalling. Nor were the dogs, named

after malt whiskies, welcome in the house at Chevening. I remember the rather snobby staff there looking on with distaste as the Foreign Secretary, clad in an unappealing nylon shell suit, tried in vain to stop his dogs chewing the legs of Lord Stanhope's priceless antique chairs. When I had to walk them, I felt very self-conscious, parading round St James's Park with two semi-feral Scotties on infuriatingly extendable leashes.

Robin Cook's relationship with Tony Blair was warily respectful rather than close. He must have known that it had taken some political courage – and confidence – for the Prime Minister to have stuck with his Foreign Secretary after the disasters, personal and professional, of his first year in office. Privately, Cook was dismissive of the 'third way' and much of the hot air associated with Blairite triangulation. What he did share with Tony Blair (at least in Blair's early years) was the belief that Britain's future lay in Europe. He worked immensely hard to generate support for the UK joining the euro, and was pleased and proud when he was elected president of the Party of European Socialists – the pan-European centre-left grouping. Even back then, he was unhappy with some of Blair's enthusiasm for the use of force, and his apparent belief that the end might justify the means. The Foreign Secretary was not properly consulted on the Prime Minister's speech in Chicago in April 1999, which set out a new doctrine of interventionism – subject to conditions. Even if those conditions were difficult to criticise, Cook confided in me, presciently, that he didn't like the tone. Sometimes, he said, Tony was just a bit too cavalier about the rule of law.

The other area where Robin Cook – ever the diligent scholar anxious to come top of the class – faulted the Prime Minister was over the latter's poor record in delivering tough or detailed messages. Whenever we flew together to European meetings, the contrast between the Foreign Secretary, conscientiously going through the briefs and writing out his own speaking notes, and the Prime Minister, gazing dreamily out of the window or gossiping about football with Alastair Campbell, was striking: of course, some of Cook's diligence was done for effect, to impress his master, but not all of it. Whereas the Foreign Secretary often came across as over-prepared, the Prime Minister sometimes seemed dangerously under-prepared. But Blair was a consummate actor, capable of entering a room, sensing what his audience needed to hear and then saying it, ad lib. He had no need of a dreary Foreign Office script. As one wag remarked, it was like Clinton without the sex. What worried Cook more than Blair's lack of interest in detail, however, was his reluctance to tell his interlocutors what they didn't want to hear. Time and again Robin would clear letters of advice from the Foreign Office to Number 10, in which the Foreign Secretary formally proposed detailed – and often difficult – points for the Prime Minister to make to Clinton, Chirac, Sharon or whichever world leader Blair was seeing next: and time and again Number 10's official record would come back suggesting that the only points the Prime Minister had made had been very general indeed. In despair, I once asked Cook why he thought the Prime Minister never seemed to pay much attention to Foreign Office briefs. 'Sherard,' he replied, rather wistfully, 'you just don't understand. Tony didn't get where he is today by ever telling anybody anything they didn't want to hear.'

Apart from the Private Office's constant contacts with our opposite numbers in Downing Street, our main intermediary with Number 10 was Michael Levy. He would constantly volunteer to Robin Cook what 'Tony' thought of the Foreign Secretary's performance. As the Government entered its fourth year, and the prospect of an election grew, Michael claimed to be working hard, and successfully, with Number 10 to secure Cook's reappointment as foreign secretary after the election. He would relay all sorts of delicious gossip about who was up and down, though how reliable it was I at least could never tell. What mattered was that Michael Levy was genuinely on Cook's side.

One of the privileges of being private secretary is that one has a better view than most senior officers of the jobs that are coming up. I had applied to be ambassador to Israel, starting in the late summer of 2001, and had been successful. On the assumption that he would be continuing as foreign secretary after the election, Robin had agreed that I could leave, to start Hebrew language training, immediately after the election. After interviews, he had chosen my successor. All seemed set. Occasionally, Robin would reflect on his plans for after the election. He was not convinced that the FCO's in-house candidate as the next permanent under secretary was the right one: he would want to consider a more independent-minded individual, who would offer the Foreign Secretary robustly objective advice.

A day or two before the general election on 7 June 2001 Michael Levy came on the phone to tell Robin Cook that Tony had once again assured him that Robin would stay on as foreign secretary. On the day after the election, Friday 8 June, I thought as the hours passed that I detected a certain shiftiness – perhaps a growing distance – in my conversations with Number 10, perhaps especially following the Prime Minister's return to Downing Street from his constituency in the north. Some time in mid-afternoon, the message came that the Prime Minister was ready to see the Foreign Secretary. With a detective and me in tow, Robin Cook set off jauntily from the Ambassadors' Entrance at the back of the Foreign Office, up the steps to Downing Street, past the pen of photographers and, with the detective, in through the famous front door. I hung about in the street, expecting him to be in and out in ten minutes. After about twenty minutes, I got a panicky call from the detective: 'Something's wrong, Sherard. The Foreign Secretary has left via the garden entrance of Number 10 and is already back in the Foreign Office.' I hurried back and up into the Private Office. The team there had heard the Foreign Secretary rush back in through the side door, but hadn't dared disturb him. Tentatively, I pushed open the great oak door and peered round. Poor Robin Cook was slumped deep in one of the ancient red-leather armchairs, slurping a glass of the brandy he kept hidden, for emergencies, in the cupboard behind his desk. 'Come in, Sherard,' he moaned. 'Tony's sacked me. I don't know what to do. I don't know what to do.' I sat down beside him. Slowly, he told me about his interview with the Prime Minister. After the assurances from Michael Levy, his dismissal had come as a thunderbolt. Tony Blair had given no reason, but had been firm. He had said that, if Robin wanted to stay in the Government, he could be leader of the House of Commons. We talked for a bit, and then I left him to make some calls – to Gaynor, to close political allies such as Jim Devine. He departed for Carlton Gardens shortly afterwards, saying that he would probably, but not certainly, accept the Prime Minister's offer of the leadership of the House.

Shortly afterwards, Number 10 phoned to say that an equally surprised Jack Straw, who had been preparing to become transport secretary, had been appointed foreign secretary. I spoke to him later, at his home in Stockwell. I explained that I was due to start language training for my next job the following Monday, and hoped that, once he had met Robin Cook's appointee as his private secretary, he would agree to take him on. Straw could not have been more accommodating. He would come over to the Foreign Office the following morning – a Saturday – meet my designated successor and, he hoped, release me. He would also start the process of briefing himself for his new job.

And so it happened. After a Saturday morning of briefing Jack Straw, and handing over to my successor, I was free to start my Hebrew training the following day. I saw Robin Cook only three times again. A week or so later he came back into the Foreign Secretary's room in the Foreign Office for a farewell party. With typical tact and generosity, Straw made the office available and absented himself from the building. As usual with such occasions, it was done on the cheap – peanuts, Pringles and cheap plonk from Tesco. That couldn't have mattered less to Robin Cook. But what I found so sad (and I expect he would have done so too, though he would never have said so) was the sense that the officials present regarded his reappearance in the Foreign Office as an embarrassing resurrection of someone who was, for them, already politically dead and buried. They had never really taken to angular, awkward Robin Cook, who did his own thing, without much time for the self-regarding equivocations of some senior Foreign Office functionaries. These officials, who a week earlier had been only too eager to please Cook as foreign secretary and would have been now, had he still been their secretary of state, hung back, preferring to chat among themselves: there was no upside in being spotted being too close or too nice to the deposed minister. They had already moved on, adjusting to a secretary of state much more to their taste, much better at being foreign secretary, not so good perhaps at doing things with his high office. Having Cook as secretary of state had been a roller-coaster ride for the entire Diplomatic Service. No one – not the Permanent Under Secretary, not one of the deputy secretaries – came forward to 'say a few words', to wish Robin Cook well. Eventually, I thought I had better propose his health, as nobody more senior would. I had no hesitation in praising a record of principled achievement unmatched by any modern foreign secretary, while glossing over the tough times we had all had at his hands. Only one official said anything to me about my remarks – Kim Darroch, who became David Cameron's second national security adviser, and who sent a much appreciated message saying that I had done and said the decent thing.

A week or two later, Robin and Gaynor Cook gave Bridget and me dinner in one of his favourite Italian restaurants, in Covent Garden. It was a jolly evening: he bore the burden of his new office much more lightly. After that, I saw him only once again, for a quick drink in his Parliamentary office in the spring of 2005. He had already been on the back benches for a couple of years, following his resignation on the eve of the invasion of Iraq. I told him how much, sitting in Israel, I had admired his resignation speech. He was cheerful and relaxed, and took a certain grim pleasure in having been proved right by the failure to find the weapons of mass destruction (which he had correctly predicted Saddam didn't have) and by the unfolding horrors of the American occupation of Iraq. He was full of ideas for the future. I was completely devastated when I heard, in Riyadh a few months later, that he had died while hiking with Gaynor on a Scottish mountainside. But I took consolation in knowing that he had gone, quickly and painlessly, doing what he liked best – walking the hills of his Highlands, accompanied by the woman he loved.

Had Robin Cook lived, Gordon Brown told me, when visiting Riyadh as chancellor of the Exchequer shortly after Robin's death, he would almost certainly have returned to the Cabinet in a Brown administration. But, in the broader balance of history, Robin had quit while he was ahead, morally as well as politically.

Of all the memories from my time with Robin Cook, my favourite concerns the occasion he stood in for the Prime Minister, Tony Blair, at a major conference on European security in Istanbul in the autumn of 2000. Robin was always proud to be at the top table, and especially so if he was representing the boss. He was not, however, a morning person, especially before he had to make a major speech. His grumpiness was increased if over-eager private secretaries tried to burden him with unnecessary information.

On the morning of the conference, the two main British tabloids both splashed one story, apparently leaked to them as an exclusive by different people in Number 10: that Mrs Blair was pregnant, and that Tony Blair would be the first British Prime Minister for 150 years to have fathered a child while in office (or at least to have acknowledged that he had done so). The whole world woke up to this news. At the conference in Istanbul as elsewhere, the political chatter was of little else.

But, knowing that Robin Cook would have been made even grumpier by this news of another Blair coup de théâtre, I decided to make no mention of it to the Foreign Secretary. He went into the conference chamber metaphorically naked. The first person he met was the Taoiseach, the Irish Prime Minister Bertie Ahern, full of bonhomie. 'This is wonderful news about Tony,' said Bertie. 'Please give Tony my warmest congratulations.' Poor Robin Cook wondered what the Taoiseach was on about. After a moment's reflection, he guessed that there must have been another breakthrough in the long-running Northern Ireland peace process. 'Bertie, of course I will give Tony your congratulations,' Robin replied. 'But you do realise that this took Tony three years of hard work.'

Ahern's reaction is not recorded. But a few minutes later the Foreign Secretary came storming out of the conference chamber. 'Sherard, why didn't you tell me Cherie was pregnant?' I said that, probably mistakenly, I had regarded it as Too Much Information. Cook grinned. And months later, when I was trying to encourage him to soften his image, he told the story at the *Spectator* Parliamentarian of the Year ceremony.

This chapter has been about how Robin Cook went about *being* foreign secretary, not what he *did* with the job. When historians start properly to examine his four years at the Foreign Office, he will go down as one of the better foreign secretaries in recent British history. His record of achievement is remarkable. From Kosovo, through Sierra Leone, East Timor, Lockerbie, the International Criminal Court, the ban on land mines, to proper controls on arms exports and much else, he really did deliver what he promised: a foreign policy with an ethical dimension. Moreover, despite his productive professional relationship with Mrs Albright, he understood that in foreign and security policy Britain has to work closely with France, above all, but also with Germany, as a true European partner. Britain on its own carries little weight in international affairs.

Robin Cook may not have been very good at the flummery and formality of being foreign secretary. But, conscientious and committed to a fault, he used his high office to do many good things. And he was courteous to those who mattered most – his foreign colleagues, with whom he built a remarkable series of relationships. One small measure of the respect which his fellow foreign ministers had for him was the handsome tribute which Madeleine Albright paid in her address at his London memorial service in December 2005.

Robin Cook's speech to the House of Commons on 17 March 2003, on the eve of the invasion of Iraq by America and Britain, is one of the few Parliamentary orations ever to have been applauded as it was delivered, I suspect in part by members on all sides who knew deep down that he was right, and felt bad that nevertheless they would still be voting for war. In it, Cook announced his resignation from a government in which he had served two happy years as leader of the House of Commons. In closing, I quote the final passages:

> What has come to trouble me most over past weeks is the suspicion that if the hanging chads in Florida had gone the other way and Al Gore had been elected, we would not now be about to commit British troops. The longer that I have served in this place, the greater the respect I have for the good sense and collective wisdom of the British people. On Iraq, I believe that the prevailing mood of the British people is sound. They do not doubt that Saddam is a brutal dictator, but they are not persuaded that he is a clear and present danger to Britain.
>
> They want inspections to be given a chance, and they suspect that they are being pushed too quickly into conflict by a US Administration with an agenda of its own. Above all, they are uneasy at Britain going out on a limb on a military adventure without a broader international coalition and against the hostility of many of our traditional allies ...

I intend to join those tomorrow night who will vote against military action now. It is for that reason, and for that reason alone, and with a heavy heart, that I resign from the government.

That speech is Robin Cook's finest epitaph.

Chapter 10

Poppies of Palestine

His Majesty's Government view with favour the establishment in
Palestine of a national home for the Jewish people, and will use their best
endeavours to facilitate the achievement of this object, it being clearly
understood that nothing shall be done which may prejudice the civil and
religious rights of existing non-Jewish communities in Palestine, or the
rights and political status enjoyed by Jews in any other country.

LETTER FROM THE BRITISH FOREIGN SECRETARY, ARTHUR
BALFOUR, TO LORD ROTHSCHILD, 2 NOVEMBER 1917

Even those Cabinet ministers most worried about Britain's decision, at
the height of the First World War, to promise a land without people (or
so we chose to think) to a people without land did not foresee the full
consequences of that historic decision – consequences still with us
nearly a century later. In the three decades which followed the Balfour
Declaration, Britain struggled to reconcile the promises it had made to
both sides with the realities in historic Palestine of indigenous settlement and mass immigration. Many mistakes were made. With the
Second World War over, Britain's moment in the Middle East was
coming to an end. Its political will, military strength and financial
resources were all weakening. Britain was no longer either willing or
able to see through to an honourable conclusion the Mandate over
Palestine which it had secured with such high hopes at the end of the
First World War.

As ambassador to Tel Aviv, I often used to tell Israeli audiences the
following story of what had in my view been one of the worst of those
mistakes. I would quote the stirring Hebrew nationalist song 'Kalaniot'

(Poppies), in which a young girl goes out to pick the poppies of Palestine for her mother.

In 1936, a full-scale Arab revolt had broken out against British rule over Palestine. At the time, the senior British officer there had been an air commodore, with little more than a flight of biplanes and a squadron of armoured cars at his disposal. They were soon overwhelmed. Massive reinforcements were sent from the Canal Zone, from Iraq and from Britain. Over the next two and a half years, British forces systematically crushed the Arab uprising. They used methods of great cruelty and effectiveness. The Royal Navy bombarded from the sea the Arab villages on the coastal plain. The Royal Engineers blasted and bulldozed patrol roads through the ancient Arab city of Jaffa. Hostages were taken, and placed on the front of the trains of Palestine Railways. By the spring of 1939, the Arab Revolt was all but over. The General Officer Commanding the 8th Infantry Division in Palestine at the time, Major General Bernard Montgomery, had served with distinction in the Great War and in Ireland. After the establishment of the Irish Free State in 1923, he had written to a brother officer that his 'own view is that to win a war of that sort you must be ruthless; Oliver Cromwell, or the Germans, would have settled it in a very short time'. In April 1939, as 'peace' returned to Palestine, he said, 'I shall be sorry to leave Palestine in many ways, as I have enjoyed the war out here.'

But, in 1945, as the war in Europe drew to a close, and as the full horror of the Holocaust emerged, a much more dangerous and desperate, cleverer and crueller, insurgency broke out in Palestine, a Jewish insurgency. By 1946, the British High Commissioner, General Sir Alan Cunningham, and the GOC, General Sir Evelyn Barker, had concluded that Britain needed to negotiate with the more moderate rebels. They were after all fighting for the national home Britain had promised them nearly thirty years earlier. The more reasonable insurgents, in the Haganah and the Palmach, should be separated off from the irreconcilable hard men of the Irgun and the Stern Gang. To strengthen the position of the moderates, military action should be restricted and surgical rather than large and sweeping. A negotiated political settlement should follow. In the winter of 1946 the High Commissioner presented this view in a paper he took to London. But the man who had commanded the 8th Infantry Division in Palestine before the war was now Chief of the Imperial General Staff: Field Marshal Viscount Montgomery of El Alamein. He rejected the advice from the men in charge on the ground. 'Viewed from a military standpoint,' the War Office stated, 'the policy of appeasement has failed.'* The CIGS advocated 'turning the place upside down'and flooding Palestine with British troops.† Britain did not talk to terrorists. The Jews would be crushed just as the Arabs had been before the war. The politicians who should have known better – the Secretaries of State for Foreign Affairs, for the Colonies and for War – deferred to the senior man in uniform.

By the end in Palestine, the British Army had deployed more than 100,000 men in a territory smaller than Wales. The paramilitary Palestine Police provided another 20,000 men. But the main force was the 6th Airborne Division, fresh from north-west Europe. They fought a bitter counter-insurgency campaign, inflicting great cruelty on the Jews of Palestine, and receiving plenty in return. And they lost.

I would remind my Israeli audiences that when the fighters of the Palmach and Haganah had sung 'Kalaniot' with such feeling they had been thinking not of poppies but of the red berets of the British paratroopers. For 'Kalaniot' – red flowers with black hearts – was the Jewish nickname for the men of the 6th Airborne Division – to be cut down just as the poppies of Palestine would be plucked in the spring.

On 15 May 1948, Britain pulled out of Palestine, earlier than planned, with our tail between our legs, leaving behind millions of pounds' worth of equipment, and a mess that bedevils the Middle East to this day. And it was all because we had failed to apply the lesson that force alone can suppress the symptoms of such problems, but it cannot solve them. For that, politics is needed. Ironically, the man who had mistakenly overruled the High Commissioner's plea for negotiations had identified the difficulty twenty years earlier, in relation to Ireland. In 1923, Bernard Montgomery's letter to his brother officer, advocating a

---

* Cabinet Defence Committee Paper DO(46)145, 'Use of Armed Forces, Part I: War Office View', 19 December 1946, Colonial Office 537/1731 quoted in David Chartres, *The British Army and Jewish Insurgency in Palestine, 1945–47*, London: Macmillan Press, 1989, p. 104.
† 'Note of a Conference at the Colonial Office', 3 January 1947, Colonial Office 537/1731 quoted in ibid., p. 105.

tough approach, had continued wisely to note, 'if we had gone on we could probably have squashed the rebellion as a temporary measure, but it would have broken out again like an ulcer the moment we removed the troops; I think the rebels would probably have refused battle, and hidden their arms etc. until we had gone'. The same, sadly, is true of almost all counter-insurgency operations, in Malaya, Kenya, Iraq or Afghanistan: the most that force can do is suppress, locally and temporarily, the violent symptoms of a much deeper disease, a disease that is, in essence, political.

There were many reasons why I had wanted to be ambassador to Israel – the first Arabist ever to serve there as ambassador. One was that I had fallen in love with the country on first visiting it, by bus from Cairo, nearly twenty years earlier: the rich beauty of the hills of Galilee and the eerie desert wastes of the Negev; the Crusader castles of the north and the ancient settlements of the south; bustling Bauhaus Tel Aviv, contrasted with the towers and spires of antique, austere Jerusalem. At the heart of three religions, Jerusalem's ancient magic is still very strong. I had long admired the way the Israelis cared for their land and its monuments, and had marvelled at their enterprise and energy. But I had been shocked at the self-deception that led them to deny the slowly shifting demographic sands on which their miracle-state was built. I felt desperately sorry for the Arabs, on either side of the Green Line, damned if they accepted Israel, damned if they didn't. And I believed, naively perhaps, and still do, that the problem is soluble, and moreover that, as with most of the world's problems, there is only one sane solution. In the case of Israel–Palestine, that only sane solution had been identified by the Peel Commission in 1937, reaffirmed by the United Nations Special Committee on Palestine in 1947, pursued at Camp David by Presidents Carter in 1978 and Clinton in 2000, and adopted, in the end, by President George W. Bush in 2002. Seventy years ago it was called partition, now it is known as a two-state solution. Just as Seamus Mallon had described the Good Friday Agreement of 1998 as Sunningdale (the 1973 power-sharing agreement) for slow learners, so I believed that a two-state solution in Palestine was essentially Peel for slow learners.

History, geography, politics, those were some of the reasons for wanting to go to Israel. But there were also more personal reasons. My mother's mother was Dutch. Many of her family, particularly the more artistic ones living in Amsterdam, had had close Jewish friends, some of whom had been taken away in the war, never to return. Her brother – my great-uncle – had been assassinated on the steps of his house, after someone had betrayed to the Germans a secret camp for Jewish children he had built in the woods on his estate near Apeldoorn in the east of Holland. His sister – my great-aunt – had hidden two Jewish children in her grand house near Utrecht. One, the boy, had been concealed in a space behind a wardrobe, the other, a girl, in a compartment under some steps out to the garden terrace. The police had turned up suddenly to search the house: the girl had escaped, and survived the war. But the boy, in his rush into the wardrobe, had left a coat caught in the door and had been found: he had been taken to Theresienstadt concentration camp and was not seen again. During the 1967 war, my Dutch family had given blood to Israel. They were enthusiastic Zionists, based on emotional engagement with their talented Jewish friends rather than any deep understanding of the rights and wrongs of the Israel–Palestine dispute. On hearing of my appointment as ambassador to Israel, my grandmother's youngest sister, my dear godmother, had sent me an emotional letter of pride, describing in vivid terms how, as a young woman in Amsterdam during the war, she had watched with sad fury as a group of Jewish women and children were herded through Amsterdam Central Railway Station by embarrassed German soldiers.

There were other family stories. As a subaltern in the Black Watch, my uncle had been in Jerusalem in 1946 when Jewish terrorists had blown up the King David Hotel, killing ninety-six people, most of them civilians. His men had dug the bodies out, taking many days. More than fifty years on he could still remember the stench of rotting human flesh: Jerusalem in July is very hot. My wife's grandfather had gone out to Palestine in the 1930s, to work as a barrister for the Mandatory Government. He had been run down and fatally injured in front of the King David Hotel, before being buried in the Protestant Cemetery on Mount Zion. What had looked like an accident was alleged years later to have been assassination.

But I did not discover the most emotional connection until I was well on my way to Israel. After briefing Jack Straw, I had left the Foreign Secretary's office for the last time on Saturday 9 June 2001. On the evening of Sunday 10 June, I had moved into my temporary lodgings in Hendon, in north London, with a kindly Israeli *kosmetikait* (or beautician) of a certain age. At my request, and with funding from the Foreign Office, Julie, a Hebrew teacher from the School of Oriental and African Studies at London University, had put together what turned out to be the best language course I have ever had. I had already spent a year grappling with the Hebrew alphabet and basic grammar – as a Semitic language, not so impossible for an Arabist. For my full-time immersion course, Julie had arranged for me to lodge with the *kosmetikait*. The beautician spoke to me only in Hebrew, and spoiled me rotten in the way that only Jewish mothers can. I slept in her treatment room, kept my bike in the garage of her flat, and cycled across north London to spend the day out at lessons at Balfour House in North Finchley. I caught only occasional glimpses of her clients – the Jewish princesses of north London – who looked beautiful enough without need of any further enhancement. Julie arranged a carefully structured programme of lessons with four separate Israeli teachers. The day started with two hours of grammar from someone who taught modern Hebrew to undergraduates at Cambridge, and who had once served as a sergeant in the Israeli Army. She imposed the discipline I needed. The rest of the day ran roughly as follows: ninety minutes of conversation, ninety minutes of newspapers and television, ninety minutes of reading. In six weeks' immersion, I learned more Hebrew more quickly than I have ever picked up any other language. By the end, I could read the front pages of the newspapers. I could sign my name in Hebrew. Most important, I could give brief television and radio interviews in Hebrew – provided I had an idea of the questions in advance. I used the trick politicians use, of saying what I had to say on a particular subject, without necessarily understanding the detail of the question. And I was able to confirm something that had bothered me ever since in 1970 the chaplain at Tonbridge School had told me that the Headmaster's signature bore an uncanny resemblance to the Hebrew for the ineffable name of God – Jahweh, or Jehovah. Yes, it was true, I now confirmed:

'MMcC' written in the script which flowed from Michael McCrum's pen did indeed look like 'God' in Hebrew. Whether McCrum (who went on to become head master of Eton as well as vice chancellor of Cambridge and died in 2005) knew it or not, I never established.

At the end of the course, I decided to write my teachers an official letter of thanks in Hebrew. Julie kindly agreed to use her car to go back to my flat to pick up some Foreign Office headed paper. While there, she collected my mail. Among the letters was one forwarded from a former head master of Charterhouse (and much else) called Sir Brian Young. Sir Brian (whom I did not know) wrote that he had been delighted to read of my appointment as ambassador to Israel for a particular reason. He explained that, as his father had been serving abroad with the Colonial Service (including as chief secretary of Palestine) in the 1930s, he and his brother had lodged with my paternal grandmother during the school holidays. He had thus come to know my father (who had died in 1968, when I was thirteen) when they had both been schoolboys just before the Second World War, Brian at Eton, my father at Harrow. In the winter of 1938–9, they and a group of school friends, mainly from Eton, had gone down to a former holiday camp at Dovercourt to help look after the Jewish children then coming over as refugees from Nazi Germany – the *Kindertransport*. As my father had learned German at school, he could communicate with the children, apparently helping them make telephone calls back to Germany. I was moved to tears: this was an aspect of my long dead father's life I had never known. For it to emerge on the last day of my Hebrew course was too much to bear.

Part of the fun of becoming British ambassador to Israel is getting to know the British Jewish community. They are not backward in coming forward. I already knew and liked Michael Levy, who regarded the new Ambassador as very much his protégé. I remember him imperiously ringing up friends in Herzliya, the beautiful coastal town just north of Tel Aviv, and instructing his former dentist – who later became a good friend – to give a dinner for me. But, even allowing for his energy and enthusiasm, there was much more to British Jewry than Michael Levy. As I prepared for the job, I came to know the people and places of our Jewish community, mostly in north-west London. Early on, Julie took me to buy a range of *kippot* or Jewish skullcaps, from a shop in Golders Green: a knitted *kippah* for the reform Jews, plain black for the more conservative. I ate kosher food and drank kosher wine. Bridget and I were invited to Friday-night meals with Jewish families of all types and conditions, welcomed without reservation into their homes. Everywhere I was met with kindness and warmth, an eagerness to explain, tolerance of my ignorance. I called on the Chief Rabbi, Jonathan Sacks. I met many other Jewish leaders, some of whom were to become good friends, ranging from Sir Trevor Chinn to Sir Ronald Cohen. In 2001, Ronnie was still running his highly success-ful venture-capital firm Apax Partners. After he left Apax, he was to spend much of his time and energy promoting Palestinian economic development. He took me completely by surprise by breaking into fluent Egyptian Arabic at our first meeting. It turned out he had grown up in Alexandria, and, like me, spoke far better Arabic than Hebrew. He and I shared a Hebrew teacher – the same one, Rachel Williams, who taught me grammar so mercilessly and effectively.

I also met some rogues and chancers, and individuals with views so conservative as to be completely detached from the realities of either Israel or Britain. But, in their way, those views were pointers to the other lesson I learned from my time with the Jewish community. That, for all their success in modern Britain, the sense of insecurity, of actual or potential exclusion, runs deep. In the leafy lanes of north-west London, it was difficult to believe that anti-Semitic attacks were still regarded as a serious threat. For a gentile, it was sometimes hard to understand why the volunteer vigilantes of the Community Security Trust would still guard the big Jewish charity dinners, or patrol outside certain synagogues at certain times. Even at home with my *kosmetikait*, in a comfortable north London apartment block, I was living in a community where all our neighbours were Jewish. I found that, for many of the Jewish friends I soon made, I was one of the few *goyim* – gentiles – they knew at all well. Most if not all of their close friends were Jewish. There was no point in being judgemental about this aspect of Jewish life: the sense of insecurity is utterly real, with roots deep in the Jewish experience. So is the sense of community, of family, of sticking together, for success and for safety in a jealous and hostile world.

That summer of 2001, we took a family holiday in Turkey, for a real break after my two tough years with Robin Cook and before embarking on what I expected to be a demanding new job – I could hardly have guessed just how demanding. We went with a friend who had worked as a journalist in Israel and knew the country. His advice was the best: if you want really to understand modern Israel, plunge into modern Israeli novels. I did, starting with Amos Oz, and learned more than all the Foreign Office briefing papers and political science textbooks could ever have told me. And we didn't just go to Turkey: we went to a Club Med where we thought there might be one or two Israelis. We got more than we bargained for: full-on immersion in Israel on vacation abroad. The noise, the exuberance, the brash self-confident beauty, of a people desperately keen to be at ease in a world which for so long had not been at ease with them. Every other guest seemed to be yelling for Yossi or Yael.

It was while I was on holiday that the Foreign Office rang to say that I would need to get out to Israel even earlier than planned: the Foreign Secretary, Jack Straw, wanted to pay his first visit to Israel in his new job in late September 2001, and I needed to be there, and accredited as ambassador, well in advance. So I had to abandon plans to drive out with my family and take the ferry from Piraeus to Haifa via Cyprus, thus retracing the route we had taken back from the Middle East eighteen years earlier. I flew out alone to Israel on 4 September 2001, with the promise that, once installed, I would catch up with my family in Cyprus. If at all possible, I still wanted to make the approach to Haifa by sea that would have been the first sight of the promised land for so many refugees from Europe. I wanted to sail back into the harbour in the lee of the great mountain of Carmel – and was later able to do so.

A limousine therefore picked me up from home in Balham and took me to the Heathrow VIP lounge. I sat there self-consciously, waiting to be driven out to the BA flight to Tel Aviv. I flew First Class – an impossible luxury in these austere days when even the Prime Minister travels Club Class. Arriving at Ben Gurion airport in the early hours of the morning of 5 September, I was greeted by the man who was to be my deputy throughout my time in Israel, Peter Carter. The first task was later that day to travel from the great coastal city of Tel Aviv (where the

Embassy and Residence are) to Israel's capital, Jerusalem, high in the Judean Hills to the east, to present the Israeli Foreign Ministry's chief of protocol with a copy of my letter of credence – my credentials – from the Queen. Once he had accepted these, I would be free to operate as an ambassador, even though I would still have to see the President of Israel for a formal credentials ceremony. As every candidate for the Presidency of the United States learns, Jerusalem, not Tel Aviv, is the official capital of Israel. But, pending the settlement of Israel's dispute with the Arabs, it is not recognised as such by the great majority of states. Only a handful of rather small states, mainly in Central America, have been persuaded by Israel to recognise Jerusalem as Israel's capital, and move their embassies there. Thus most countries, including the United States and the United Kingdom, keep their embassies in Tel Aviv. Apart from the Defence Ministry, however, the Government of Israel sits in Jerusalem. To reach Jerusalem from Tel Aviv there is a choice of routes: one is the old road, twisting and turning past the ancient armoured personnel carriers left where they were hit as they sought to break the siege of Jerusalem in 1948. The other, much faster, much newer road leaves Green Line Israel by the new town of Modi'in and snakes gracefully across the Occupied Territories straight into the heart of West Jerusalem. I never knew if Palestinian Arabs were formally banned from using that road, but you never saw them on it.

Not surprisingly, the Israeli protocol chief was rather less stuffy than those in many other foreign ministries I had come across. He not only accepted the informal copy of my credentials, but said that, if I didn't mind the short notice, I could be slipped in at a credentials ceremony the following day, 6 September. Of course, I accepted with alacrity. And so, a day later, I found myself marching along a red carpet, past a guard of honour, into the President's House in Jerusalem, flanked by my Defence Attaché, Colonel Tom Fitzalan Howard, and Peter Carter. I handed President Moshe Katsav the formal letter from the Queen, introducing me as Her Majesty's latest Ambassador Extraordinary and Plenipotentiary to the State of Israel, and made a short speech in halting Hebrew. Katsav and the line of officials behind him broke out into broad grins: it was some time since a gentile ambassador to Israel had addressed its President in his own language.

There was one other thing I knew I must do, on returning to Israel as ambassador: visit the haunting halls of Yad Vashem, the memorial to the victims of the Holocaust. I had last been there with Robin Cook, and the Foreign Secretary had been invited to rekindle the eternal flame. Now it was my turn, in a small act of acknowledgement of the idea that explains – and for many justifies – the Jews' need for a state of their own.

In those rushed first few days in Israel, I hardly had time to absorb the fact that I had at last become what all diplomats aspire to become: an ambassador. Finally, I was my country's representative, the official link between my own government and my host country. Just as twenty-four years earlier, I had realised at my first lunch with the Irish Embassy that everything I said and did even as a junior diplomat would assume a special weight in the eyes of my interlocutors, so now, as an ambassador in post, I realised I was on almost permanent exhibition. In the country to which I was accredited, Israel, I could never be completely off duty – as I was to be reminded time and again during the terrorist campaign of the next year. But there were big compensations: the British Government provided me with a car – a choice, in fact, between a Jaguar and, for the tough areas, an armoured Range Rover – and a superb driver, a Christian Arab from Jaffa; and my family and I were looked after in a large and comfortable residence – a pleasant bungalow on a small hill in a mixed suburb of Tel Aviv – with a talented Israeli woman chef and a team of devoted house staff. I felt very lucky.

After my third full day at work in the Embassy, I was driven back to the Residence, for what I had expected to be a quiet evening on my own, a chance after the first few hectic days to catch my breath. I had hardly got in the door, when my mobile phone rang. It was Tom Fitzalan Howard. 'Turn on the television, Sherard,' he urged. 'Something terrible is happening in New York.' It was. I was just in time to see the second aircraft smash into the World Trade Center. I watched transfixed, as first one tower, then the other, collapsed in on itself. In scenes straight out of my childhood nightmares, thick clouds of debris and dust rolled after petrified people running up the canyons of Manhattan and swallowed them up. I knew at once that this was Al Qaeda. I knew at once that the world would not be the same again. I called Peter Carter: we needed to get together in the Embassy that evening, to assemble our thoughts on how the Jewish state would react to this outrageous assault on America. We would send a telegram to London that night. In the meantime, I managed, somehow, to speak on the phone to the heads of both the Mossad (Israel's external intelligence service) and the internal security service, known colloquially as the Shin Bet after its Hebrew initials. Both had the same view. This assault, which also included an attack on the Pentagon and a planned attack on, probably, the White House, was too ambitious to be other than state-sponsored terrorism. Neither would say which state. But each was clear that even a terrorist organisation as sophisticated as Al Qaeda could not have mounted an operation of such terrible complexity: it had to have come from a state. How wrong they were.

9/11 did change everything, for a while. But at the same time it didn't change anything fundamental. For Israel, the event served mainly to confirm their view of Islamic *terroor* (a Hebrew word). We forget now that Prime Minister Sharon's initial efforts to use it to enlist the Bush Administration's support in a single fight against such 'terror' met a cool reception: on a post 9/11 tour of the Middle East, the US Defense Secretary, Donald Rumsfeld, deliberately avoided Israel, presumably out of fear of offending the moderate Muslims whose support the US sought in attacking Al Qaeda in Afghanistan. The Blair Government took a wiser view: in times like these, Israel needed to be embraced and encouraged towards peace, not ignored and isolated. The Foreign Secretary, Jack Straw, decided to proceed with the visit he had planned to make to Israel at the end of September. And, with my strong support, but against the advice of some in London, Tony Blair included Israel in one of the swings through the Middle East he made in a frantic round of post 9/11 diplomacy: a month or so after the Foreign Secretary, the Prime Minister came to Israel from Jordan, before going on, via Gaza and Amman, to Damascus.

Neither visit was without incident. Jack Straw's visit began disastrously. As had happened with Robin Cook on his first official visit to Israel, the Israelis chose to take offence at something the Foreign Secretary had said or done. In Straw's case, it was a press article in which he asserted – rightly – that anger over 'Palestine' was one of the factors breeding Islamic terrorism. Unfortunately, the piece appeared while he was in Tehran, en route to Israel. The Israeli Government chose to see his 'abominable' words as blaming them for 9/11. They promptly cancelled Straw's meeting with Sharon, just as Netanyahu had cancelled his meeting with Cook three and a half years earlier. Only a calming phone call from Blair to Sharon, and miraculous behind-the-scenes work by Lord Levy, reinstated Straw's meeting with a tetchy Sharon.

A month later I stood on a helipad in Jerusalem waiting for Tony Blair. In he swept. As instructed by the advance team from Number 10, I rode with the Prime Minister in the car straight to the King David Hotel to prepare for his meeting with Sharon. It was there that an incident as amusing as it seemed trivial occurred. Michael Levy was apparently upset that Blair had invited the brand new Ambassador, rather than his Middle East envoy, to be in the car with him for the short ride to the King David. None of us could quite believe his ears or eyes (and Alastair Campbell rolled his upwards) as Michael rushed into the hotel suite after us, grabbed the Prime Minister by the lapels and cried, only half-jokingly, 'Tony, do you still love me, do you still love me?' Blair quickly reassured Michael, and all was well. I for one never quite understood the chemistry between the Prime Minister and his Middle East envoy: on more than one occasion, Jonathan Powell had told the Foreign Office that the Prime Minister would shortly be telling Michael Levy that his services as Middle East envoy would be required no longer, but afterwards Michael was heard to say that his 'relationship with Tony had never been stronger'. Michael had many strengths, not always obvious to those who did not see how tenacious he was in his Middle Eastern diplomacy; but, as I told him, he could sometimes be rather high maintenance.

The underlying situation across Israel and the Palestinian Territories was bad, and getting worse. Early on 17 October, I had been in the gym at the Hilton Hotel on the Tel Aviv seafront when my mobile phone had rung – how I came to dread those phone calls from the Embassy Duty Officer – with the news that the Israeli Tourism Minister had been assassinated, while staying in the Hyatt Hotel in Jerusalem. Despite his innocuous portfolio, Rehavam Ze'evi was something of an icon for the

Israeli right. He favoured population *transfair*, the Hebrew word for ethnic cleansing of the Palestinians out of historic Palestine. He had opposed the Oslo accords.* He wore the names of missing Israeli soldiers on an identity disc round his neck. He regularly based himself in the Hyatt in (Arab) East Jerusalem in order to assert Israel's claim to Jerusalem as its eternal undivided capital. The leader of the team of Palestinian gunmen who shot him was later sentenced to 125 years in prison.

By October 2001 the second Palestinian *intifada* had been under way for over a year and was really starting to get going. Almost every week saw a terrorist incident of one kind or another. But the single worst attack of them all did not come until Passover – 27 March – 2002. I was on my way back from a Passover celebration in northern Israel when the Embassy Duty Officer rang with the terrible news. Somehow, a suicide bomber disguised as a waiter had slipped into the Passover meal at the modest Park Hotel in Netanya, a dormitory city on the coast between Tel Aviv and Haifa. The guests, mostly elderly, had fought for places in the sunken area in the centre of the dining room, closest to the rabbi. No one had wanted to be shut off behind the pillars without a view of the top table. But those shielded by the pillars turned out to be the lucky ones. Thirty people were killed, 140 wounded, in the single worst atrocity of the second *intifada*. When I visited the Park Hotel the day after the massacre, the central well of the dining area was still a small lake of blood and gore. Everything movable had been blown out and away. The false ceiling had come down. A single cheap metal table knife was stuck in the concrete ceiling, driven there by the force of the explosion.

That attack provoked a chain of events from which the Middle East has yet fully to recover. Sharon reacted two days later by sending the

---

* The Oslo accords grew out of the Madrid Conference of 1991 and were signed at the White House in September 1993, between Israel and the PLO, and the United States and Russia. They were the result of the first open face-to-face contact between Israel and the Palestinians, and created the framework for a permanent peace based on two states. But the Oslo process gradually unravelled in the face of rising violence from extremists on both sides, culminating in the assassination of Prime Minister Yitzhak Rabin of Israel by a Jewish militant in November 1995.

Israel Defence Forces back into the Occupied Territories. He called it Operation Defensive Shield (*Homat Magen*), but it was anything but defensive. The centre of the Palestinian town of Jenin was cordoned off and then largely flattened. My friend the late Marie Colvin of the *Sunday Times* rang from inside Jenin as the tanks closed in: her reports led me to call my friend Zvi Shtauber, the Israeli Ambassador in London, to protest at what Israel was doing. I thought that, as a former general with moderate views, Zvi would understand. Tom Fitzalan Howard got in there after the damage had been done: his courageous report was read out in the Commons by a Foreign Office minister.

As part of *Homat Magen*, Arafat was besieged in the Muqata'a, the old British Mandate fort outside Ramallah which served as the West Bank headquarters of the Palestinian Authority. With him were six men wanted by Israel for Ze'evi's murder. That siege was lifted only after joint efforts by the American Ambassador, Dan Kurtzer, and me to persuade Sharon to allow the six men to be transferred to a Palestinian prison in Jericho which would be placed under the supervision of a team of international monitors, mostly UK prison officers. A late-night meeting at which I introduced a sceptical Sharon to the former Governor of HM Prison, Brixton, did the trick. As the British prison Governor explained how convicted terrorists were subject in British jails to the same strict regime as ordinary serious criminals, Sharon relented.

But, as one siege ended, another had begun. Over 200 Palestinian militants had taken refuge in the Church of the Nativity in Jerusalem. Once again it was Dan Kurtzer who got Sharon off his self-imposed hook. After a month, the Israeli Prime Minister was persuaded to grant the most wanted Palestinians safe passage out of the country. At my suggestion, they were flown to Cyprus. An RAF Hercules arrived at Tel Aviv airport to pick them up, with an RAF doctor and a detachment of Royal Military Police on board. I felt proud of the small part British forces played in this episode.

It was not long, however, before Sharon reimposed the siege on the Muqata'a. Arafat was effectively a prisoner in his own country, remaining there until in late 2004 he was allowed out to be treated in France for his final, fatal illness. In June 2002, I went with Michael Levy to see Sharon, in his tiny office at the back of the Prime Minister's block in

West Jerusalem. Sharon was accompanied only by Dubi Weissglas, his lawyer and chief of staff. Sharon had one thing on his mind: we were to stop seeing Arafat. If we did see him, we were supporting 'terror'. Never lacking courage, Michael pushed back. Was Sharon suggesting that, in dealing with Arafat, Tony Blair had blood on his hands? No, said Sharon, but just don't have anything to do with Arafat. Twice more Michael came back at Sharon. The third time, Sharon had had enough. His massive fist came thumping down on his desk. 'Nigmar ha Mandaat,' he shouted in Hebrew. 'Nigmar ha Mandaat.' I translated: 'The British Mandate is over.' The meeting was over too, and we had to get out. After that, Sharon kept his dealings with Blair's Middle East envoy to an absolute minimum.

In October that year, the Foreign Secretary instructed me to go to see the Israeli Administrator of the Occupied Territories, Major General Amos Gilad, to protest at the restrictions being imposed on the Palestinians. To prepare for the meeting, Tom Fitzalan Howard and I toured both the West Bank and Gaza. We did not like what we saw. At the northern end of the West Bank, for example, we came across an IDF roadblock. The Israeli Army had closed the road. But the insouciant IDF conscripts were sitting there watching as the Palestinians were forced to trudge through the muddy fields around the roadblock: the Army weren't stopping the movement of Palestinians, merely humiliating them. Seeing the peasant women struggling with their baskets through the mud was deeply upsetting. I tried to speak to the Israeli soldiers in Hebrew, in Arabic and in English. But they replied in Russian. In the Gaza Strip, things were even worse. At the southern end of the Strip, in the town of Rafah, Tom and I got out of our armoured Range Rover, with the Union flag flying on the bonnet. We were wearing shirts and ties. We could hardly have looked more British. I spoke to some Arab children. Suddenly, shots rang out. 'Get down,' shouted Tom. 'Get back in the car.' The IDF had opened fire, for no obvious reason. They had also done so earlier in the day, as our car had approached a checkpoint in the centre of the Gaza Strip. Our subsequent protest made no obvious impact, especially as the incident at Rafah was a foretaste of the shootings of two Britons that were to disfigure my last few weeks in Israel.

At my meeting with Gilad, I said that, with the Territories locked down and the Gaza Strip under siege, Israel was in danger of creating the largest detention camp in the world. I made some suggestions for easing the restrictions on the Palestinian people. The Israeli Foreign Ministry official scribbled furiously. A few days later a selective account of what I had said was leaked by sources in Jerusalem – the Foreign Ministry, I guessed. I received scores of messages from Israelis, and from Jews around the world, mainly in America. Most of the Israelis expressed support for what I had said. Most of those from outside Israel were more hostile, and used the identical language which betrays an organised campaign. And then the Simon Wiesenthal Centre in California piled in, claiming – quite falsely – that I had spoken of a concentration camp, that therefore I was anti-Semitic and that therefore I should be recalled. They did have the grace to retract when told the truth. But by then the word was out. Curiously, however, the episode did me more good than harm: everyone who knew me realised that I was a true friend of Israel, and that true friends speak the truth, in private, as I had tried to do.

All these events within Israel were unfolding as the drums of a wider Middle East war were becoming more insistent. It was becoming clear that attacking Iraq, and dislodging Saddam, was the Bush Administration's overriding priority in the region. It was also clear that Britain would be alongside America in that enterprise, more or less whatever happened. At a Middle East Heads of Mission Conference in Cairo that summer, the Foreign Office's Middle East Director told us, in the garden in order to avoid being overheard, that in his view war against Iraq was inevitable, and that Britain would be part of it. To his credit, Blair did have some success in persuading Bush to offset his lunge against Baghdad with compensating activity on the Middle East Peace Process. In a speech on 4 April 2002, Bush called on Israel to halt incursions into Palestinian-controlled areas and begin withdrawing from those cities it had recently occupied.* While paying lip-service to

---

* In the same speech, delivered at the White House, Bush made the following point: 'When an eighteen-year-old Palestinian girl is induced to blow herself up, and in the process kills a seventeen-year-old Israeli girl, the future, itself, is dying.'

what the American President had said, in practice the Israeli Prime Minister ignored his request. Ten years later, the IDF were still in many of the areas of the West Bank they had re-entered in April 2002. Using an Israeli businessman based in New York as a go-between, Sharon had sent Dubi Weissglas to the White House with intercept material designed to convince Bush that Arafat was a liar. The detention in the Red Sea in January 2002 of the *Karine A* cargo ship allegedly carrying Iranian weapons for the Palestinians had been the beginning of the end for Arafat in Bush's eyes. By the summer of 2002, the Bush Administration was refusing to deal with him direct on anything of substance – not the easiest stance to adopt if you are trying to promote Middle East peace. Nevertheless, in June, Bush announced the principles of a Road Map for Middle East peace, promising a Palestinian state by 2005, thus making him the first American President explicitly to support a state for the Palestinians. There followed nearly a year of stalemate, however, while Bush focused on attacking Iraq, Israel refused to budge, and Arafat sat holed up in Ramallah.

Meanwhile, the violence continued. Over 200 people died as a result of *intifada*-related violence in 2002. One of them was Yoni Jesner, a young Jew from Glasgow who was killed with five others on a bus in Tel Aviv in September 2002. His cousin was also on the bus, much closer to the bomber, but escaped with only a scratch. That lottery of death was something I was to experience in my next post as well. Yoni suffered a critical head injury which put him into a coma. His family came out from Scotland and had to take the awful decision of whether or not to keep him on life support. They bravely faced the fact that he would never again be conscious and told the doctors to turn the machine off. But out of the death of a young boy who had wanted to become a doctor came life: one of his kidneys was donated to a seven-year-old Palestinian girl from East Jerusalem who had suffered kidney failure from birth. It was the most noble of gestures. It was a privilege to put the Ambassador's Residence in Tel Aviv at the disposal of the family as they coped with these appalling issues.

In November that year, Israel's former Foreign Minister Abba Eban died. With him died something of the old Israel. He was a man of immense courage and civilisation – and had of course been the first

Chief Instructor at MECAS. I recorded the funeral and my feelings in an emotional telegram.

As Britain's ambassador to Israel, I had two jobs. The first, and more important, was to act as Britain's official representative in Israel, reaching out not just to those who governed the country, but also to as many parts of Israeli society as possible. It was the extraordinary variety of background and talent that made the country so exciting and interesting. Whether it was watching Shakespeare in Hebrew and in Haifa, or visiting an archaeological site in the Negev, or driving down a trail along the Lebanese border observed by rock hyraxes, or speaking at an orthodox *yeshiva* (religious school) in one of the more conservative suburbs of Tel Aviv, I was always welcomed with open arms, and with amazement that I spoke even a few words of Hebrew. Sometimes, though, the latter could be a liability: once, at a rural restaurant near Haifa I decided I would order 'chicken breast' in Hebrew. I knew that the Hebrew for chicken was *off*, and for breast *shad*. So *shad off* was what I ordered, only to see the waitress collapse in giggles: I had asked for the bosom of a chicken. The breast/chest of a chicken is something completely different in Hebrew.

But I also saw myself as Israel's ambassador within the British system. I made sure that Israel's views were heard around Whitehall. I would remind colleagues in London and other Middle East posts of the iron truth that there can be no peace between Israel and the Arabs unless the Israeli people, or at least their Knesset, can be persuaded to vote for it.

I went to great lengths to welcome groups of visiting British Jews to the Residence whenever possible, so that they could see their taxes at work, but also so that they could hear how we saw the situation – not always the same way as their Israeli hosts. I would also do my best to accept invitations from Jewish organisations back in Britain to visit them, and speak where and when asked to do so. In doing this, I wanted to help Israel's friends in Britain deal with the dilemmas of being both Jewish and British. I wanted to help them see that, just as true love for a child is not giving him the keys to the car, the gun cupboard and the drinks cabinet all at once, so support for a country and a concept as dear to many British Jews as Israel should not be wholly unconditional.

I wanted to help them use their influence, and their British values, to encourage Israel to make the compromises for peace that were in its long-term interest.

In this, I had only limited success. Like their American cousins, and like Jews elsewhere in the Diaspora, many British Jews feel, deep down somewhere inside them, a bit bad about not living in Israel. Sharon used mercilessly to exploit that feeling of guilt, by teasing delegations of visiting Jews about their failure to make *aliyah* (literally, 'going up') to Israel. Many assuage their 'guilt' by visiting Israel as often as possible, by buying second homes there and by sending their children there for gap-year Israel experiences. They are also reluctant to criticise Israel, in public or even in private. Leaders of the Jewish community in Britain take the line that they have no right to criticise the elected government of Israel, and that their policy must be to support it, whatever one's private feelings about the policies they are following. I never thought that such an approach was quite enough: being Jewish, loving Israel and feeling bad about not living there should not be reasons for leaving British values at home. If Israel was breaking international law, by, for example, transferring its population to territories occupied as a result of war, then it should not be immune from criticism – private if necessary – from friends who want the country to survive and succeed.

On one or two occasions I appeared on the same platform as the Chief Rabbi of the Commonwealth, Jonathan Sacks, later Lord Sacks. Jonathan is a man of high intellect, great fluency and deep spirituality. But I could not help wondering why, faced with fundamentalist criticism of the first edition of his book *The Dignity of Difference* for saying that 'no one creed has a monopoly on spiritual truth', he had deleted that phrase from the second edition. My doubts about Jonathan's willingness to face down his own fundamentalists were reinforced when, at a public meeting with him, I had argued passionately that compromises for peace were in Israel's overwhelming long-term interest, but received no public support from the Chief Rabbi. In my view, for a range of different reasons, too many leaders of the British Jewish community somehow couldn't find the courage to tell Israel – even in private – the truths it needed to hear from its real friends overseas. To his great credit, Michael Levy was one of those friends: he had no hesitation in speaking to Israeli or Jewish power the truth about the damage the occupation was doing to Israel.

Even in Israel the spring of 2003 was dominated by preparations for the war against Iraq. Based on what had happened in the first Gulf War, in 1991 there was a real fear of Iraqi Scud missile attacks on Tel Aviv. Embassy families were evacuated. We reduced the Embassy staff to a small skeleton team. We were given anthrax injections and provided with charcoal-lined chemical and biological warfare suits. Sitting in Tel Aviv, I saw most of the intelligence which purported to show that Saddam had weapons of mass destruction. I confess that I was convinced: based on what I read, I judged that he probably did have such weapons. What I wasn't convinced of was the reasons for going to war then: I knew that that had more to do with the American political timetable than with realities in Iraq. I didn't see why the inspectors couldn't be given more time. Containment was working. And, when we failed to get a second UN resolution, I thought our legal cover for going to war was flimsy: using a 1991 Security Council Resolution ending the first Gulf war to justify a second, twelve years later, smacked of legal expediency. But, as ambassador to one of the few countries positively to welcome the invasion, it was not for me to reason why. I kept my head down and went along with government policy.

In the immediate run-up to the war, on 23 February to be precise, I got into the office at 8 a.m., my usual time, and opened up my email inbox. One message stuck out: the subject line read 'Congratulations' and the text read simply 'The Prime Minister has agreed.' It was from my successor as principal private secretary in London. I was flummoxed: to what had the Prime Minister agreed? I pressed the reply button, typed in 'To what?', and pressed send. Two hours later, just after 8 a.m. in London, the answer came: 'Your appointment to Riyadh.' At first I thought this was a joke. As ambassador to Israel, I had assumed that I was immune from being posted to Riyadh. Moreover, on his most recent visit to Israel, the Foreign Secretary himself, Jack Straw, had told me that he wanted me to stay the full four years in Tel Aviv. Thereafter I might return to London, to a director's job in the FCO. Now, without my knowledge let alone consent, I had been posted to Riyadh. The Prime Minister had agreed. I just could not believe it. I made further enquiries. The FCO Human Resources Director, Alan Charlton, was apologetic. The FCO Administration had simply forgotten to ask me if I was prepared to be considered when they had drawn up a list of Arabists eligible to be ambassador to Saudi Arabia. The PUS was vague about it all. Had I been more suspicious, I would have detected conspiracy, but the reality was, as it usually is, cock-up. After considering my options, I decided to accept. Riyadh was a big promotion at my age, and a huge challenge. If I left Israel in the summer of 2003, I would have had nearly two tough years there. Riyadh might be more restful. And it was the most senior post in the Middle East. Had I been more calculating, however, I would have turned the posting down: in accepting Riyadh, I was ignoring the advice Trevor Mound had given me twenty-five years earlier, to spend as much time as possible in London. But, out of vanity and ambition, and curiosity, I accepted.

There was plenty more to do in Israel, however, between early spring and late summer 2003. With the war in Iraq behind him, or so he thought, Bush turned his attention back to peace in the Middle East. In May, he set out the details of the Road Map he had announced almost a year earlier. By then Arafat had been persuaded to appoint Mahmoud Abbas as his prime minister, thus enabling the United States to work around its self-imposed ban on dealing with Arafat. Israel set a number of other conditions for agreeing to the Road Map, among them a complete cessation of Palestinian violence and no imposition of a settlement freeze on Israel.

But those conditions disguised an evolution in Sharon's attitude. At the end of May 2003 he shocked the Israeli people by using the word 'occupation' to describe the Israeli presence in the West Bank and Gaza, saying that it was a 'terrible thing' that could not continue endlessly. In addressing the central committee of the Likud party he spoke of the need for 'painful compromises' for peace. In this hopeful atmosphere, Bush met Abbas and Sharon at Aqaba in Jordan, on the Red Sea. At Passover that year, I had arranged for Tony Blair to give an interview to Israel's largest-circulation paper, *Yediot Aharonot*, in which he had reassured the people of Israel that they had nothing to fear from peace. Blair understood better than most that Israel was a democracy – albeit a flawed one – and that there could be no real peace in the Middle East unless one took the people of Israel along as well. And he knew that Sharon, with his hard-line record in peace and war, was better equipped than any other potential Israeli leader to persuade his people to make those 'painful compromises'. At the end of July 2003, Sharon came to London: as a special mark of favour, we arranged for the Prime Minister to take him up to the Downing Street flat alone, while the Number 10 foreign policy adviser, David Manning, entertained separately the talkative Dubi Weissglas (who, as Sharon's ever diligent lawyer, was apt to interrupt meetings to explain what his boss 'really meant'). With Arafat in balk, and Bush and Sharon committed, the peace process seemed at last to be gaining traction. I returned to Tel Aviv from London, full of hope, for a round of farewell parties. It was good to be leaving on an upbeat note.

But, as so often in Israel, there were darker clouds in what looked like a blue sky. In March 2003, an IDF bulldozer had killed a courageous young American, Rachel Corrie, who had been protesting against Israeli behaviour in the Gaza Strip, as part of the International Solidarity Movement. In April, a British photography student, Tom Hurndall, who was also working with the ISM, was shot in the head by an Israeli sniper while protecting children in Rafah – the border village where Tom Fitzalan Howard and I had been shot at. Hurndall was left in a deep coma, and died in London nine months later. And then in May a British film-maker, James Miller, was also killed in Rafah by a single shot from an Israeli sniper while working on a documentary about Gaza. I was determined that the British Government would do more to press the Israelis for justice over what had happened to the two Britons than the US Government seemed willing to do in the case of Rachel Corrie. Just as we had supported the Jesner family when they had come out to Israel to cope with the aftermath of the attack on Yoni, so I was clear that we should do all we could to help the family and friends of both Tom and James. We did our best, but, looking back, I am not satisfied that that best was good enough. Perhaps partly it was because I was leaving a few weeks later. But mostly it was because I knew that, in the IDF even more so than in most armies, there was a culture of impunity for soldiers suspected of unlawful killing. Overturning that would require Herculean efforts. In both cases, it was the unflinching determination of the families to secure justice (or something close to it) for a loved one unlawfully killed that in the end won through. Thanks largely to their efforts, the soldier who killed Tom was eventually court-martialled, and, although the officer alleged to have killed James was never indicted, the Israelis did, six years after the event, finally pay compensation. One of the sadder aspects of both terrible cases was the fact that the snipers responsible were bedouin Arabs serving in the army occupying their lands.

My family and I flew back to London at the end of July. Israel had been an unforgettable, unmissable experience. For all its many and obvious defects, the Jewish state was indeed a *nes* – a modern miracle. But its hopes of surviving as a place worthy of the Jewish people depended on it making those 'painful compromises' for which Sharon was then calling. Otherwise, its long-term prospects, as a liberal democracy, were bleak. Within a decade or two, Israel's six million Jews would be outnumbered by the Arab populations between the Jordan River and the Mediterranean Sea. Of the four options for the Jewish state – *transfair* (or ethnic cleansing) of the Arabs, the present course of keeping the Palestinians walled up in the Occupied Territories, a single binational state, or two states living side by side in peace and security – only the last would deliver a decent democracy with a Jewish majority. In a binational state, the Jews would soon become once again a minority, defeating the object of the Zionist enterprise.

Back in England, ready to relax and prepare for Riyadh, there was one Israel-related duty to perform. It wasn't so much a duty as a pleasure. My friend and colleague the Israeli Ambassador to London, Zvi Shtauber, had once told to me that he had grown up on an agricultural *moshav* (settlement), on which Friesian cows were raised and milked. I was determined to invite Zvi to my family's small farm in Devon, just as I had invited him to my home in Balham before leaving for Tel Aviv. It was more of a performance than I had imagined. The Metropolitan Police Close Protection Team who accompanied him everywhere insisted on doing a reconnaissance, although the threat from Palestinian terrorists in rural Devon must have been close to zero. They caused a minor sensation when they appeared at the local cottage hospital, to check that it had supplies of the Ambassador's blood group. They strode over the farm, frightening the cows. But all was set. The Ambassador's great armoured Jaguar crawled up my mother's stony drive. Zvi climbed out, in his best farm clothes. A bevy of detectives, clad inconspicuously in brand-new Barbour jackets and Hunter boots, surrounded him. My mother offered everyone lunch. And then she dropped the bombshell. 'Ambassador,' she said, 'in your honour, I ordered one of our best local hams.' Zvi was too polite to say anything, and the detectives – who emphatically didn't keep kosher – wolfed it, and a lot else, down. I explained to my mother only later that Israelis are Jews, that Jews don't eat pork, and that ham is pork.

Chapter 11

In the Heart of Arabia

One of the perks of becoming a senior Ambassador is that you are granted a private audience of the Queen: more junior Ambassadors are received in batches. In July 2003 I was at Buckingham Palace for a Royal audience before setting off as Her Majesty's Ambassador to the Kingdom of Saudi Arabia.

You are not supposed to repeat what the Queen says in private conversation. But the story she told me on that occasion was one that I was also to hear later from its subject – Crown Prince Abdullah of Saudi Arabia – and it is too funny not to repeat. Five years earlier, in September 1998, Abdullah had been invited up to Balmoral, for lunch with the Queen. Following his brother King Fahd's stroke in 1995, Abdullah was already the *de facto* ruler of Saudi Arabia. After lunch, the Queen had asked her royal guest whether he would like a tour of the estate. Prompted by his Foreign Minister, the urbane Prince Saud, an initially hesitant Abdullah had agreed. The royal Land Rovers were drawn up in front of the castle. As instructed, the Crown Prince climbed into the front seat of the front Land Rover, with his interpreter in the seat behind. To his surprise, the Queen climbed into the driving seat, turned the ignition and drove off. Women are not – yet – allowed to drive in Saudi Arabia, and Abdullah was not used to being driven by a woman, let alone a queen. His nervousness only increased as the Queen, an Army driver in wartime, accelerated the Land Rover along the narrow Scottish estate roads, talking all the time. Through his interpreter, the Crown Prince implored the Queen to slow down and concentrate on the road ahead.

Three months after my audience of the Queen, I had my first audience of Crown Prince Abdullah of Saudi Arabia.* He began, as he always did, by enquiring politely after the health of the Queen, the Prince of Wales, the Duke of York and other members of the royal family, and then of the Prime Minister. I replied that I brought greetings from HM the Queen, who had shared with me fond memories of their drive through the Highlands. Abdullah grinned broadly. 'Yes,' he said in Arabic, 'I was rather nervous. I did tell your Queen not to look at me, but to look at the road.' On cue, his Princeton-educated Foreign Minister, Prince Saud al Faisal, interjected, 'I suspect, Ambassador, that Her Majesty steers the Ship of State more steadily than she drives a Land Rover.'

I had worried that my service in Israel would have counted against me with my new host government. But I was talking to the Arab leader who, at the Beirut Summit in March 2002, had persuaded every Arab state, including Saddam's Iraq and Qadhafi's Libya, to support 'normalising' relations with Israel, in return for perfectly negotiable concessions on Jerusalem, borders and even refugees. Abdullah of Saudi Arabia held no brief for the Palestinians. He wanted a just peace in the region, of which he accepted that Israel would be part. It was a tragedy that President Bush, with other things on his mind in the spring of 2002, had failed to respond. But, more than a year later, Abdullah and Saud were still interested in my honest assessment of what was happening in Israel and among the Palestinians. They recognised that there could be no peace unless the Israeli people – and the US Administration – supported it. Moreover, in trying unsuccessfully to undermine me by leaking my discussion with General Gilad, the Israeli Foreign Ministry had unintentionally done me a favour. My comments about the danger that the Territories would become the world's biggest detention camp had been relayed around the Arab world, including to Riyadh.

Since the shock of discovering, in February 2003, that I had been posted to Riyadh later that year, I had come to terms with the move. Riyadh would be a serious job. Britain was still a big player in Saudi Arabia, and, after America, the country's closest Western partner. With

---

* He had become king on his brother Fahd's death in August 2005.

three diplomatic missions, three military missions, vast commercial and defence interests, and a British community some 30,000 strong, much was at stake. Riyadh was the senior diplomatic mission in the Middle East, and the natural culmination of any Arabist's career. I also sensed that there was work for an ambassador to do – in both directions: helping the British Government better understand Saudi Arabia, and helping the Saudis better understand Britain. It would be good to be in a country where I would meet the top leaders and speak to them in their own language. And it was a bonus to be refurbishing my rather dilapidated Arabic, not used seriously since I had left Cairo twenty years earlier.

So I started actively to prepare for re-entry into the Arab world. As part of that, with help from the political officer in our Embassy in Amman, Jonathan Layfield, I spent time with the bedouin in eastern Jordan. The idea was to reprogramme my Arabic from the wheedling elisions of the Levant to the cleaner, clearer, harsher sounds of the deep Arabian desert. Jonathan arranged for me to stay at 'H5' in eastern Jordan, the former pumping station on the Haifa branch of the old Iraq Petroleum Company's pipelines to the Mediterranean. H5 (as it is still known by the bedu) was the home of an air base and of a desert agricultural research station. Alongside was the little town of Safawi. I made my home with the desert researchers, almost all of them from local tribes, living in one of the old basalt blockhouses of the pumping station. From the small hill behind an Arab Legion fort watched over us. I imagined the British commander of King Hussein's Arab Legion, General Glubb, Glubb Pasha, visiting the fort in the 1940s or 1950s. Alone among Arab armies, the Arab Legion had held Israeli forces at bay in 1948, keeping the old British Mandate fort at Latrun – now the museum of the Israeli armoured corps – under Arab sovereignty, until it fell in the Six Day War of 1967. Britain's IPC had spared no expense in building its chain of pumping stations across the desert. Each was a small fortified village, and H5 even included what had once been a refrigerated mortuary. I was living among the jetsam of Britain's moment in the Middle East.

I arrived at H5 six months after the invasion of Iraq, when there was still hope that the American assault had brought a better future. The main road past H5, up to the frontier at H2, was chock-a-block with trucks and long-distance taxis conveying people and goods towards 'liberated' Iraq: it wouldn't be long before the flow was in the other direction. Already, the fuel in Safawi was mostly smuggled Iraqi petroleum, conveyed across the region's wholly artificial, British-imposed borders by tribes whose reach extended across large parts of Syria, Iraq, Jordan and Saudi Arabia.

The couple of weeks or so I spent in and around H5 brought my Arabic rushing back. Once again, I lived and breathed, and ate, Arabia. I danced the *dabka* (a sort of tribal line dance) at a bedouin wedding. I plugged my ears as, illegally, the sheikhs of the tribe discharged their Kalashnikovs in the air in celebration. I travelled out on to the black volcanic rocks of the Hauran, on the borderlands between Syria and Jordan, to work on experiments in harvesting rainfall, and even dew, thus turning barren desert into rangelands capable of supporting sheep or goats. I helped gather up the tomatoes grown in the wadis. I drove east towards Iraq, and found the old IPC pipeline half buried in the rock and sand. A bad moment came late one evening when I had been sitting, drinking coffee, round a fire with my bedouin colleagues. I got up to go to bed and, without pausing, wished them all 'Leila tov' – the Hebrew for good night. I realised at once what I had said and wanted the ground to swallow me up. But the word *Leila* – the same in Arabic as in Hebrew – saved me: my hosts just assumed my Arabic was even worse than it was, and cheerily wished me a good night's sleep, using the Arabic formula.

One weekend, a Palestinian working on the research project invited me back to his home village in western Jordan, high on the Jordanian (or eastern) escarpment of the Great Rift Valley. He lived near the ancient town of Gadara, now Um Qais, one of the ten cities of the Decapolis, on the eastern frontier of the Roman Empire. The towns that are now Amman, Damascus and Beit She'an in northern Israel were all members of the informal league of the Decapolis. From Um Qais, I looked down on the Sea of Galilee and on Israel, only a few miles away as the crow flies, but a thousand feet below, and another world entirely. My past was indeed another country.

I had left Israel in July 2003 hoping that I had put the miseries of terrorism behind me. But those hopes were soon dashed, and my three and a half years in Saudi Arabia were to be dominated by a terrorist campaign of exceptional viciousness, mounted by Al Qaeda in the Arabian Peninsula.

The first sign of the horrors to come had been the attacks – while I was still in Israel – on the expatriate compounds around Riyadh in May 2003, in which a number of brave Britons who were later to become friends only just escaped with their lives. Those attacks had had the traditional AQ hallmark of using suicide bombers, on foot or in vehicles, to breach the target's defences, followed by an infantry assault by individuals who were prepared to, and usually did, die. Thirty-five people had been killed, and some 160 injured. Somehow, I hoped that that terrifying series of assaults would have been a one-off, AQ's last gasp after the damage then being done to it in Afghanistan and Pakistan. Only later did the world realise that the May attacks were the opening salvo in a campaign intended to bring down the Saudi state.

Only a month or so after arriving in Riyadh, in early November 2003, I was due to fly back to London on a 3 a.m. flight to attend a management course. As I lay in bed waiting for the alarm to go off, the Residence was shaken by an enormous explosion which I judged to have been a mile or so away. We soon discovered that it had come from the Muhaya compound, inhabited mainly by Lebanese and other Middle Eastern expatriates, but once used by the Boeing Company. As soon as dawn broke, I drove down to the site of the explosion, and did what I could to assess the damage. It emerged that a Lebanese employee of the Embassy, a member of our public affairs team, had been in her house next to the first car bomb. She and her husband had just put their baby daughter to bed and had been preparing to turn in themselves. A massive blast had demolished the ground floor of their villa, blown the tiny girl out into the back garden and pushed an air-conditioning unit and a shower of glass on to the young couple. The first floor of their house had simply subsided on to the remains of the ground floor. The baby was found sitting in the rubble in the back garden, smiling and unscathed. But our employee had sustained bad laceration wounds, and her husband had been hurt by the flying air conditioner. As they picked up their child and made their way to safety in bare feet over the broken glass and concrete around their villa, they heard their neighbours on both sides groaning and calling out for help. They had been buried alive, as their villas had been completely demolished in the blast. Not one of the neighbours survived. Curiously, the proximity of the Embassy family's villa to the car bomb had saved them. It was not the first or, sadly, the last time I was to see the curious ways in which blast behaves following a bomb explosion.

The compound attack proved to be the just the start of a campaign that was to rock Saudi Arabia to its foundations and do severe (but temporary) damage to confidence in the Kingdom. A British community of some 30,000, divided roughly in thirds between the two coasts and Riyadh, shrank to nearer 15,000. Against my wishes, I was obliged to accept a team of eight bodyguards provided by the Saudi Interior Ministry. They were brave bedouin warriors, and became the best of friends and travelling companions. But in the autumn of 2003 I wasn't convinced they were necessary. We also took steps to reinforce our diplomatic posts, and stationed armed expatriate guards – provided by a leading British security company – inside the perimeters of our Embassy in Riyadh and our Consulate-General in Jeddah. The Saudis would not allow foreigners to carry weapons, or to use them, on Saudi soil, but they accepted the need for us to have them within diplomatic premises.

The next main attack in the series came at Yanbu, the Red Sea port where T. E. Lawrence had stayed in 1916 as he started to stir up the Arab Revolt against Turkish rule. But there was nothing romantic about Yanbu now: the old fishing port was bound on the landward side by a heavy necklace of refineries and industrial plants, with an outer ring of accommodation of various kinds for the expatriate workers, from the West and from Asia, who manned the facilities. On 1 May 2004, we were sitting down to the morning meeting in my office in Riyadh when the phone rang: it was our Consul-General in Jeddah, reporting that there were rumours that some foreign workers, including several Britons, had been killed in what sounded like a characteristic Al Qaeda assault on a petrochemical plant in Yanbu. I told the Consul-General that he should immediately send staff up there, and that I would set off in parallel with a team from Riyadh, flying to Medina in Saudi Arabia's western mountains and then driving down to the coast from there. I was joined by the officer from the Metropolitan Police's Anti-Terrorism Branch who was then permanently stationed in the Embassy in Riyadh, in anticipation of exactly this kind of attack on British citizens.

The reality, when we finally arrived in Yanbu later that day, was more gruesome than the first reports had suggested. Using false car passes, an AQ assault team had simply driven through a lightly guarded gateway in the perimeter fence around a camp for those building an extension to one of the refineries. The attackers had then entered, from both front and back, a complex of Portakabins in which the engineers responsible for the project had their offices. Any Westerner they encountered either had his throat cut or was gunned down.

We arrived at the camp, to find it deserted. The sights we saw within those drawing offices will never leave me: in one room a morass of congealed blood, with the victim's torn British passport protruding from the bloody swamp on the floor. Blood and gore were spattered on the corridor walls, in front of which some of the victims had been shot. All that was missing were the bodies of the victims. No attempt had been made either to secure the site for evidential purposes or to clean up the mess. We moved on to the mortuary in the small local hospital in Yanbu. The floor was awash with blood and water and other ghastly detritus. The hospital staff were in shock, unable to cope with the horror suddenly visited upon them. The Scotland Yard officer quietly took photographs of the bodies, and calmed and guided me as the drawers were pulled open for me formally to identify the victims. Just as we were finishing this gruesome task there was a scuffle and shouting in the corridor outside: the FBI had arrived, from the US Embassy in Riyadh, and were forcing reluctant Saudi staff to grant an American posse immediate admittance to the mortuary.

Worse, far worse, was to come. Only a few weeks later, on 29 May 2004, our Trade Representative in the Eastern Province rang to say that reports were coming in of multiple terrorist attacks on Western individuals and assets in and around the city of al-Khobar. From what he said it sounded as though dozens of terrorists were on the loose. I decided immediately that I had to get down to the Eastern Province. But I would not be welcome while the fire fight was continuing, and decided to stay away until the next day. I set off before dawn, racing at

110 mph down the great highway between Riyadh and the Gulf, and was in al-Khobar by 11 a.m.

What I found when I arrived was that the surviving terrorists had been holed up in the luxurious Oasis compound owned by the Saudi businessman Sheikh Ma'an al-Sanea. Earlier that morning they had somehow fled the compound and evaded arrest. But they had left behind a trail of destruction. It turned out that the attacks had been carried out by one dedicated team, who had struck hard and quickly at a variety of targets and moved on rapidly before the Saudi security forces, in their confusion, could catch up with them. The first target had been the offices of the Arab Petroleum Investment Corporation on a wide boulevard on the seaward side of the town. In an appalling piece of bad luck, a British investment banker, Michael Hamilton, had been driving through the security chicane into the offices when the terrorist team arrived. He was shot dead through the window of his car, and his body pulled out and tied to the rear bumper of the pickup truck in which the terrorists had arrived. The attackers then ran up the steps into the main building, shattering the plate-glass doors with Kalashnikov fire. Most of the few employees who were there at that hour in the morning followed the security procedures and ran up on to the roof, closing the trap door behind them. Their lives were saved. But two who did not, and ran downstairs towards the commotion at the front door, were gunned down.

The terrorists did not stay at APIC for more than a few minutes. They moved on to another set of Western company offices, towards the centre of town, dragging Michael Hamilton's body behind them for two miles, before cutting it loose beneath a flyover. Afterwards the APIC management ordered all their employees to scour the whole route, in order to find Michael's signet ring – which, amazingly, they did. It was a kindly gesture, but no consolation to his devastated widow, Penny. The bitterness of the whole tragedy was increased by the fact that Penny and Michael had been planning shortly to leave Saudi Arabia, for their longed-for retirement at their beloved house in Sussex. I had already come to know them as pillars of the classical music scene in the Eastern Province, bringing much-needed cultural refreshment to thousands of thirsty expatriates and Saudis alike.

The final act of this awful drama was played out in the Oasis compound. The terrorists bluffed their way in and proceeded to cause mayhem. They ran from house to house, office to office, asking the occupants to identify themselves as Muslims or non-Muslims. The non-believers were usually murdered, or gravely wounded, in a variety of gruesome ways. A Swedish cook walking down the main street of the compound was beheaded. As these events unfolded behind the high walls of the compound, the Saudi security forces – police, army, navy commandos and many other disparate units – started to mobilise and cordon off the area. But it was some hours before they were able to enter the compound.

One man to venture into the compound during this period was its owner, Ma'an al-Sanea. He donned a helmet and flak jacket, and, as the closed-circuit television footage which he proudly played me later showed, walked into the hotel area to lead to safety a couple of US military personnel, in uniform, who had been hiding, terrified, in the ventilation ducts of the hotel. The siege ended with the departure or escape of the surviving terrorists – no one knew exactly how or where – and the world breathed a sigh of relief. But the casualty toll was dreadful: some twenty-five killed, and many more injured, all in the heart of the area that produces a good proportion of the world's hydro-carbons. The world's press converged rapidly on the Eastern Province, among them the BBC Security Correspondent, Frank Gardner, and his experienced cameraman, Simon Cumbers. Frank filed a memorable report, standing in front of a Saudi petrochemical plant flaring gas. I gave him an interview in my hotel suite in al-Khobar. After Frank had gone, I had a long talk with Simon as he packed up his equipment.

Back in Riyadh, my first preoccupation was convening what I had hoped would be the first annual Heads of Post Conference for the heads of our three diplomatic missions in Saudi Arabia – the Embassy in Riyadh, the Consulate-General in Jeddah and the British Trade Office in al-Khobar. I wanted to use this conference to bring together the three groups, along with the substantial UK military presence in Saudi Arabia, to take a collective view on where our interests lay. And I wanted to use the meeting for some team-building. As a part of that, I had arranged a dinner at the Residence on the first night, to be addressed by

Britain's foremost expert on Saudi Arabia, St John Armitage. As we were gathering for drinks before dinner, the Embassy Duty Officer came hurrying into the Residence drawing room. Reports were coming in that two Western journalists, possibly Britons, had been shot in south Riyadh. Nothing else was known. I asked our political and intelligence teams to find out what they could from their Saudi contacts. We warned the Resident Clerk at the Foreign Office in London that we might be facing another consular incident. Within minutes, there was more grim news. The Interior Ministry were telling us that those shot were indeed British journalists. They had been taken to a hospital in a notoriously rough area of south Riyadh. An awful fear began to creep up on me. Over a drink in the Residence the evening before, Frank Gardner had told me that, following his despatches from the Eastern Province, he was planning to file another piece from Riyadh on Al Qaeda in the Arabian Peninsula. I took an instant decision. I would head down to the hospital myself, to find out what was happening. We would have to abandon the dinner, and Armitage's long-awaited talk.

As I drove south at high speed in my armoured BMW, accompanied by my Saudi bodyguards in two SUVs, I kept in touch with the Embassy by mobile phone. They told me that they had now heard that the body of one of the victims was already in a hospital mortuary. I asked the driver to go straight there. The mortuary was deserted. But, using my most insistent Arabic, I begged a sleepy gate guard to let me in. As I entered the building, I turned right, and there, on a gurney in the corridor, lay, quite serenely, Simon Cumbers's body, with a single small bullet wound in the head, still dressed in a check shirt and jeans. My heart almost stopped. Feeling quite sick, I rushed on to the Al-Iman hospital in South Riyadh, where we believed that the other victim, who I knew by now was almost certainly Frank Gardner, had been taken. Chaos greeted me. Frank, I managed to discover, was already in the operating theatre. Amid the shouting, and ringing of mobile phones, with soldiers with guns, and doctors and nurses, rushing back and forth in all directions, I came across a quiet South African trauma surgeon, Peter Bautz. He and a team from the King Faisal Specialist Hospital had been sent to Al-Iman, on the orders of the Governor of Riyadh, Prince Salman. In a strong South African accent, Bautz said that we had to stop the hospital operating on the patient, stabilise him and move him as quickly as possible in a mobile intensive-care unit to the King Faisal Hospital for sustained skilled attention. If the local surgeons carried on, they would kill the patient. Frank had lost a lot of blood, and his temperature had dropped to 30 degrees centigrade. Operating on someone, however fit, still in shock was likely to be fatal: he needed to be stabilised, and only then operated on. We didn't know it, but Frank had received half a dozen serious gunshot wounds in a diagonal line across his torso, breaking his right thigh, doing serious damage to his abdomen and bladder, and leaving him paraplegic. After a bit, Bautz's advice prevailed. Frank (whom I was able to recognise as he was brought out, unconscious) was taken by ambulance, under police escort, to the King Faisal Hospital in central Riyadh. I followed immediately behind. As we left, Bautz murmured under his breath, 'That's one sick boy. It's touch and go.'

Frank lay in a medically induced coma for more than a week. The doctors kept him heavily sedated as part of the process of recovery. In the meantime, Simon's poor widow, Louise, and his parents, Bob and Bronagh Cumbers from Ireland, had flown to Riyadh, along with Frank's wife, Amanda, and a team of senior BBC executives. Our house was full of those mourning the departed, and those hoping for the recovery of the survivor. It was a time heavy with emotion and a sad echo of the times in Israel when the Residence had been filled with the Jesner and Hurndall families.

There followed a series of attacks on individual Westerners, but nothing on the scale of the al-Khobar attack. In early December, however, came what was potentially the worst assault of all, on the US Consulate-General in Jeddah. Once again the terrorists blasted their way through the defences of a walled Western compound. This time they tailgated behind an official vehicle passing through the heavily guarded main gate. Luckily, the alarm was given just in time, and the Consulate's main office building was locked down, with a detachment of US Marines inside, as the terrorists approached. They tried to blast through the armoured glass with concentrated Kalashnikov fire, but the Marines discharged tear gas, causing the terrorists to withdraw. The terrorists then ran amok in the compound, asking everyone they came across whether he or she was Muslim. Those who weren't were killed. Eventually, the security forces got into the compound and hunted down the terrorists one by one. Chillingly, they were found to have with them plasticuffs, long knives and a video camera, presumably for use had they been able to take any Americans hostage. I had always assumed that the US Marines who guard American diplomatic missions around the world were there to protect the mission as a whole. But I learned from the Jeddah incident that they are under strict instructions to defend only the secure area – the Chancery or its equivalent – and the people and secrets therein. Jeddah showed the wisdom of that policy: if the small detachment of Marines had ventured out, there would have been a good chance that some of the terrorists would have found a way into the Chancery, perhaps taking hostages there. As it was, five locally engaged US Consulate staff were killed.

It was the Jeddah attack that caused British Airways to cease serving Saudi Arabia. Management had already been coping with pressure from the cabin-crew unions, worried about their members' security. Now, the airline's security 'experts' said that, in their view, Saudi Arabia would never again be a safe destination for the airline. Only a few weeks earlier those same 'experts' had judged that Saudi Arabia was now safe enough for cabin crew to stay there overnight. Top management had no option but to cease flying, early in 2005. It was a bitter blow to the thousands of Britons whom we had worked so hard to encourage to stay on in the Kingdom. I was summoned to see the Saudi Defence and Civil Aviation Minister and was reprimanded severely for allowing BA to go. My explanation that BA was a private company, with commercial independence, cut little ice.

I decided to do what I could to encourage other British airlines to fill the gap which British Airways would leave. I approached four. Richard Branson was enthusiastic, until his Managing Director pointed out that they didn't have the spare capacity. If Virgin had flown to Saudi Arabia, I wondered what we would have done about the half-naked women who adorn the sides of their aircraft. From the start, the most enthusiastic, and the one who eventually took over the route, was Michael Bishop of bmi, and his buccaneering Managing Director, Nigel Turner. Michael had aviation in his blood. He had helped establish, among others, Kuwait and Sudan Airways, and was up for a challenge. The energy which bmi brought to launching their service, first to Riyadh, and then to Jeddah, was a real boost to morale among travelling Britons and Saudis alike. Less sedate than BA, and perhaps more agile, they won many friends in Saudi Arabia by flying to the Kingdom when others wouldn't. And, so far as the routes between London and Saudi Arabia are concerned, all's well that ends well: BA returned to the Kingdom on its own in March 2009, and its takeover of bmi should mean that the routes are secure for the foreseeable future.

The Jeddah attack was the last full-scale attack on a Western facility in my time as ambassador. But Al Qaeda didn't give up. They set off a bomb outside the Saudi Interior Ministry in December 2004, and, nearly five years later, tried to kill the Saudi Counter-Terrorism Minister, Prince Mohammed bin Naif, by sending a suicide bomber in to see the Minister in his office in Jeddah. Prince Mohammed was lucky to escape with his life: his would-be assassin was just beside the Minister when he self-detonated. Potentially the attack with the most economic significance occurred in February 2006, when Al Qaeda nearly succeeded in disabling the huge oil-processing facility at Abqaiq in the Eastern Province south-west of Dhahran. Luck and courage stopped an attack that, had it succeeded, would have taken out a substantial proportion of world oil output and sent the price surging: as it was, oil jumped $2 a barrel in the wake of the attack.

The final AQ attack in this series was perhaps the most horrifying. In February 2007, just as I was preparing to leave Saudi Arabia for Afghanistan, a group of nine French tourists stopped for a picnic lunch near the road on their way back to Jeddah after a desert camping trip to the wondrous ruins of Medain Saleh in western Saudi Arabia. They were spotted by a terrorist cell. The killers approached the family group, separated the four men off from the women and children, and shot them.

Surprisingly, perhaps, Saudi Arabia is one of the few countries to have dealt successfully with a serious terrorist threat without over-reacting. Of course, the Saudi authorities took tough security measures. But, much more important than that, they adopted a policy of outreach to the families of actual and potential terrorists. They addressed head on the causes of radicalisation, promoting moderate Islam and marginalising the extremists who fed the hatred which nourished the terrorists. They clamped down on sources of terrorist finance and monitored closely the movement of funds and people across the Kingdom's borders. With my strong encouragement, Saudi experts in deradicalisation were invited to seminars with the British police and security services to show us how it could be done. The result today isn't that there is no terrorist threat in Saudi Arabia – no one in authority in Saudi Arabia would be foolish enough to claim that – but that the problem has been contained and calmed in ways that other countries, which have reacted more hysterically, would do well to follow.

The lessons of how Saudi Arabia tackled a threat that seemed at one time to endanger the stability of the state are not new. The most important is that the terrorist wins when he provokes from his target a reaction far larger and more irrational than the objective facts of the threat justify. The second is that terrorism can never be tackled successfully by force alone. Any successful counter-terrorist policy needs to address the political, economic and social sources of terrorism. In many ways, tough action against its symptoms – violence – is the least difficult part. Most of us would accept that this is no more than common sense. But, provoked by terrorist outrage, we still seem to ignore those lessons of history at least as often as we apply them.

One Friday morning in Riyadh in the spring of 2004, in the middle of the frenzy of the terrorist campaign, the Embassy's chief communications officer contacted me. It was the Saudi weekend, but there was an urgent 'DEYOU' telegram from London which I needed to see. My heart leaped. I started to imagine for what emergency, probably linked either to Iraq or to Al Qaeda, or to both, London was calling me out during the Saudi weekend. And then I saw the telegram: 'Her Majesty the Queen is minded to appoint you a Knight Commander of the Order of St Michael and St George, and I [that is the head of protocol at the Foreign Office] need to know if you will accept.' I was gob-smacked. I was aware that my predecessors as ambassador to Riyadh had been knighted. I had thought that, in times when honours were fewer, I might be offered a knighthood at the end of my time, provided I put in a decent performance. But being offered one before I had been there even a year was, like so many of the best things in life, utterly unexpected. Of course I accepted, mainly out of vanity, partly because of the pleasure I knew that this would give my whole family.

Awkwardly for me, the news broke, in the 2004 Birthday Honours List, in the immediate aftermath of the appalling attack on Frank Gardner and Simon Cumbers. I felt very embarrassed to be receiving messages of congratulation on something so essentially trivial when I had a house full of people coping with things really serious and sad. The counterpoint between their grief and my ephemeral honour put the latter in proper perspective.

People often say that the best bit about receiving an honour is the flood of congratulatory letters which follows. It is, though answering all the messages, especially those that are less than sincere, or sent through the written equivalent of gritted teeth, takes some of the gilt off the gingerbread. But I think a close second is the journey to Buckingham Palace, for the investiture ceremony. That really is special, not just for the person honoured, but for the family and friends who go with him or her. What I found so humbling about such occasions was the flood of 'ordinary' people collecting MBEs, behind the senior civil servants and generals and occasional showbiz personality. They come from all corners of the United Kingdom, and from every kind of background, often literally from dukes to dustmen. They reminded me what a small part of our national life is the diplomatic world which I had inhabited for so long.

As ambassador to Saudi Arabia I was often asked to give talks in Britain, and on several occasions in the United States, about a country that 9/11 had made more mysterious and more important than ever. Particularly with American audiences, I used to invite those present to imagine a country of continental proportions, with vast natural resources. A country addicted to cheap oil, and cheap imported labour, much of it illegal. A country with an eighteenth-century system of government that still executed its criminals. A country with a liberal elite, open to the wider world, on its two coasts, but a population in the interior that is deeply conservative, deeply religious and rather ignorant of that wider world. And then I would say that I was referring not to the

Kingdom of Saudi Arabia – though all those descriptions applied to it – but to the United States of America. In my view, today more than ever, that deep religious devotion, that fundamentalist conservatism, that ignorance about the world beyond its shores, apply to 'fly-over' America as they do to the heartlands of the Arabian Peninsula. Of course, there are huge differences, but, face to face after 9/11, these two young countries ought to have been able to spot more of themselves in each other than they did.

With honourable exceptions, most Western politicians don't get Saudi Arabia. It used to infuriate me as ambassador that, for all the words about the country's importance in the Middle East, ministers still preferred to visit other, easier-to-digest places in the region. I pointed out to London that in one year British ministers had paid some thirteen official visits to Oman, but only three to Saudi Arabia. Western democrats found it difficult to understand that, in pushing social and political reform, Crown Prince, later King, Abdullah might have been ahead of the conservative majority of his people. Nor could they accept that, for all the obvious imperfections, the links that the thousands of members of the Al Saud had across Arabia made for more representative and accountable government than existed in the Arab republics further west. Only a few understood that, just as Saudi Arabia was a swing producer of oil, so too was it – is it – the swing producer of moderate thinking on Middle East peace and, given its experience of Al Qaeda, on tackling militant extremist Islam. I used to cringe as visiting ministers, who would have no hesitation in making robust statements at Westminster on democracy in the Middle East, would suddenly lose their courage when confronted with senior Saudi interlocutors in Riyadh. Somehow, it was easier to lecture the House of Commons on human rights in Saudi Arabia than it was even to mention the subject to men whose active engagement in Middle Eastern politics dated back to before the visiting politician was born. The visitors didn't understand – and in part it was probably my fault for not briefing them robustly enough – that, like most people, the Saudis respect colleagues who say what they mean, and mean what they say. They are more than willing to accept tough messages, provided they are delivered with courtesy and in private. Thinking Saudis know that their young country – some eighty years old – faces tough challenges in the decades ahead, and needs quiet help in meeting them without the violent disorder that has plagued other Arab countries.

One visitor who did understand this was the Prince of Wales. Almost alone of all the official visitors I had from Britain in nearly four years as ambassador in Saudi Arabia, HRH would speak truth to Saudi power, but he would do so with great courtesy, and strictly in private. Prince Charles's visits were always something to which I looked forward, because his eagerness to understand the realities at the heart of Islam and Arabia built bridges, and gave us – me – access to parts of the Saudi Kingdom it would have been difficult otherwise to reach. One special example of the Prince of Wales's value to British interests was a speech he gamely agreed to give in March 2006 at the al-Imam Muhammad ibn Saud Islamic University just outside Riyadh. This deeply conservative institution had been unfairly described by some American neoconservatives as 'the terrorist factory'. Prince Charles was the first Christian ever to lecture there. His message, born of deep sympathy with the basic tenets of Islam, broke down barriers. In his words, as well as in the deed of going to a university feared and hated in equal measure by many outsiders, he showed that the fundamental message of all three monotheistic religions – 'do unto others as you would be done by' – is the same.

At times, the Prince's search for simplicity was more complicated than he imagined. On one earlier visit he had said that he wanted to spend some time 'simply painting in the desert'. He wanted no fuss to be made. Just a tent and a view of the desert. The Saudis duly obliged. On top of a vast dune, with nothing but more dunes stretching to the distant horizon, they installed a traditional goat-hair tent, with rugs, cushions and a coffee pot bubbling on a fire. The Prince of Wales duly started work on his painting. What he didn't see, or hear, was that behind the dune on which he was sitting lay a vast trailer park, set up specially for the honoured guest from Britain. There were enormous caravans with hot and cold running water, a small field hospital, satellite dishes, mobile phone masts, local wi-fi and a battery of muffled diesel generators humming noiselessly away. In Saudi Arabia simplicity could mean hiding the complexity.

Some of the happiest times I had in Saudi Arabia were in the desert, preferably the deep desert. The best way of escaping the pressures of Riyadh – the vast and rapidly growing metropolis at the crossroads of the peninsula – was to drive out into the dunes around for a night or two under the stars. Even better were long desert journeys across the Empty Quarter or following the line of the great Turkish pilgrim railway from Tabuk in the north to Medina in the south. These expeditions, often lasting a week or more, were usually planned and led by active or retired British Army officers, with great thoroughness and a real sense of fun. In the school or university holidays, our children came along as well. And my bodyguards, desert bedouin at heart, were always enthusiastic participants. They knew so much better than we did how to travel long distances across arid areas. Not for them the mountains of absurd equipment – folding beds, chairs and tables, portable showers, portable lavatories, inflatable mattresses – which we namby-pamby Europeans piled into and on to our overloaded Land Cruisers. Instead, the Arabs took a couple of rugs, a barrel of water, a barrel of petrol, firewood, coffee and coffee pots, and plenty of bread, dates and olives, plus canned food for emergencies. They then tipped the lot into a couple of old-style open Toyota pickups – the 'chassis' beloved of the bedouin – and went up and over dunes, and through depressions, that we would never dare approach. When they set up camp, it was done in ten minutes, while we Europeans took an hour. But best of all was half-dark before dawn, when the bodyguards would rise, and, with the sergeant as imam, and the corporal as muezzin, say the dawn prayer to the stars. Hearing and seeing that small band pray in the desert in the way the bedouin have done for centuries made me feel I really was in the heart of Arabia.

In the deep desert, we had all sorts of excitements and excursions. Once, 200 miles from the nearest road, we came across a small 4x4 bogged down in soft sand. Some of the party went over to investigate. We found an eccentric British teacher of English from Riyadh. He was entirely on his own, in a flagrant breach of the first rule of desert travel. Every seat except the driver's had been removed from his car, to give him extra space for cases of bottled water. Sounding rather like a bizarre

Arabian version of an AA patrolman, I explained that I was his Ambassador and could give him a tow if he wanted. He didn't, and preferred to spend the next thirty minutes revving himself deeper into the sand, as we withdrew and watched from a discreet distance. I went over again, and this time he relented. If we had left him there, he would quite probably have died.

In preparation for one of our expeditions into the Empty Quarter, I made contact with a geography professor from my old college. He was one of the world's leading experts on dune formation – probably the leading expert – and sent me some wonderfully learned papers on how all the sand in the Arabian Peninsula gradually collected in its south-eastern corner, and on the difference between mature and adolescent dunes. Crossing them in a 4x4, even with the tyres deflated for better traction, one soon knew the difference without being told. Traversing the great dunes was more art than science, and had its terrifying moments: a jeep rolling over with jerry cans full of fuel on the roof, some of which burst; or a desperate day spent plunging again and again into impossibly soft sand, and each time laboriously digging ourselves out under a blazing sun. Once, not far from the border with Oman, we came across a suspicious-looking party of Emirati Arabs, carrying guns. Another time, in the north, near Jordan, just as we were all turning in for the night, my bodyguards thought they spotted raiders – in fact it was the local undercover police spying on us. On both occasions my bodyguards insisted on immediate evasive action, which involved rapid strategic movement to a safer part of the vast desert.

For all the giant grandeur of the Empty Quarter, it will be the monuments of the deserts of western Arabia – both natural and man-made – that will provide my most lasting memories. First among them must be the Nabatean tomb city of Medain Saleh, a place to rival Petra or Palmyra. But unlike those cities, which also peaked as part of the entrepôt civilisation that rose and fell on the commercial frontier of the Roman Empire in the early centuries after Christ's birth, Medain Saleh is largely unknown and unvisited. The Koran tells of the violent fate which befell the people who had 'hewed out houses on the mountains' and whose elders told believers 'we deny all you believe in', before killing a she-camel sent as a sign from God.* Perhaps because of the wrath this invoked, most Saudis have never been to the most magnificent monument from their country's pre-Islamic past. But what really marks out the tombs of Medain Saleh, carved mostly in great pillars of sandstone rising out of the desert floor, is what lies around them: to the west, towards the Rift Valley (filled by the Red Sea), a great basalt plateau, still pockmarked with the husks of hundreds of extinct volcanoes; to the east, the desert, but of dunes and shale, of infinitely greater variety than the Great Sand Sea.

Medain Saleh's natural surroundings are not all. Improbably, incredibly, nestling among the ruins is an ancient railway depot, and a station, Germanic in design, but wholly Middle Eastern in appearance. And in the shed stands, on rails, one of the original locomotives, supplied by Germany to Turkey before the First World War, to equip the narrow-gauge line south from Damascus to Medina: the Hejaz Railway, which I had first ridden while on language training in Damascus in 1978. One of the great civil engineering projects of its time, the railway constituted a Turco-German *Drang nach Osten* that was dead before it was finished. In the first years, the railway's builders had to fight off bedouin raiders, angry at a Western intrusion that would threaten their monopoly of the Hajj traffic. And, then, not a decade later, the bedu were again attacking the finished railway, this time encouraged by British officers, of whom T. E. Lawrence was one. The trains he and his comrades derailed lie today like beached whales in the sand, perfectly preserved by the dry desert air. The rails were stolen long ago, but the track bed – and the graves of the Turkish soldiers who died defending it – are still there. Today you can drive along the line of the old railway through tunnels and over viaducts now almost exactly a century old. The Hejaz railway offers a wondrous intersection between the modern political history of the Middle East and its ancient pasts. With Medain Saleh, it is one of the best things about historic Saudi Arabia – and one of its best-kept secrets.

---

* *The Koran*, trans. N. J. Dawood, London: Penguin, 2000, pp. 158–9 (7:73–81). Sura Al A'raf (Verses 73–81) mentions the fate of the unbelievers of Thamud (Medain Saleh): when they refused to heed the warnings of the prophet Saleh, 'the earthquake felled them, and when morning came they were crouching lifeless in their dwellings'.

We were lucky enough to have been invited out into the deep desert by the descendants of the man who had conquered it, Ibn Saud, Abdul Aziz, the founder of Saudi Arabia, and one of the giants of modern Middle Eastern history. In the first three decades of the twentieth century, Ibn Saud had led his bedu fighters to all corners of the peninsula and unified it – apart that is from Yemen and the Gulf sheikhdoms kept independent by British protection, as one of Ibn Saud's sons who had travelled with his father on those campaigns used to remind me. Early on, the India Office's political agents in the Gulf had spotted Ibn Saud's potential. Less wisely, the Foreign and Colonial Offices had backed his rival, the ill-fated Sharif of Mecca and ruler of the kingdom of the Hejaz in the west. On one such expedition, we watched desert bustard being hunted with falcons up near the Iraqi border. As we sat with our host in his tent afterwards, I was foolish enough to express my admiration for his surprisingly ordinary Browning shotgun, and Bridget said how beautiful she found the falcons. That evening, there was a knock on the door of our caravan. The Prince's falconer was there, with a great white bird on his arm and a gun slung over his shoulder. He said, in rough bedu Arabic, that His Royal Highness wanted us to have both. I was horrified and tried to refuse. But my wife wisely said we had to accept.

So the next day we flew back to Riyadh with a gun and a live falcon. I was wondering how on earth I was going to explain this to the Foreign Office's Conduct and Discipline Section: at the time, diplomats were not allowed to accept gifts worth more than £140, and then only with permission. We had just accepted a gun worth – I had no idea – probably several times that, and a Siberian Gyr falcon worth perhaps £150,000. Moreover, we had to house and feed the falcon, apparently on live quail. Luckily help was at hand. We rang an old Cairo friend and colleague who had written a book on falconry in Arabia.* He put us in touch with a professional falconer, who came round at once and reassured us. We found that the Riyadh suq had a ready supply of live quail, which we bought by the crate. And, most important of all, we found that Hassan, the quiet Pakistani with a genius for looking after

---

* Mark Allen, *Falconry in Arabia*, London: Orbis Books, 1980.

the Embassy garden, also had a talent for handling birds of prey. I squared the Conduct and Discipline Section by agreeing with them that I had accepted the falcon on behalf of the Embassy, and that I would in due course have the gun valued and pay the Foreign Office the relatively small difference between that and £140.

For the next three years, falcons became part of the life of the Embassy. Bridget devoted many hours to caring for our first bird, and his three successors. Saudi guests were hugely impressed. British visitors said they were impressed, but only at a distance. A ritual with British Cabinet ministers who came to stay was to persuade them to pose with one of the great birds on their arm. Most did, quaking. The Lord Mayor of London was braver, which is probably why he later became lord lieutenant of London. The Embassy children used to love the gruesome spectacle of the evening feed. A wretched squeaking quail was tipped out on to the lawn in front of the falcon on its stand. It would start to peck around, quite unaware of its fate. Seconds later, the great bird would pounce, and break its little victim's neck, before devouring it whole. All this to whoops of delight from the watching children. This was feeding time with guts, our mini-version of the Roman Games. I heard an appalled mother reassuring her wholly unconcerned child that he needn't worry – he wasn't at all worried – the quail would go to heaven. The next morning we would find on the lawn regurgitated pellets of the bits of the quail the falcon couldn't digest – mainly the feet.

Thanks to the foresight of my predecessors, the British Embassy in Riyadh has a well-equipped Residence and a beautiful garden, including a small swimming pool and an amphitheatre. All were built in the mid-1980s, when foreign embassies were allowed to move from Jeddah to the interior of the Kingdom. A Diplomatic Quarter was constructed on the outskirts of Riyadh, in which individual nations were encouraged to build embassies to their own designs. Britain's, in an international modern style, is not beautiful, but it works. The climate in central Arabia is such that the gardens can be used most of the year, although in summer night time is best. I did my best to ensure that the house and garden really were a 'corporate entertainment facility' for the whole British community. That community had stayed on when many others had left, and the Embassy played a part in keeping them together and in good heart. With the help of dedicated volunteers, we organised concerts by visiting performers, charity balls and all kinds of other events for Britons and Saudis alike. It really was an embassy at the service of a British community of which I felt proud.

There were, however, some elements in that community about which I was more doubtful. Following the precedent set by my predecessors, I allowed Protestants to worship in the Embassy on Friday mornings, and Catholics on Sunday evenings. The Catholics were fine: in my first few months in Riyadh, my deputy, Dominic Asquith, was a Catholic, and he took charge of their services, even reading out a weekly sermon which he found on a Vatican internet site. But the Protestants troubled me, as there was no one from the Embassy keeping a watchful eye. As an Anglican, and ambassador, I used occasionally to attend their Friday-morning services. Every few weeks, with the knowledge of the Saudi authorities, a priest would visit to take their services. And twice a year the Anglican Bishop of Cyprus and the Gulf would pay a low-key pastoral visit: he had spent most of his working life in the Middle East and was a middle-stump Anglican of wisdom and real holiness. But it was when the official priests weren't present that things went off the rails. The services were hijacked by American fundamentalists of a somewhat intolerant variety. I agreed that they could use the Ambassador's private pool for the occasional baptism by total immersion. Some of them really did think of themselves as the persecuted Christians of ancient Rome, with the Embassy as the modern equivalent of the catacombs. One Friday, I went along and heard the American 'pastor' say, 'And now we pray for Rowan Williams, the Archbishop of Canterbury, that he may return to the True Path, and be saved.' I was horrified, and rang the 'pastor' the next day. Why had he suggested that the Archbishop of Canterbury needed to be saved? His reply was unequivocal. Rowan Williams was no longer a true Christian, because he had said that both Muslims and Jews could go to heaven. But the Bible said clearly that only those who had taken Jesus Christ as their personal saviour could be saved. Everyone else was lost – including apparently the Archbishop of Canterbury. Here, in the heart of the British Embassy, among so-called Christians, was the kind of literalist fundamentalism for which we criticised the Saudis, and with which I had seen the Chief Rabbi having to contend. I warned the 'pastor' that I did not want that kind of divisive language used again.

By the winter of 2006 I was starting to think about my next job. In three years in Saudi Arabia, much had happened – much more than can be recorded in a short chapter. The Kingdom had weathered, better than most, a ferocious series of attacks by Al Qaeda. Following his brother Fahd's death in August 2005, Abdullah had become king, and started gradually to speed up the process of political, economic and social reform. As a contribution to opening the country up, Britain had provided Saudi Arabia with practical support in meeting the criteria necessary for it to join the World Trade Organisation, which had finally happened in December 2005. The Embassy had also supported quiet dialogue between Human Rights Watch and the Saudi authorities. On the commercial front, we had done all we could to encourage British exports. In the sensitive areas of defence and security co-operation, the Embassy had played a full part in both securing success and avoiding disaster. We had launched the Two Kingdoms Dialogue, covering political, economic, commercial and defence relations. We had increased the flow of Saudi students to British universities. On a professional level, I could look back on a tough but fulfilling time – very different from the easy boredom I had half expected when I had been posted to Riyadh. What had made the job so rewarding was the fact that Saudi Arabia was indeed a country where an ambassador had real work to do, explaining each side to the other, in their mutual interest. It was somewhere where local knowledge – of language and culture, politics and personalities – really could make a difference, for Britain.

Before leaving for Tel Aviv, I had remarked to a rather angular member of the Foreign Office camel corps that, to be effective in Israel, I judged that it would be important to show the Israelis that I was on their side. He disagreed angrily: after all that the Israelis had done to the Palestinians, no one decent could ever possibly be on their side. But he was wrong: in their different ways my postings in both Israel and Saudi Arabia each underlined the importance for a diplomat of showing both understanding and affection for the country to which he is accredited. Only then does the diplomat have a chance of making a difference. If he doesn't see the good – however limited – in his host country, he has very little to work with. As Mrs Thatcher might have put it, effective bilateral diplomacy means accentuating the positive, while keeping a clear view of the negative.

But none of that – the *intifada* in Israel, the Al Qaeda campaign in Saudi Arabia – prepared me for the scale of the challenge I was to face in my next, and final, post, Kabul.

Chapter 12

Afghan Afterword

My farewell audience of King Abdullah of Saudi Arabia in February 2007 had a sense of déjà vu all over again. When I had first met him, on my arrival in Riyadh in the early autumn of 2003, I had told him of the good things we were planning to do in and for the Iraq we had just invaded. Now, nearly four years later, I was telling him of the good things we were planning to do in and for Afghanistan, as NATO was taking over responsibility for security across the whole country. On both occasions he gave me that look of politely sceptical pity that he reserves for naive Westerners whom he likes, but with whom he fundamentally disagrees. Nevertheless, his good manners meant that he wished me well in my new mission, and thanked me for what I had done in my time in Saudi Arabia. I had already told his chief of protocol that I was sorry but British rules – Elizabeth I's dictum 'My dogs shall wear only my collars' – prevented me from accepting His Majesty's offer of the Order of King Abdul Aziz First Class. The King was especially grateful for the solidarity Britain had shown when the Kingdom had faced what had seemed at times like an almost existential threat from Al Qaeda. Abdullah had every reason to detest Al Qaeda. But, unlike many Americans, he knew the difference between AQ, with their commitment to global *jihad*, and the Taliban, who in most cases were deeply conservative, devoutly religious nationalists determined to resist with force the presence in their homeland of Western armies but who themselves posed no direct threat to Europe or America – contrary to what politicians trying to justify the war in Afghanistan liked sometimes to pretend.

As *Cables from Kabul*, my book about my three and a half years working in and on Afghanistan showed, like many others, I soon discovered how right the King was, and how misguided the whole Western 'strategy' in Afghanistan really was. As I look at the West's Afghan adventure in the rear-view mirror, two things make me especially sorry: how all the mistakes we made could so easily have been avoided, had politicians and those who advise them done their job; and, second, the utter waste of lives and limbs – mostly Afghan – and of money and effort – mostly Western.

As I have travelled around Britain and even parts of Europe and America, speaking about Afghanistan, I have been struck by a paradox: never, at least not since the Second World War, have our armed forces been held in higher regard by the British people; and yet, by contrast, that respect comes at a time when those same armed forces have been fighting, with iron courage and unquenchable enthusiasm, a war in which almost no one – certainly not the senior politicians – really believes. As Churchill might have said, never in the field of human conflict have so many fought for a cause in which so few believed. Privately, from the White House to Downing Street, from the Bundeskanzleramt to the Elysée, our political leaders are intelligent enough to see that a 'strategy' based on garrisoning selected parts of Afghanistan first with Western troops, and then with Western-trained Afghan troops, without any serious attempt to deliver a political settlement within Afghanistan, or between Afghanistan and its neighbours, has been, to put it mildly, unlikely to succeed. In the case of the Obama Administration, both Bob Woodward* and David Sanger† have revealed that, from the start, the White House had no illusions about the likely success of the Afghan surge. Private contacts with senior British politicians of all three parties suggest that they are equally clear-sighted. But somehow political leaders on both sides of the Atlantic have found it easier to let the military campaign run on for a year or two or three, and then call time, rather than do the right and responsible thing straight away: either make a serious effort to deliver a political strategy into which a largely tactical military campaign could be

---

* Bob Woodward, *Obama's Wars*, New York: Simon & Schuster, 2010.
† David E. Sanger, *Confront and Conceal: Obama's Secret Wars and the Surprising Use of American Power*, New York: Crown, 2012.

folded, or stop the whole pointless waste much sooner. As the future Senator John Kerry said in 1971 about Vietnam, 'How do you ask a man to be the last man to die for a mistake?'

In an essay which the former US Treasury Secretary Larry Summers cited in the *Financial Times** in relation to the euro crisis, Dr Daniel Ellsberg summed up this tendency of political leaders to take the line of least resistance in deciding what to do about an earlier war in Asia. That essay – 'The Quagmire Myth and the Stalemate Machine'† – showed that 'the best and the brightest' who advised President Kennedy in 1961–2 knew that a successful policy in South Vietnam required one of two approaches: either full-scale intervention or withdrawal. Instead, they muddled along through the middle, gradually adding small numbers of military advisers, knowing that the policy wouldn't work, but telling the public that all was well. Ellsberg's point was that America didn't stumble blindly into a quagmire in South Vietnam. Those around JFK were well aware that, without a decisive change of policy, they were marching into a quagmire. But somehow in the short term stalemate, at not too obvious an immediate cost, was politically easier than doing the right thing immediately. Some fifty years later, those around another young Democratic President took a similarly sceptical-cynical view of the prospects of success for a 'strategy' for winning another land war in Asia recommended by an over-enthusiastic, but under-informed, US military machine.

As with Vietnam, so with Afghanistan: privately the policy-makers have had no illusions, sharing the doubts of a deeply sceptical public; but, publicly, they have never ceased to affirm, without any sense of irony, that progress is being made – while challenges remain. It is right that we should be stopping fighting in Afghanistan. It is right that our forces should be leaving. But it is wrong that we should be going without the slightest serious effort on the part of the West, meaning the United States and its key allies, to broker either some kind of regional agreement between Afghanistan's neighbours, some of whom are

---

* Lawrence Summers, 'The world must insist that Europe act', *Financial Times*, 18 September 2011.

† Dr Daniel Ellsberg, 'The Quagmire Myth and the Stalemate Machine', in *Papers on the War*, New York: Simon & Schuster, 1972.

fighting a proxy war in that country, or one within Afghanistan. The Russians did both before they departed in 1989, leaving behind a regime that not only survived, but actually defeated the insurgency. That regime, led by a credible Pashtun placed in power by the Kremlin, Najibullah, collapsed only when the Soviet Union itself folded, ending the external support, in money and kind, upon which any modern Afghan government must depend. Neither a new internal settlement nor a regional one would be easy to secure. But nor would they be impossible, given two facts: first, each and every one of the regional powers would benefit from a gradually stabilising Afghanistan that was no longer exporting terrorism and terrorists, drugs or refugees, and was once again the commercial and cultural crossroads of South-west Asia; and, second, all Afghans know that wars end through talk – through sitting down in a *jirga* – and that the Taliban, who were not defeated in 2001, but were still excluded from the subsequent 'peace', need somehow to be accommodated in a new Afghan political settlement.

Right across Britain, I have found that it is the audiences with the closest connections with our armed forces and with Britain's imperial past who are most sceptical of the whole Afghan enterprise. In Cheltenham, true to caricature, it is a retired colonel, with grandsons in an Army of which he remains immensely proud, who explodes with rage: what on *earth* do we think we are doing invading Afghanistan, and then compounding the error by trying to garrison parts of it? In the English shires, in the Scottish Lowlands, in the Welsh marches, it is always the same: no one in the audience can explain what the strategy is, let alone justify it. All of us are full of praise for what our armed forces have done in Helmand. But each of us knows that it has been like cultivating an allotment in a jungle: once the gardeners leave, it won't be long before nature takes over again. An analogy closer to home comes from Ireland. The NATO 'strategy' in Afghanistan has been as though Britain had tried to solve the conflict between Protestants and Catholics in Northern Ireland without a Sunningdale-style political process, and without either the United States or the Irish Republic, and as if we had then proceeded to boast that we were going to deal with the Provisional IRA by killing or detaining as many of them as possible, while garrisoning only parts of Armagh (= Helmand), Belfast (= Kabul) and Londonderry (= Kandahar), without doing anything about the rest of the province or the sanctuaries across the inner Irish border. The US Army's own *Counterinsurgency Field Manual* says it all: counter-insurgency is 'mostly politics', and you cannot deal with an insurgency without cutting the insurgents off from the sanctuaries into which they withdraw when put under military pressure, or without dominating militarily the whole, not just parts, of the insurgency-infected area. Boasts that we are defeating the insurgents on the battlefield are beside the point: the battlefield is the last place the insurgents will want to fight. In any case, given our massive technological superiority, it would be rather worrying if we couldn't defeat the Taliban on the battlefield.

All the above is so obvious, so much part of the British imperial experience, so much in the very bloodstream of Britain. And yet we have ignored those lessons and been complicit in an exercise that no one serious really believed could have succeeded without a dual-track political strategy. Of course there have been Alliance and Army reasons for sending British troops to Helmand, in ever increasing numbers. But that cannot excuse the failure by political leaders and those of us who advised them to look the facts in the face. Symptomatic of this failure was my experience of having a senior Foreign Office official tell me that the Embassy in Kabul shouldn't report the facts about Afghanistan because it 'will upset the MOD', and the Foreign Office needs 'good relations with the MOD'.

None of this would matter if the policy issue was the route of a new by-pass or the closure of local libraries. But much more has been at stake in Afghanistan. When I left government in 2010, the Treasury representative was warning that the annual cost to the British taxpayer was 'getting on for £6 billion' a year. If that is so, recent suggestions that the whole project has cost Britain £20 billion look like an underestimate. More than 400 British servicemen and women have been killed, and hundreds more have suffered what the MOD coyly calls 'life-changing injuries'. Thousands of American and Allied soldiers have been killed or seriously wounded. And tens of thousands of Afghans, in and out of uniform, have lost their lives, limbs and much more: for them no Help for Heroes, no Headley Court rehabilitation centre, no Bluetooth-equipped prosthetic limbs at £17,000 a time. And, while we ship our Mine Resistant Ambush Proof vehicles back to Salisbury Plain, we leave the poor Afghan National Police still roaring around in un-armoured pickup trucks, to be blown sky high at first contact with an IED.

Perhaps the most striking monument to this latest bout of neo-imperial folly will be the great Anglo-American legionary fortress of combined Camps Bastion and Leatherneck, in the Helmand desert north-west of Lashkar Gah. In the spring of 2010, when I last visited, concrete was being poured and girders swung into place as contractors hurried to build huge new 'permanent' maintenance hangars for NATO forces. Imagining a Congressional delegation visiting ten years from now, I could not help paraphrasing Shelley's *Ozymandias*: 'Look on the West's works, ye mighty, and despair!'/Nothing beside Bastion remains. Round the decay/Of that colossal base, boundless and bare/The lone and level sands stretch far away.'

Britain's own record of accelerated imperial withdrawal does not bode well. In August 1947, we left India earlier than planned, without having settled the problem of Kashmir; in May 1948, we gave up our Mandate over Palestine early, leaving the two sides to fight it out, with consequences still with the world today; and in November 1967, we pulled out of Aden early, having failed to establish durable political arrangements for South Yemen, again leaving a problem still with us today. In all three cases, the reason we left in a hurry was not that it was the right thing to do – at least not without having addressed the politics – but because our imperial stamina, and funds, were exhausted. We must hope that, in extracting its armies from Afghanistan, America leaves behind a country in better order than Britain did in those three earlier cases.

But it's an ill wind that blows nobody any good. I would not have missed my Afghan experience for anything. I left full of admiration for a proud people and a truly beautiful country. So have thousands of other Westerners, all now friends for life of their beloved Afghanistan. Despite the lack of a serious strategy, or perhaps because of it, at a tactic-al level our soldiers have had a good war. When they finally march off the battlefield, they can do so with their pennants flying, and their heads held high. They have received the honours and awards they so richly deserve. We now have a generation of officers with experience of command in real war unmatched in recent times. For the British forces, and their NATO counterparts, Afghanistan has been a live-fire exercise of unmatched value. Given the resources, British forces have shown once again that they really are good at counter-insurgency. I also saw for myself that military personnel are generally better at delivering 'civilian effect' to post-conflict areas than civilians, however dedicated. Soldiers, or sailors or airmen, are simply braver, more pragmatic, more can-do, than civilians subject to 'duty of care' constraints. But there's little new under the Afghan sun: that was, of course, why a century ago most of the Political Agents on the North West Frontier came from the Indian Army; and why in my view some of the most effective 'stabilis-ers' in twenty-first-century Afghanistan have been the high-achieving officers from the United States Navy and Air Force sent to man American Provincial Reconstruction Teams.

What I have admired most about the British military, however, has been their willingness to learn. *Cables from Kabul* cannot have been easy reading for many who served so bravely in Afghanistan. And yet I have had countless messages of congratulation and agreement, and, to the consternation of some in the MOD Main Building, I still receive scores of invitations to speak to military and paramilitary audiences.

I often remind such audiences that, when you walk down Whitehall from Trafalgar to Parliament Square, you pass a small green in front of the old Air Ministry, now the MOD's forbidding Main Building. On that green are statues of three of our greatest generals. On the left, the man who was in my view the finest British field commander of the Second World War, General Bill Slim of the Fourteenth Army. It was he who referred to Kipling's poem when he addressed his victorious men in the great fort of Dufferin at Mandalay, and told them that their war was now about the road *from* Mandalay, as the Fourteenth Army would go on to roll the Japanese Empire up and out of South-east Asia. On the right, perhaps the most populist of generals, the commander of the 21st Army Group, Bernard Montgomery, who, when he arrived at the head-quarters of the Desert Army to take command in August 1942, allegedly began his address to his officers with the immortal words 'God said – in my view, rightly'.

But in the centre is the greatest commander of them all, General Sir Alan Brooke, later Field Marshal Viscount Alanbrooke. As Chief of the Imperial General Staff for most of the war, Brooke had to contend with a Prime Minister who was a supreme tactical commander, forever wanting vicariously to relive his experiences as a young officer in South Africa, in Sudan or on the North West Frontier. Almost every week of the war (or so it seemed) Churchill would have some barmy tactical idea or other: reinvade Norway, land in Sumatra, strike up through Salonika. But Brooke knew that only one strategy would win the war in the West for the Allies: to land troops in enough strength on the coast of north-west Europe in the spring or summer of 1944 to strike a mortal blow at the heart of the German Reich. And he stuck to that through thick and thin. He had the courage, and the sense of national duty, to say 'No, Prime Minister.' That is why, I suppose, three words adorn the pedestal of his statue: 'Master of Strategy'. And it is why, metaphorically, I doff my hat to the stubborn Ulsterman every time I walk up Whitehall.

Which brings me to my final point about Afghanistan. However enthusiastically our troops have embarked on their Afghan adventure, the civilians responsible in a democracy for directing them owe our armed forces more than just sending them into battle with the best body armour, or the latest Mine Resistant Ambush Proof vehicle. Apart from the waste of blood and treasure at a time when our nations' resources are stretched to the limit, the real tragedy of Afghanistan for America and its loyal allies – Britain first among them – has been that we have sent our soldiers to a distant land to fight for their country without a strategy worthy of the name. We have sent them to do and die: we should have been able to offer them a credible reason why.

Chapter 13

Envoi

Both during my time in the Diplomatic Service and afterwards, I have often been asked two questions: first, would I do it again; and, second, what advice would I give a young person considering a diplomatic career today?

The answer to the first question is an unqualified yes. For more than three decades, I had the rare joy of actually looking forward to going to the office – or its equivalent – almost every working day, and often, to the dismay of my family, at weekends as well. I had a career of immense variety, real intellectual challenges, working with colleagues of high ability and great dedication to public service. In London and abroad, I went to interesting places and met interesting people. I dealt with issues of real national importance. Long before it became fashionable for management gurus to talk about team-building, British diplomats worked in teams, sharing tasks and information and credit. All of us knew that, in general, ability and effort were fairly acknowledged and rewarded. Except at the very top, where politics and ambition overlap, promotion was on merit. When I joined the Diplomatic Service in 1977, about half my group of seventeen fast-stream entrants came from Oxford or Cambridge, and only three were women. Four of us had read classics at Oxford. Today about half the policy-level entrants are women, and a minority from Oxford and Cambridge. The image of the Foreign Office as dominated by products of Oxbridge and the public schools is completely out of date. Sadly, though, it is an image which endures, wrongly deterring many who should apply. In Saudi Arabia, the most effective diplomat on my team was a woman who had joined the Diplomatic Service as a clerk straight from school with only GCSEs to her name. But she had risen far and fast, and worked the Saudi ministries far more effectively than many men. The reason was that she was a natural diplomat, with both confidence and ability. Interestingly, she was one of a handful of Diplomatic Service colleagues in three decades whose drafts I felt I could never improve. In both Tel Aviv and Kabul, the Embassy's best political officers were women.

It was only shortly before I joined the Foreign Office that the rule obliging women members of the Diplomatic Service to resign on marriage had been abolished. In 1977, evidence of homosexuality led to withdrawal of security clearance. By the time I left, such offensive restrictions, and many others, had long gone. In 2010, the Foreign Office postings system was truly open to all, with allowances payable for partners, irrespective of gender or sexual orientation.

As a student, I had toyed with the idea of applying for a job with British Leyland, out of interest in engineering and manufacturing, and a perhaps misplaced sense of economic patriotism; I was offered jobs in merchant banks which would have brought me significantly greater financial rewards than a career in public service; and I made serious plans to read for the Bar. But I knew, deep down, that what I really wanted to do was to serve my country as a diplomat. I never had the slightest reason to regret that choice.

That is why I tell young people – and not so young people – that, if they are interested in a varied and demanding career in international affairs, they should apply to join the Diplomatic Service, at whatever level they think right for them. Given the numbers who apply, the chances of getting in are small. But that is not a reason for not trying, and trying again. The Foreign Office doesn't need the finest academic brains: what it does need is able individuals who take an intelligent and an active interest in abroad, who are adaptable and who can express themselves well orally and in writing. And, as Harold Nicolson suggested, in addressing the new entrants to the Foreign Service in 1946, it needs people with a sense of proportion. It needs people who can be relied on in a crisis. Sitting in the PUS's office or the Foreign Secretary's office, I was continually amazed, when a crisis blew up in a small and faraway country to which the Foreign Office had not

necessarily posted its brightest stars, how those in post – almost always
– rose to the occasion. I would also argue that we need diplomats of
courage, the courage to tell their political masters or military colleagues
unpalatable truths about Britain's place in the world and in Europe,
and, increasingly, the courage to work in some dangerous places.

As I hope this book has shown, at the heart of effective diplomacy lie
clarity of thought and clarity of expression. Diplomatic telegrams
should be the embodiment of such clarity. In 1998, Robin Cook
announced with a great flourish that the Foreign Office had finally
abolished the diplomatic telegram – another overdue reform, delivered
by New Labour, on the march towards Cool Britannia. In reality, Cook
was both right and wrong. The telegram, in the sense of a diplomatic
message, usually encrypted, conveyed by telegraph wire and printed out
on rolls or strips of thin paper, had long vanished from the Foreign
Office. It had been replaced by messages composed on, and conveyed
by, computer. But the telegram, in the sense of a collective message sent
to London by an overseas diplomatic post, analysing events in the host
country and making recommendations for policy, had certainly not
gone. Neither had the telegram of instructions from London, still bearing the name of the current Foreign Secretary at the bottom.

When I started in the Foreign Office in 1977, the first thing we did
each morning was read a buff folder full of carefully sorted paper telegrams from different posts, held together by an India tag. It was the
same in Cairo in 1980. The communications staff would get in early,
print off the overnight traffic from London and posts around the
region, and from Washington, the UK Mission to the UN in New York
and other posts involved in Middle East business, and prepare a number
of telegram folders. We read them before the daily Chancery meeting,
at which the first item on the agenda was 'the telegrams'. Thirty years
later, when I was in charge of one of Britain's largest and busiest embassies, at the epicentre of the conflict in Afghanistan, the first item on the
agenda of my morning meeting with the whole Embassy team was 'the
telegrams'. Nowadays, telegrams are called eGrams and flash around the
world in real time. They are encrypted automatically: gone are the one-
time pads and crude cipher machines. Special software pulls together
in a rich daily menu the summary with which each message begins,

enabling busy readers to dine à la carte. Gone too are the banks of teleprinters clattering away in the bowels of the Foreign Office main building in Whitehall, coming to life and subsiding back into silence as the working day moved round the globe. Gone are the 'scheds' when communicators at our posts overseas would make contact with the London Comm Cen for the daily, sometimes twice-daily, intercourse with headquarters, setting teleprinter talking to teleprinter.

As for what a diplomatic telegram actually says, the art of producing something worth reading is not yet quite lost. But it is in need of care and attention. Producing a carefully crafted description of the situation in a particular country at a particular time, and offering views (if required) on where Britain's interest lies, and how that interest might best be promoted, is not easy. Producing a report that will be both read and remembered, let alone acted on, is even harder. But, in a profession that is in the end about honest communication, getting such exchanges right is at the heart of successful diplomacy.

I give those considering a diplomatic career one health warning, and point to two possible drawbacks. The health warning is 'Don't enter the Diplomatic Service if you want to be even vaguely wealthy.' As the head of recruitment said to us when we joined in 1977, the only way to retire from the Diplomatic Service with a small fortune is to have entered it with a large one. In the same year, a colleague in the Republic of Ireland Department said he couldn't bear to read *Country Life*, as he knew that even after a working lifetime in the Foreign Office he could never hope to afford any of the houses advertised there. But there are plenty of compensations, especially when living abroad, which make life comfortable, financially and in other ways. Both the drawbacks are the flip side of what can be attractive aspects of a diplomatic career. The first is that the requirement to move around the world can be very disruptive of family life, sometimes terminally so. Especially in a world where both partners have careers, continual moves can be tough. And, remote though the possibility may seem to young new entrants, when children come along, as they usually do, family life is even more complicated. Boarding school is not for everyone, especially if the Foreign Office no longer subsidises the fees. On the other hand, modern communications and flexible postings policies, often including double postings for partners, make manageable what only a few years ago seemed impossible. The second drawback is working for ministers. Here today, gone not long afterwards, they are not the most consistent or caring of employers: one very grand Tory minister used to treat his officials rather as he treated the upper reaches of his estate staff – I ranked as an assistant land agent, I think; while a Labour minister from the other end of the social spectrum used constantly to mock me as the out-of-touch toff I hoped I wasn't. And yet working at the interface between domestic politics and international relations is one of the most exciting and interesting parts of a career in the Diplomatic Service.

People often ask if modern communications mean less of a role for embassies, and if therefore the Foreign Office isn't what it was. In fact, overseas posts are now linked to London and each other by secure email and voice, and video, channels. That makes them part of a single global Foreign Office, and a single global machine for making and delivering policy. It makes working overseas even more interesting than it already was. Office Meetings now include ambassadors on the spot, beamed direct into the Foreign Secretary's office. And as the world globalises and contracts, countries and governments will have more not less to do with each other, meaning more not less business for those who manage the relations between states. However much it may change, diplomacy is not going to go out of business any century soon.

But while embassies – HMG's overseas offices – are as important as ever, it may be true, however, that the Foreign Office isn't quite what it was, or should be. The rebranding of the overseas and defence policy committee of the Cabinet as a National Security Council, and the designation of the senior official who services it as the National Security Adviser, hasn't changed as much as it should have done. In practice, the net result has been to give the Prime Minister not one but several self-appointed national security advisers, among whom the Foreign Office may struggle to make its voice heard. Ministers boast about the number of times the NSC has met, confusing quantity of meetings with quality of decisions. With more brainpower, more international reach and deeper understanding of the world as it really is than any other Whitehall department, the Foreign Office should be the dominant department in setting national security strategy. But it has lost ground to Number 10 and the Cabinet Office, to the intelligence agencies and DFID (with its continually increasing resources) and to an MOD packed with confident generals. A wise Australian diplomat at the top of his country's 'national security' structure recently put his finger on the problem: for several reasons, but most of all the American-led expeditions into Iraq and Afghanistan, there is too much bogus talk of 'national security' and of 'strategy', and not enough genuine foreign policy. By that he meant that 'national security' puts misleading emphasis on hard power, and 'strategy' suggests greater capacity to shape the world than Britain or any other country actually has. In reality, in a world where Britain's relative standing, and that of our allies, continues gradually to decline, a wiser course might be a bit more emphasis on the soft power of traditional foreign policy. But that is not for this book.

I have only one, concluding observation about the Foreign Office as an institution: that collectively it is sometimes too eager to please, its political masters in particular. There are a number of reasons for this: partly a lack of institutional self-confidence, deep doubts about what the Foreign Office is for; but also a professional deformation that comes of years trying to get on with people you may not really like – making good relations an end in itself, rather than a means to an end. Senior politicians, including both Tony Blair and David Cameron, complain from time to time that civil servants obstruct ministers' efforts to drive through new policies. That may be true of the Home Civil Service. But my experience of the Diplomatic Service is the opposite: that sometimes it is too anxious to make ministers' ideas work, somehow, however madcap they may be. The grand Victorian building, built at the zenith of British power, doesn't help. (Professor Sir Michael Howard once observed acidly to me that the surest sign of an institution beginning its decline is when it was well housed.) The magnificent offices in which Foreign Office ministers receive their visitors, and from which they set out with their red boxes across the road to the Prime Minister or to Parliament, or around the world, feed delusions of grandeur long past. If the Foreign Office ever sank to piped muzak, it would have to be 'Pomp and Circumstance'. In such surroundings, it can take a brave official to confront an ambitious politician in a hurry with home truths about the world as it is, not as he would wish it to be.

In my career, I had direct experience of only three major strategic mistakes in foreign policy. Each was avoidable. Each was in large part the result of senior officials failing to furnish their political masters with the full but unwelcome facts about the venture on which they were about to embark. Of these the least damaging in the long-run was the Government's decision in 1992 unilaterally to invade (metaphorically) post-1997 Chinese territory, in ignorance of the agreements that had already been made between Britain and China, and of the likely reaction to our proposals. Chris Patten's personal courage and political skills, and surprising Chinese restraint, meant that we soon recovered from that unforced error, and even reaped some benefit at Westminster and in Washington for our 'crusade' for democracy in Hong Kong. Quite probably ministers would have gone ahead anyway. But, as I have pointed out, it is a stain on the Diplomatic Service that the Governor in Hong Kong and ministers in London were not told in advance of the exchange of letters between the British and Chinese foreign ministers, or formally warned of the likely Chinese reaction to the package cooked up in a hurry in Hong Kong over the summer of 1992.

Tony Blair's decision a decade later to join George W. Bush's 'crusade' for democracy in Iraq was much more serious, and much more damaging. It is a stain on the Diplomatic Service that only two of its members – the Deputy Legal Adviser Elizabeth Wilmshurst and a young diplomat in our UN Mission in New York, Carne Ross – had the guts to resign over a decision that those closest to the action should have known in their hearts was both immoral and of doubtful legality, as well as deeply unwise. As recently as 2011, one of the officials most intimately involved told me that he salved his conscience by assuring himself that, thanks to the Attorney General's last-minute sophistries, the invasion, while illegitimate, was technically legal. For the sake of the Diplomatic Service, there should have been somewhere on the record a minute formally warning ministers of the folly of joining the American invasion of Iraq. That might just have given other wavering ministers the cover and courage they needed to do the right thing. Tony Blair might well have gone ahead anyway, as he was entitled to do. But the Foreign Office should have done its national duty.

The third mistake was the Foreign Office's enthusiastic endorsement of Britain's half-baked effort to occupy Helmand in 2006. The mission sent out to assess the prospects for stabilising the province reported to Number 10 that it would take at least a decade to stabilise Helmand. A senior member of the Diplomatic Service who should have known better told them that it had to be done in three years, because that was what the Prime Minister wanted. The FCO official to whom I observed, before leaving for Kabul in early 2007, that invading Helmand had probably been a strategic mistake merely shrugged his shoulders. All the while the FCO Director most responsible knew that, in sending troops to Helmand without a serious political strategy, we were stirring up a hornets' nest, making things worse, not better.

That really is my only significant criticism of the Diplomatic Service: that, close to political power, senior officials, with many honourable exceptions, occasionally tend to behave a bit like the policy equivalent of the butler in *Remains of the Day*.* They find it easier to serve up more or less whatever their masters want, when a better model of true national service would be General Brooke, the real Master of Strategy. Being too eager to please is not an accusation often levelled at the Foreign Office's great departmental neighbour and rival, HM Treasury. Sometimes the Foreign Office would do itself good by being slightly less politely complaisant, with its own side as well as the opposition.

In early 1977, the late Geoffrey Moorhouse published a book about the Foreign Office, called *The Diplomats*,† which I saved for as soon as I had finished my university finals and then savoured. Even today, it is a pretty fair portrait of my beloved Diplomatic Service. In it, Moorhouse quotes an MOD official seconded to an embassy overseas as saying that diplomatic life was a bit like having Christmas every day of the year. That comes close to capturing the almost unalloyed pleasure I took in three decades spent as a member of Her Majesty's Diplomatic Service.

---

* Kazuo Ishiguro, *Remains of the Day*, London: Faber & Faber, 1989.
† Geoffrey Moorhouse, *The Diplomats*, London: Cape, 1977.

Index